THE STORM ON
OUR SHORES

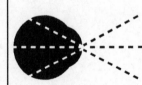

This Large Print Book carries the
Seal of Approval of N.A.V.H.

THE STORM ON OUR SHORES

ONE ISLAND, TWO SOLDIERS, AND THE FORGOTTEN BATTLE OF WORLD WAR II

MARK OBMASCIK

THORNDIKE PRESS
A part of Gale, a Cengage Company

Farmington Hills, Mich • San Francisco • New York • Waterville, Maine
Meriden, Conn • Mason, Ohio • Chicago

GALE
A Cengage Company

Copyright © 2019 by Mark Obmascik.
Thorndike Press, a part of Gale, a Cengage Company.

ALL RIGHTS RESERVED
Thorndike Press® Large Print Nonfiction.
The text of this Large Print edition is unabridged.
Other aspects of the book may vary from the original edition.
Set in 16 pt. Plantin.

LIBRARY OF CONGRESS CIP DATA ON FILE.
CATALOGUING IN PUBLICATION FOR THIS BOOK
IS AVAILABLE FROM THE LIBRARY OF CONGRESS

ISBN-13: 978-1-4328-6610-5 (hardcover alk. paper)

Published in 2019 by arrangement with Atria Books, a division of Simon & Schuster, Inc.

Printed in Mexico
1 2 3 4 5 6 7 23 22 21 20 19

For John Obmascik,
my father, who served.

CONTENTS

7

PREFACE

Laura Davis was confused. In the living room of her home stood a fidgety old man, but she did not know what the visitor wanted. He talked about his grown children. He talked about his Arizona retirement. And he talked on and on about his beloved orchids and all their beauty and their fragility and their rewards. Davis had little patience for exotic flowers or idle chitchat. She was an intensive-care nurse scrambling at home with five-year-old fraternal twins, her live-in elderly mom, and an increasingly rocky marriage. She tried to be polite, but really, wasn't it time for this guy to go?

Finally it was. As Laura walked the man outside to his car, he paused, then wheeled around. "By the way," he told her, "I'm the one who killed your father."

Laura reeled. Was this some kind of a sick joke? *By the way?* What kind of talk was that — so casual, yet so devastating? With his

9

black frame glasses and shock of white hair, the visitor looked like a lanky grandfather, not some demented prankster. He seemed nervous, too. His face was ashen and grim.

Before Laura could ask a question, the man dropped into his driver's seat, checked his rearview mirror, and drove away.

He left Laura so stunned she felt dizzy. She had been through a lot — crushing childhood poverty, a life-changing move from Japan to the United States, the birth of her beloved children — but she had always had one deep hole in her life. She had never met her father. He died when Laura was a baby, before she had babbled even her first word. The little she knew about her father came almost entirely from her mother, who wasn't saying much. Laura had been too busy raising her own family to spend time researching the past of a man who only existed as framed photographs on a wall.

With the few brief words uttered in front of a house in Sherman Oaks, California, the lives of Laura Davis and her visitor were changed forever. Laura would spend the next years scrambling to uncover her family's past. The visitor would struggle to overcome his own past.

They would each learn about honor and

courage, anger and forgiveness, the duty of a man to serve his country even if the result was a pain that would not go away. They would become enmeshed in a military battle long forgotten, on a miserable island far from civilization, a place that claimed thousands of lives but ultimately yielded no prize for its conquerors. Davis and the visitor would discover the secrets that had ruined lives and the truths that had helped to heal them. They would find fathers who soared with joy and others who shouldered burdens that grew unbearable. They would learn about scars that could heal only with atonement.

At the center of all these revelations would be the diary. In his last eighteen days on earth, when Laura's father was doomed and knew it, he had written a diary — his final farewell to the family he had just started and the daughter he had never met. That diary had been recovered by the stranger at Laura's door. It had been passed around to thousands of servicemen. How the diary would change hands — and change the hearts of so many who read it — would be the greatest lesson of all to Laura.

Decades later, this diary started me on the long path of reporting this story. I first found out about it while researching an unrelated book. I was chasing a story about competitive birdwatching. It turned out that the greatest spot in North America to spot the rarest avian species of the 1990s had been amid the shrapnel of one of the most deadly firefights in all of World War II.

Attu Island was a forbidding outpost in the far western Aleutians of Alaska, a treeless crag that natives called the Cradle of Storms — the place where weather was born. In June 1942, exactly six months after the attack on Pearl Harbor, Japan invaded and conquered Attu and several other of the barren Aleutian Islands. It was the first time since the War of 1812 that the United States had lost territory in war. To win it back, more than 100,000 United States soldiers were called into an Alaskan military campaign that culminated in the ferocious Battle of Attu. By comparison, that's roughly equal to the total size of the U.S. force dispatched decades later during President Barack Obama's surge in the Afghanistan War.

The Alaska campaign had been a significant part of World War II. How had I grown up without hearing about any of this?

Despite their numbers, Aleutian veterans remained largely unrecognized in both the United States and Japan. In the depths of

World War II, propagandists in Washington and Tokyo were not anxious to publicize a military campaign so stained with agony and blunder. While Midway, Iwo Jima, and Okinawa headline chapters in every history of the Pacific War, the location of the determining battle in the Aleutian campaign is known mainly today as the answer to an obscure clue in a difficult crossword puzzle. (Four letters, a Near Is., Westernmost USA pt — Attu.)

Though fascinated by the history and military significance of Attu, I kept coming back to the war diary of Laura Davis's father. He was a Japanese surgeon who graduated from medical school in California and returned home to Tokyo only to be forced into a war he did not support against the United States. I was struck by his valor and dignity. His writings made many Americans think twice about the true nature of their foe in the Pacific. U.S. soldiers were told during training that the Japanese military man was a bloodthirsty savage who had engineered the outrageous sneak attack on Pearl Harbor. The diary, however, raised the possibility that the enemy might also be a homesick father torn between his love of family and country. The writing and the situation in the diary were so heart-wrenching that it went on the 1940s version of going viral — countless copies were transcribed and mimeographed and passed among United States soldiers.

Over the years, I worked on other projects, but the messages of the diary pulled at me. I wondered how I would confront similar circumstances. Could I fight in a war I deeply opposed? What if the nation I lived in and admired had tried to kill me? If I knew my end was near, what would I write to my wife and children?

Little by little, I traced the path of the diary, as well as the soldiers and families who saved it. I followed it from the military bases of Alaska to the document depositories of the War Department in Washington, D.C., and Maryland, from family rooms in Los Angeles to kitchens and courtyards in Tucson, Arizona, and Las Cruces, New Mexico. I found people still moved by the diary in Atlanta, Boise, Boston, Dallas, Denver, Orlando, New York, San Francisco, and rural Oregon, plus Hiroshima, Osaka, and Tokyo. I learned that the first translator of the diary, a Japanese American soldier fresh off the battlefield in the Aleutians, had been so taken by the writing that he wept.

I also learned that the U.S. Army, whether

by accident or design, had lost the original diary.

Nevertheless, the surviving English translations had become so popular among American soldiers that I found at least ten different versions of the document. They were filed in the cabinets of windowless rooms on military bases, the stacked boxes of the National Archives, the microfiche libraries of several universities, and the personal collections of soldiers and their families. Some had only minor spelling changes, but others featured the addition or deletion of whole phrases. As a result, the exact meaning of some key entries in the diary remains under dispute, which I point out when it is applied. Otherwise I rely heavily on the judgment of Emory University professor Floyd Watkins, an Aleutian war veteran who studied extensively the similarities and differences in several versions of the diary.

No matter the interpretation of the diary, everyone seemed to agree on a few things: The Battle of Attu was fought by ordinary men thrust into extraordinary circumstances; soldiers on both sides were young, scared, and subjected to a relentless cascade of man and nature at their worst; and few sought glory, but many emerged as heroes, though in very different ways.

After conducting dozens of interviews and reviewing thousands of pages of letters, documents, photographs, and journals, I came away from this project in awe of the overwhelming dedication and humility of the men who froze and fought in Alaska.

I also admired the families back home who had to live with the difficult peace. The children of soldiers faced daunting problems, but the younger generation also crafted some of the most moving solutions. These American and Japanese families were linked by combat, and they toiled hard to transcend it.

All this work stretched well ahead of Laura Davis and the elderly stranger on that afternoon in front of her house in Southern California. As his car faded from view, Laura shook with worry. It felt as if an asteroid had hit. This man had come out of nowhere to reveal something about her father — something about her life — that she could not even fathom. How could someone unleash a thunderclap and then just exit?

Laura rushed back inside the house and found her mother, Taeko, who declined to talk with the man.

That man, Laura told her, just told me

that he killed Father.

Her mother sat silently.

From her work as an intensive care nurse, Laura knew that people displayed their grief in different ways. Some dissolved into wracking heaves of sorrow; others stayed stoic. Laura tried to read her mother, but her own emotions blocked the way. She felt overwhelmed. Raising twins, having her mother move in with her — Laura's life already felt so chaotic. The startling news about her father only deepened her vulnerability.

Taeko could see the doubt on Laura's face. She moved to reassure her daughter. Your father, she said, was a good man, a devout Christian and gifted surgeon who did the best he could for his family and his country. He believed in the Bible. He was killed in war. How exactly that happened, she didn't know. Did Laura want to know?

Laura thought. She didn't especially want to know how her father died. She did, however, want to know how he lived.

Growing up fatherless, she had always watched her friends with their dads and wondered what might have been. Laura's mother had been determined and brave, and her grandparents had helped out, but there were stretches when Laura and her

17

sister lived in third-hand clothes and went to bed shivering and hungry. They certainly could have used a father's financial support.

But her father sounded like more than a provider. Even in her own tense marriage, Laura could see how a man could offer love and guidance. What kind of man was her father?

"The more I think about this," Laura told her mother, "the more I want to learn about my father. What would you think if I pursued this?"

"If it brings you peace, then do it," her mother replied.

The visitor had given his phone number to Laura. At the moment, however, her five-year-old son and daughter were squabbling in the backyard. Laura folded the sheet of paper with the man's name and phone number, and pledged to call him later.

Eventually Laura did make that call. She set about her difficult journey of discovering the man who helped start her family, as well as the man who shattered it. The story that follows is built upon discoveries by Laura and her family, plus much outside reporting by me and other researchers. The passage of time may have dimmed some memories, but many important events remain vivid years later to family members, friends, classmates, and other witnesses. Whenever possible, I double-checked the recollections of these people with the recorded statements of letters, documents, and film. When the sequence of events is uncertain or disputed, I have noted that and tried to say why.

History isn't always pretty, especially in wartime. One person's truth may be another's rumor or lie. Learning about the past can hurt, but it also can offer an unparalleled opportunity to heal and to grow.

■ ■ ■ ■

PART ONE:
TATSY

■ ■ ■ ■

1
DELIVERY

Paul Tatsuguchi needed a baby.

As a medical resident at White Memorial Hospital in Los Angeles in 1938, he could complete his training only by delivering a newborn. Three times he traveled to the home of an expectant mother only to discover that the reports of labor were false alarms. A fourth time, he and a nurse stayed with a laboring mother in her home for two full days. When the exhausted trio finally retreated to the hospital for the grand finale, the baby was delivered not by Tatsuguchi, but by a resident physician who pulled rank. Tatsuguchi wondered if he were jinxed. Would he ever supervise the miracle of birth?

He dreamed of becoming a doctor in California. Twelve years earlier, he had moved from his family home in Hiroshima to attend Pacific Union College in Napa Valley. He struggled with English but excelled at science, and he won admission to medical school at Loma Linda University of Southern California in 1933. He had spurned the Shinto religion native to his homeland and grew up as a Christian. He learned to love ice cream, the open road, and the Sierra Nevada. His classmates and teachers even gave him a Westernized nickname — Tatsy. By the time he started at White Memorial Hospital, Tatsuguchi seemed as much of an American as a doctor.

If only he could find a baby to cooperate.

Tatsuguchi's friend and roommate, Harold Stout, who also was a medical resident, took pity on him. When a promising call for a home childbirth was phoned in to the hospital, Stout rushed into his car with a nurse to handle it. Then he saw Tatsuguchi, dejected after weeks without a baby delivery and trudging up the hill to work.

It was time for a change of luck. "Tatsy," he called, "this is your case and it sounds like a hurry-up one. Take my car and go!"

Tatsuguchi jumped into the driver's seat and rushed away with the nurse. Together they were finally able to deliver Tatsuguchi's first baby. Mother and newborn were fine. Tatsuguchi rejoiced. He was one step closer to becoming a full-fledged doctor.

The next day, however, the delivery nurse confronted the man who had set it all up.

"What did I ever do to you?" she demanded of Stout.

The roommate was confused. "What did I do to you?"

"You turned me over to Tatsuguchi yesterday," she said.

Stout knew some people weren't comfortable working with foreigners, especially ones from Japan, the source of much recent political tension with the United States. "He can't help that he's Japanese," he told the nurse. "He pays tuition just like I do. It was his turn."

"I didn't mind that he was Japanese," the nurse shot back, "but he had never driven a car before, and this is Los Angeles!"

Classmates loved to tell that story about Tatsuguchi, because it showed his grit and determination. A mere driver's license would not stand between Tatsy and a required medical accomplishment.

But the same story also highlighted something darker. No matter how much Tatsuguchi shared with his new country — his medical training, his religious beliefs, his love of California — he was often viewed as different, an outsider. America might have been established on the shared ideals of the

Constitution and the Declaration of Independence, but on the streets in the 1930s, skin color mattered.

He was insulted as a Jap, a yellow, a Chinaman. Never confrontational, he let the slurs slide, except for the last one. Tatsuguchi was precise and proud. He quickly corrected the classmate who called him a Chinaman.

In his first years in the United States, the animosity against him seemed racial. As his decade overseas progressed, however, the prejudice turned political. Though he tried to spend even his free time talking about the best ways to repair internal organs, Tatsy faced uncomfortable questions from classmates about the government of his home country.

Why had Japan invaded China? Did the Japanese really believe that Asia was only for Asians? Why was Japan allying itself with the likes of Hitler and Mussolini? What should the rest of the world make of Hitler's declaration that the Japanese were honorary Aryans?

Truth was, Tatsy could answer few of these questions. He was interested in medicine, not politics. Yes, he was proud of his Japanese homeland and culture, but Paul Nobuo Tatsuguchi loved the United States. He wore American eyeglasses and an American wristwatch, and he slept, American-style, on a mattress with sheets, not on a futon. He excelled at Western music — classmates always circled around whenever he played Mozart or Bach on the school's Steinway piano — and he loved Hollywood movies. He had lived more of his adult life in the West than the Far East. He even had learned to cook a few basic American meals, though he still preferred the miso soup and ramen of his homeland to the steak-and-potatoes of the California roadhouses.

In fact, he had acclimated to his new country so well that one of his medical school classmates, Joseph Mudry, concluded that Tatsy "was quite an American."

In Japanese schools, Tatsy scored in the top of his class with grades in the high 90s, but in America, the challenges of learning technical terms in his second language of English knocked down most of his scores to the 80s. He worked harder and refused to complain. When Stout, his American roommate, lamented the difficulties of memorizing such medical terms as sternocleidomastoid, acromioclavicular, and brachioradialis, Tatsy shrugged and replied, "No different than rough, through, threw, ewe, you, yew, to, two, too, knew, gnu, new, speak, and speech." Like the great movie star of the times, Ginger Rogers, who did everything Fred Astaire did except backwards and in high heels, Tatsuguchi was matching every move of his classmates, but in an adopted language thousands of miles from home and in a culture that would not fully accept him.

Classmates loved his wry sense of humor. While in a neighborhood Japanese grocery, his roommate found a bottle of soy sauce, at the time a rare ingredient for California cuisine, and called across the store to Tatsy: "Shall I get some of this beetle juice?" Stout had tried soy sauce once and hated it. Tatsuguchi's tendency to add it onto so many different foods became a running joke between the roommates. Tatsuguchi responded in jest the next day by pouring the soy sauce into a glass-stoppered bottle usually reserved in the chemistry lab for nitric acid. Before placing the bottle on their tiny dining table, he added this label: SNAKE'S BLOOD.

Tatsuguchi remained acutely aware that most Americans did not know anyone Japanese, and that his actions would sometimes be seen as representative of his entire native country. He convinced himself to put on a good show. When Tatsuguchi's roommate brought home some papaya nectar,

Tatsuguchi felt obligated to try it. Not a good idea. The taste was so disgustingly sweet that Tatsuguchi ran to the sink, spit it out, and spent much time at the faucet rinsing out his mouth. The roommate chided Tatsuguchi: That papaya nectar doesn't taste nearly as bad as the other stuff you brought home from the Japanese grocery store. Replied Tatsuguchi: "Yes, I know, but that was Japanese stuff. You ate it. So I had to, too." To Tatsuguchi, fair was fair.

He kept in touch with life back home by subscribing to a Japanese newspaper and using his shortwave radio to tune in news broadcasts from Tokyo. He knew far more about world events than most of his classmates, who had little reason to focus on life outside the United States. Still, he genuinely enjoyed his fellow students and medical residents, who were open and friendly and helpful. They banded together in misery under the brutal around-the-clock hours of a medical residency that left little time for much outside the hospital. White Memorial was a hectic but comfortable cocoon. Dedicated to becoming the greatest possible surgeon, Tatsuguchi centered his life around his career. No one ever disputed his work ethic.

Life outside the hospital was more complicated. Resentment of Asians in general, and the Japanese in particular, was building. Starting in 1913, fifteen Western and Midwestern states, including California, had enacted alien land laws, which banned Japanese immigrants and other Asians from owning real estate. (As a reflection of the prejudiced times, California continued enacting other anti-Japanese laws through the 1920s that, among other things, banned the leasing of farmland to Asian immigrants and even their American-born children.) In Washington, D.C., and Sacramento, race-baiting politicians warned of the rising Yellow Peril that would lower wages for whites and destroy the values of Western Civilization. Congress in 1917 had overridden President Woodrow Wilson's veto of the Asiatic Barred Zone Act, which denied citizenship to "all idiots, imbeciles, feeble-minded persons, epileptics, insane persons" — and most Japanese (as well as most other Asians). That law was followed by a series of other anti-Asian laws, including the Emergency Quota Act of 1921, the Cable Act of 1922, and the national origins quota of the Immigration Act of 1924. When a Berkeley, California, high school graduate named Takao Ozawa applied for U.S. citizenship by claiming he was as light-skinned as any white man, the United States Supreme Court disagreed, issuing an ugly ruling saying the man "is clearly of a race which is not Caucasian and therefore belongs entirely outside the zone on the negative side."

The anti-Japanese laws were just a symptom of the racist sentiment in the street. Japanese Americans were routinely denied the ability to rent an apartment, shop in some stores, attend certain schools, join labor unions, and work some jobs. White mobs in Portland, Oregon, and Coeur d'Alene, Idaho, harassed and chased out Japanese railroad workers. Another mob in Toledo, Oregon, evicted thirty-five Japanese working at the Pacific Spruce Corporation. There were forced evictions of Asians in Tacoma, Seattle, and Rock Springs, Wyoming. The Anti-Alien Association railed against land ownership and citizenship for Asians. The San Francisco Labor Council organized a boycott against all Japanese-owned businesses.

Many Americans did not distinguish between Japanese, Chinese, Koreans, or Filipinos. Popular books like *The Insidious Dr. Fu-Manchu* — "the greatest genius which the powers of evil have put on the earth for centuries" — only reinforced the perception

31

of Asians as crafty, shifty double-dealers bent on world domination.

Tatsuguchi could not ignore the contradiction: Inside the hospital he saved the lives of white people with emergency surgery, but outside in the parking lot he was persecuted as a Jap. He was winning his career dream. He was struggling to win cultural acceptance.

Many days Tatsuguchi felt like a lonely atoll in the Pacific, buffeted by conflicting winds from the east and west. He was an L.A. guy who shunned cars, a man who prized the modesty and dignity of Japan, but still craved the fun and energy of Southern California. He would never fit in perfectly in either the East or West, but he wondered who lived as more of an outsider — the Jap in America, or the gaijin in Nippon.

He longed for someone who knew what he felt, a friend who loved the best of both countries, a confidante who could join him to chart a new, wonderful, blended life.

What he longed for was a girl named Taeko Miyake.

2
LOVE

He hadn't realized how much he had missed her — until he couldn't see her. Paul was supposed to meet Taeko at her ship in Los Angeles. She had spent weeks sailing across the Pacific, from Tokyo to her new college and life in California, and Paul intended to meet her at the dock. But now Paul stood at the Port of Los Angeles, a long passenger liner stretching in front of him, and Taeko was nowhere to be seen.

Paul worried that he wouldn't recognize her. He had known her more than twenty years, when they were both schoolchildren in Japan, but since he had moved to the United States they had kept in touch only by letter. He certainly had changed during his years in America. He was more confident, more open, more accepting of new things. But what about Taeko? He knew she was no longer a girl. She was a woman, an excellent student, who was both thrilled and

33

a little scared to be moving to a new country for classes. In the United States, Paul felt sure that he and Taeko would be friends. As he scanned the docks searching for her, though, he felt they might be something more. Where was she?

Not at the port, it turned out. Taeko's ship had arrived hours earlier. She had come and gone from the docks.

Paul scrambled and found Taeko later that day at the home of a mutual friend. Paul apologized for missing her at the port. Taeko said she was just grateful that he found her. They started talking and did not stop. She was enrolling in a Seventh-day Adventist college, La Sierra Academy in Riverside, where she planned to study the Bible, English, and the violin. She was the daughter of a minister from Tokyo. He was the son of a Hiroshima dentist. Both families were dedicated to Jesus Christ and the Seventh-day Adventist Church.

They talked about old times and new, family and friends, hopes and dreams. And for the first time in a long time, he was overcome with a singular, fantastic realization: Taeko Miyake *knew* him.

For starters, she didn't call him Tatsy, the nickname all his classmates used. To Taeko, he was Paul, the apostolic name his parents had given him to signal the Tatsuguchi family's deep faith. Like Paul, Taeko knew what it felt like to be outside the mainstream. They had both grown up Christian in a Japan dominated by Shinto and Buddhism, a country suspicious of most things Western. As part of a scorned religious minority, Paul's parents, like Taeko's, deemed it important to learn about life outside the Japanese cultural island. They had sent Paul years earlier to study for his undergraduate degree at Pacific Union College, a Seventh-day Adventist school in Northern California.

While he was away at college, however, both his parents died within a month of each other. Following Japanese tradition, the Tatsuguchi family inheritance went to the oldest son, not Paul.

Taeko was the only person in the United States who knew just how devastating this turn of events had been to Paul. The Tatsuguchi family was extremely wealthy — so rich that Paul and each of his five siblings had been assigned two servants. (The cooking, cleaning, and gardening was left for ten additional family servants.) Paul grew up with the best clothes, the best food, and the best tutors. His parents were major contributors to the Seventh-day Adventist Church in Japan and prime backers of a church tuberculosis sanitarium in Tokyo. His parents had shown him the good life as well as the Christian philanthropic obligations that came with it.

The death of Paul's parents meant the end of his financial support. Stranded on the other side of the Pacific Ocean with no clear way to pay for anything, Paul pleaded with his older brother for money to let him finish his medical studies at Loma Linda University. Weeks passed, and Paul grew more nervous. Would he be forced to return to Japan without a medical license? Could he even cover his current school bills? And what would happen to his younger brothers and sisters still home in Japan? Eventually the older brother agreed to give Paul the family house, which was sold quickly, at a cut-rate price, to pay for his medical school tuition, plus other expenses for his brothers and sisters.

It was a testament to Paul's own sense of dignity that his medical school roommate, Harold Stout, had never heard about his financial crisis. In the minds of Stout and other classmates, Tatsy was a quiet, sincere, and modest medical student. They never knew that he was rich, because he didn't tell anyone, and they didn't know that Tatsy was now poor, because he didn't say any-thing about that, either. What they did know was this: Tatsy was a skilled surgeon who performed top-quality appendectomies faster than anyone. In the true American spirit, he was working harder to get ahead faster.

Taeko, however, knew more. She knew all about Paul's problems back home because her family had helped him through his money woes. Her parents were religious missionaries from Tokyo, now living in Hawaii, who had contributed a modest sum to help continue Paul's schooling. Others in the church had donated as well. Seventh-day Adventists were all about community and sticking together during times of adversity. If the orphaned son of a church committee member needed help to pay for medical school in America, then the church would deliver that help. It was expected that Paul would pay back the favor someday.

Paul liked that Taeko knew all this about him. America was invigorating, but it also could be lonely. He wanted someone to confide in. Yes, Taeko was an antidote to homesickness, a connection to the customs and culture of a native land far away. As they talked on their first evening together in a new country, she started to become something more. She understood his problems. She might even offer some solutions.

Taeko soon learned there was no such thing as a simple date night with Paul. In the same way he memorized the McBurney, Lanz, and Pararectus incisions for surgeries, Paul also felt compelled to classify and categorize the natural world around him. A walk around the block turned into a quest to identify the moths fluttering at the streetlight. He prided himself on his ability to pick out constellations in the night sky; no evening stroll was complete without finding the Sagittarius tea pot in summer or Orion the hunter in winter. A lunch by a lake was more than just a picnic — Paul always collected water samples to examine later with a microscope for amoeba, paramecium, and other protozoa. Every finding was recorded with detailed notes. In Paul's world, everything had a purpose, and he was determined to figure it all out. He was like a grown-up Huck Finn exploring a new land. There were exotic plants and birds and landscapes, and, especially, people.

In Japan, so many people had the same background and beliefs. Southern California, by contrast, was a hodgepodge of races, religions, and economic class. It was both frightening and thrilling, and the more he explored with Taeko, the closer they grew.

Paul was also deeply devoted to his faith. He did more than just attend their Seventh-day Adventist church on Saturdays. At home he pored over the scriptures and memorized many favorite verses. The margins of his personal Bible were filled with notes and interpretations. He worked hard to be virtuous and set a good example. In a letter home to her parents, Taeko wrote that she was impressed by Paul's dedication to, as she put it, "living a good Christian life." Paul clearly wasn't going into medicine to build a fat bank account. He was doing it to help others. He was genuinely devoted to improving the lives of the less fortunate.

Smart, enthusiastic, sincere — and a surgeon in the making — Paul was quite the catch for the marriage-minded coed, and he had attracted much notice on La Sierra's Seventh-day Adventist campus. Still, Taeko never felt any competition. She genuinely enjoyed being around him. Yes, Paul was a little quirky, but he also was a man who took on hard challenges and persevered. Though Taeko's botched arrival day at the Port of Los Angeles proved Paul could sometimes live in his own world, he still had a good heart.

He also knew how to pick the right spots. On a long weekend, he had organized a trip to Yosemite National Park, one of the planet's great cathedrals of nature, and one of the most beautiful places either he or Taeko had ever visited. She was taken by the vast waterfalls, and the granite domes, and the rolling green meadows. He was taken by her. In fact, he was so focused on her that he had neglected to dip into the Merced River for water samples.

He looked at her and she at him. In Taeko, Paul could see a future together, a shared journey of children and church, and a life that balanced the best of the United States and Japan.

In the shadow of Yosemite's iconic Half Dome, Paul dropped to a knee and asked Taeko to marry him. She had a quick certain answer. She said yes.

Their engagement was cause for celebration, but also fraught with complications. For starters, Taeko's college did not allow married women. Though she had crossed the Pacific for an American undergraduate degree, Taeko would be forced as an engaged woman to leave school without a diploma. Still, she knew there were worse fates in life than becoming a surgeon's wife.

Planning the wedding was not straight-forward. The fight over Tatsuguchi family money had left some hard feelings among Paul's siblings. With both parents dead, Paul saw little reason to return to Japan for a marriage ceremony. Besides, Taeko's mother and father had been living and working as missionaries in Hawaii, or, as Taeko put it, "on this side of the globe." In 1938, less than a year after Taeko had arrived in California, the couple married in Los Angeles.

There was little debate about what to do for a honeymoon. Paul and Taeko admired America, were fascinated by America, and wanted to see America. But how?

They didn't have enough money for plane or rail travel. And the truth was that the traumatized baby-delivery nurse at White Memorial Hospital had not exaggerated: Paul really was an awful driver. A car trip across the country with him at the wheel would not be a honeymoon. It would be a death wish.

Luckily, Hollywood had just popularized another way to see America. In 1934, Clark Gable and Claudette Colbert had rolled up the East Coast on a Greyhound bus for their blockbuster romantic comedy, *It Happened One Night.* It was the first film to have won all five major Academy Awards — best

41

picture, director, actor, actress, and screenplay — and, even more amazingly, it made bus travel look fun. If Greyhound spelled love for Gable and Colbert, then why not also for the newlywed Tatsuguchis?

And so Paul and Taeko set off on bus for their great adventure across America. They could not imagine sights more breathtaking. The ocean around Japan always inspired awe, but nothing prepared Paul and Taeko for the majestic open spaces of the Grand Canyon. A single place in Colorado, Rocky Mountain National Park, had forty peaks higher than Mount Fuji, the tallest mountain of their homeland. Rolling through the endless farmland of Nebraska and Iowa — two states that, combined, nearly matched the total area of all of Japan — made the Tatsuguchis realize that America should never go hungry. And it was hard to tell which man-made creation appeared more impressive: Chicago and the sprawling stockyards that made it the Hog Butcher for the World, or Detroit and the massive factories that turned out more automobiles in a year (3.3 million) than Japan's second-largest city, Osaka, had people.

The more the Tatsuguchis traveled, the more they fell in love, with each other and with their adopted country. On their honeymoon, they even traveled to the ultimate newlywed destination — Niagara Falls. When the vast cataract was illuminated at night, they had to ask: Could there be a more all-American honeymoon? In Japan, the Tatsuguchis had always felt safe and secure, but in the United States they felt exhilarated. Americans were not pre-occupied with avoiding embarrassment or failure. They dodged conformity. They took risks. They were optimistic. They believed they could control their own destiny and even change it. Plus, for Paul, the United States had one other big advantage: excellent ice cream.

On their grand cross-country honeymoon tour, no place left the Tatsuguchis as amazed as New York City. Paul stood at the base of the Empire State Building, at 1,250 feet the world's tallest, and gaped upward until his neck hurt. The highest building in all of Japan stood one-tenth as tall. Manhattan was almost incomprehensible.

Paul and Taeko Tatsuguchi were taken aback by the wealth of a country that could create such magnificent structures. They could not imagine how Japan could ever match such an economic colossus in either war or peace.

They would soon find out.

Sometime after their return to Los Angeles from their honeymoon, Paul and Taeko were confronted by a terrible turn in Paul's family life in Japan.

According to his family, Paul's oldest brother had sold a sister into prostitution. Few details were clear to Paul. Suffering from a mix of shame and horror, family members were reluctant to discuss it. Paul could not understand how any human being, especially his own brother, could do such a thing. The sad truth, however, was that famine and economic hardship across rural Japan in the 1930s had led many families to sell daughters into the sex business. Still, Paul's brother was neither poor nor a farmer. Why had he done it? The more Paul pressed his family for information, the less he learned. Adding to the frustration was the slow pace of communications. Paul's letters took weeks to travel from California to Japan, and the family's responses took weeks in return. The whole situation was so shrouded in shame and secrecy that, even decades later, the couple's daughter, Laura Davis, was unable to learn much about it.

Still, the reality was that Paul's sister was living in a brothel in Manchuria, China. The more he thought about it, the more he grew angry, heartbroken, and disgusted. Five thousand miles away, however, he could do little. The horror gnawed at him in the morning when he said his prayers and in the evening when he prayed again.

Finally he could take it no longer. He had to rescue his sister. After ten life-changing years in America, Paul and Taeko Tatsuguchi boarded a ship in California and sailed west three weeks across the Pacific. The Tatsuguchis were returning home.

3

HOMELAND

With a new wife, a new medical license, and a new appreciation for life outside Japan, Paul Tatsuguchi knew he was returning to Japan as a new man. What he hadn't realized was how much his home had changed, too.

When he had left Japan in 1929, the country was in distress. Six years earlier, an earthquake, tsunami, typhoon, and firestorm lashed together on the same day to create the worst natural disaster in the history of Japan, and one of the worst of the modern world. Just before noon on September 1, 1923, as cooks across Tokyo stoked lunchtime stoves, a 7.9 magnitude temblor rocked the Kanto Plain of western Japan for fourteen seconds. Thousands of buildings collapsed. Cooking fires jumped from houses to streets to neighborhoods. Tens of thousands of refugees from the fires fled for the wet safety of the Sumida River, which had flooded in the aftermath of a forty-foot-high tsunami. Alas, at that very moment, ferocious winds from an offshore typhoon whipped dozens of smaller city fires into a pillar of flame. The three-hundred-foot fire tornado, called a dragon twist, consumed all available oxygen and burned alive as many as 44,000 people.

Between the fire, flood, and building destruction, the Great Kanto Earthquake of 1923 killed at least 140,000. Nearly half the structures in Tokyo, the capital city, were destroyed; two million people were left homeless; and the nation's most important port city, Yokohama, was reduced to cinder and rubble. "The city of almost half a million souls had become a vast plain of fire, of red, devouring sheets of flame which played and flickered," wrote Henry Kinney, editor of *Trans-Pacific* magazine, after a tour of Yokohama. "Here and there a remnant of a building, a few shattered walls, stood up like rocks above the expanse of flame, unrecognizable. . . . It was as if the very earth were now burning. It presented exactly the aspect of a gigantic Christmas pudding over which the spirits were blazing, devouring nothing. For the city was gone."

At the time, the Tatsuguchi family was living 400 miles away in Hiroshima, but the earthquake and firestorm had devastated the nation's economy. With the port shut down, few goods could get in or out of the country, and the modernization and industrialization of Japan ground to a halt. False rumors spread that foreigners were poisoning wells and profiteering from the disaster. Japanese vigilante mobs responded with mass murders of as many as ten thousand Koreans and Chinese. After weeks of pointless hate and distrust, Tokyo and Yokohama finally turned to the formidable task of rebuilding. First shanties and then permanent structures had to be built for the two million homeless. Typhoid fever raged in the unsanitary conditions. One of the world's largest cities required a total overhaul of its water, sewer, electric, and transportation lines. Reconstruction boomed, aided by Japanese wages that in the 1930s were about one-tenth of those in the United States.

When Paul and Taeko returned to Yokohama in 1939, the newlyweds hardly recognized it. There were few signs of earthquake misery. Instead, the rebuilt port now bustled with new docks, vast warehouses, and an unending parade of merchant ships that filled the island nation with new goods and, even more importantly, the confidence that came from a frenzied construction drive. Few people had been subject to a natural fury as fearsome as the Great Kanto Earthquake. The Japanese, however, had seen it, survived it, and, in many ways, been strengthened by it. At the same time, in the United States and Europe, the Great Depression had crushed hopes and fortunes. In Japan, the earthquake had exacted a far worse human toll, but the recovery set the country on the path to becoming a modern industrial juggernaut. In some ways the earthquake worsened relations with the West. The United States donated millions to Japan for rebuilding, but American officials complained that Tokyo was ungrateful. At the same time, many Japanese officials believed the Americans were trying to profit from their misery. The seeds of distrust had germinated.

The Tatsuguchis could feel the difference in the neighborhoods of Tokyo, which brimmed with confidence. New construction and prosperity seemed to have taken root everywhere. What other nation could have withstood such a calamity? Japan had always been a proud nation, but the remarkable Kanto comeback seemed to infuse the country with a wash of hubris.

The nation had become the region's preeminent power, both militarily and in business, but it carried a serious chip on its shoulder.

Patriotism can be a fine balance between pride and belligerence. On the streets of Tokyo, Paul and Taeko could feel the scales tilt in a way that made them uncomfortable. Dissent was quashed, conformity expected. Yet the Tatsuguchis had lived long enough in the United States to value their independence. While Japanese neighbors carried watches from Seiko and Citizen as a point of national pride, Paul stubbornly stuck with his American timepiece, on a flexible wristband, because it was easier to put on and take off for surgeries. He kept his American eyeglasses because they felt more comfortable. In California, the couple had grown accustomed to sleeping on a mattress with sheets and pillows, so they kept the same arrangement in Japan.

Neighbors and co-workers could sense there was something different, something foreign about the Tatsuguchis. They had become the object of curiosity, and, sometimes, derision. Paul and Taeko didn't understand it. In their hearts, they still felt Japanese, even if they loved America.

Yet they didn't always help themselves

blend in. Surrounded by crowds on the street, or in a garden, or at a shop, Paul and Taeko sometimes guaranteed themselves some privacy by conversing in English. In Japan of the 1930s, few things were more jarring than a countryman who spoke an alien language.

Paul and Taeko were set apart by their religion, too. Even in the United States, the birthplace of Seventh-day Adventism, their faith was considered unusual. Adventists attended church on Saturday. Secular work and sports were discouraged on Saturdays, though nature walks or hikes were permitted. (Just as they loved visiting Yosemite National Park in California, the Tatsuguchis in Japan loved to hike and check for wildflowers around Lake Chuzenji at Nikko National Park.) Most Adventists also followed the Old Testament kosher dietary rules, eschewing pork and shellfish, while many gave up meat altogether and became vegetarian.

One major tenet of their faith: Seventh-day Adventists were pacifists. Through the Civil War, the Spanish-American War, and World War I, Adventists were either conscientious objectors or, if drafted, noncombatants. They could work behind the lines of combat, or in medical service, but they could not bear arms.

If their religion was considered unusual in the United States, it was even less understood in Japan, where the Adventists represented only a small minority of Christians, who themselves comprised less than one percent of Japan's population. The dominant faith in Japan was Shinto, which at that time was used by the state to promote nationalism and worship of the emperor. The Tatsuguchis, like all schoolchildren in Japan, had grown up memorizing and reciting the Imperial Rescript on Education, a kind of Japanese Pledge of Allegiance that promised, among other things, to "offer yourselves courageously to the State; and thus guard and maintain the prosperity of Our Imperial Throne coeval with heaven and earth."

How exactly could anyone square a belief in a Christian God with a Japanese leadership connected directly to heaven? Paul and Taeko did not preoccupy themselves with philosophical concerns. They had more pragmatic worries.

The biggest nightmare continued to be Paul's sister in the brothel in Manchuria. Details of her ordeal were scarce. Paul worked steadily, but quietly, to get her back, working through intermediaries and sending along money when he had it. His single biggest sum of cash came when he imported a Steinway piano from California and sold it. How and why she eventually won her freedom remains unclear even to family members — neither Paul nor the sister would speak of it. One day, however, she returned to Japan. She was sullen and hurt, and, according to some family members, changed forever. But she was home, and for that both she and Paul were extremely grateful.

Her return allowed Paul and Taeko to readjust to Japanese life. They had settled in Tokyo, Taeko's girlhood home, and Paul started work at the Adventist sanitarium for tuberculosis patients that had been funded generously by his philanthropist parents.

In his new job, Paul missed performing surgeries, but felt that his new service was crucial. As more Japanese moved from open farms to cramped cities and factories, tuberculosis spread quickly. The sickness carried a deep stigma, and few people wanted to risk any contact with the afflicted. Helping the desperate and the unwanted, Paul Tatsuguchi believed, was an essential Christian value. He not only loved helping — he loved showing what Seventh-day Adventism was all about. He considered himself to be more than a doctor. He was a medical missionary. He devoted himself to healing not just the body, but also the soul. Faith gave him purpose, community, and hope.

It also set Paul and Taeko apart from their neighbors. In 1939, Japan was not focused on charity. After centuries of isolation and subjugation, Japan was transforming itself into something new and powerful.

4
ISOLATION

Japan had always chosen a different path than its neighbors. Like almost every other Asian country, Japan had been descended upon in the Sixteenth Century by Europeans bent on plunder and colonization. Yet when Portuguese sailors were blown off-course by a storm in 1543 and landed on the southern Japanese island of Tanegashima, something odd happened.

The Japanese did not surrender to the Europeans. Instead, they adapted and learned.

The local territorial warlord, or daimyo, grew fascinated with the strange but powerful exploding rods that were wielded by the Portuguese sailors. The daimyo traded for two, and commissioned his swordsmith to replicate them. When islanders couldn't figure out how to make the copies work correctly, they negotiated more trades for new lessons in craftsmanship. Two hundred years after guns and cannons had begun to dominate warfare in Europe, firearms had arrived in Japan.

Initially the warlords thought they were getting a fantastic deal. For the mere price of some local silk, or fish, or hand-carved curios, a daimyo received the weapons to keep his peasants in line and his rivals at bay. Subsequent Portuguese ships were welcomed enthusiastically.

Over time, however, the Portuguese began introducing more than just guns to Japanese society. They also packed another powerful force — Christianity.

By the end of the sixteenth century, dozens of Roman Catholic missionaries, mainly from Portugal and Spain, had spread across the nation and introduced native Buddhists to Western religion. Japanese warlords viewed the first Christian evangelizers as a necessary evil. The only way to get European guns was to put up with European proselytizing.

After a few years, however, the exotic religion had spread even more rapidly than the revolutionary weapons. More than 100,000 Japanese, including at least eighty daimyos, were baptized as Roman Catholics. Though many daimyos embraced Catholicism for reasons of faith, large numbers also converted for more practical reasons. From the Europeans, Christians in Japan gained better access to saltpeter, a crucial ingredient of gunpowder.

Alarmed that so many natives were becoming loyal to a pale-faced and mitered pope in Rome, Japanese authorities launched a major crackdown on the two Western innovations. In 1587, the Supreme Commander of Japan, Toyotomi Hideyoshi, forbade peasants from owning guns. Then he expelled the missionaries and officially banned European religion.

Guns receded from everyday life, but the pope's religion was too strong to wither. Japanese peasants, especially, appreciated a faith that offered the promise of heaven after a life of oppressive serfdom. Jesuits remained influential in western Japan, and Franciscan missionaries continued to enter the country through the southern port city of Nagasaki. The Church estimated the number of Catholics in Japan had more than doubled, to 220,000.

With growth came excesses. Some daimyos forced peasants to convert to Christianity under threat of death. In Kyushu, Catholic converts even helped the Portuguese sell off their poor Japanese neighbors as slaves to Europe, Africa, and India.

Finally, the supreme commander of Japan had enough. Six months after the arrival of Japan's first Catholic bishop, Hideyoshi ordered the arrests of twenty-four Catholic converts and ordered their left ears chopped off as a warning. When the one-eared Christians were paraded through the streets of Nagasaki, two Jesuits arose to defend them. The two Jesuits and the maimed men were all chained to crosses, slashed with swords, and left to hang for eighty days. The crucifixions made Christians across Japan cautious about professing their faith.

After that gore and several other incidents like it, Christianity vanished from Japan. So, too, did almost all contact with the West. For the next 250 years, Japan became Sakoku, a chained country, an island of both geography and policy.

The first five points of the Sakoku Edict of 1635 stated:

- Japanese ships are strictly forbidden to leave for foreign countries.
- No Japanese is permitted to go abroad. If there is anyone who attempts to do so secretly, he must be executed. The ship so involved must be impounded

and its owner arrested, and the matter must be reported to the higher authority.

- If any Japanese returns from overseas after residing there, he must be put to death.
- If there is any place where the teachings of the [Catholic] priests is practiced, the two of you must order a thorough investigation.
- Any informer revealing the whereabouts of the followers of the priests must be rewarded accordingly. If anyone reveals the whereabouts of a high-ranking priest, he must be given one hundred pieces of silver.

Limited trade was allowed with some Chinese merchants and the Dutch East Indies Company through the port of Nagasaki. By and large, though, the outside world was cut off from Japan, and Japan was cut off from it. For more than two centuries, the outside world knew less about everyday life in Japan than it does today about everyday life in North Korea.

At the same time, few Japanese knew much about anything beyond their islands. And the little they did know only bolstered their decision to seal off themselves. Across Asia, nation after nation had been forced to submit to the humiliation of European colonization. India, Singapore, Burma, and swaths of China fell to Great Britain; Vietnam to France; Indonesia and the Spice Islands to the Netherlands; and the Philippines to Spain.

In its isolation, however, Japan remained independent and free. Why did Japan stand virtually alone among Asian countries in resisting colonization? One reason was that the country had few natural resources to attract outside invaders. With no gold, silver, coal, oil, spices, or rubber, Japan was not an inviting target for Western plunder.

Japan was also well-protected. The same samurai who preserved order for the supreme commander presented a formidable warrior defense against would-be colonizers. Any European who doubted the fighting spirit of Japan had only to remember the twenty-six crucified Catholics of Nagasaki. Would-be invaders stayed away.

For more than two centuries, Japan became convinced of its own greatness, because it was the only greatness it knew. With little exposure to outside ideas, the country under Sakoku believed it had the smartest thinkers, the fiercest warriors, and the greatest leaders. They were a chosen people, a superior people, favored with special grace from the deities.

Problem was, the rest of the world didn't stand still. The period of Japan's greatest isolation, roughly from the 1630s to the 1850s, coincided in the outside world with one of the greatest explosions of knowledge in the history of mankind.

Beyond the closed harbors of Japan, the Scientific Revolution transformed intellectual life. Isaac Newton unveiled calculus and the laws of motion; Antonie van Leewenhoek discovered the unseen with the microscope; and astronomers such as William and Caroline Herschel uncovered the vast beyond, including the new planet Uranus and moons of Saturn. John Harrison eased the dangers of transoceanic navigation with his invention of a marine chronometer, and Charles Morse revolutionized communications with his invention of the telegraph. Charles Darwin set off on the HMS *Beagle* to chart the course of evolution.

At the same time, the Industrial Revolution churned out the fantastic machines that spun textiles, mixed cement, mined coal, hauled incredible loads, and pushed back the night sky with dependable brilliance from gas lamps.

Inside Japan, a single man could travel only as fast as a galloping horse; outside Japan, the steam engine transported hundreds of men and women across continents.

Outside Japan, arts and letters changed the world as never before. With *Don Quixote,* Miguel de Cervantes gave birth to the modern novel, which inspired Voltaire, Goethe, Austen, and Dickens to write for thousands of readers. When educated Westerners were not reading at home, they filled great halls to hear the masterworks of Beethoven, Mozart, Haydn, and Schubert. A revolution in painting was led by Rembrandt, Rubens, and Velázquez.

The most potent transformation outside Japan, however, came in the realm of politics. When Japan shut itself to foreign ideas in the early 1600s, the Ottoman Empire of Constantinople was the world's greatest multinational and multilingual power, controlling much of southeast Europe, the Caucasus, the Middle East, the Horn of Africa, and North Africa. Absolute monarchs, such as Louis XIV of France, Peter the Great of Russia, and Frederick the Great of Prussia, built up strong central governments and vast armies. While Japan was locked down, China surrendered in the

First Opium War to Britain, losing control of Hong Kong in the process.

In the meantime, Napoleon waged the greatest war campaign in the history of Europe. The subsequent French Revolution upended the entire continent, beheading monarchs and buffeting churches while promoting radical ideas like democracy and meritocracy. All this tumult, all this upheaval — because of Sakoku, Japan missed it all. Amazingly, the country knew little about most of the political revolutions to the west. The bigger threat, however, rose from the east.

On July 8, 1853, Japanese residents along the Uraga Channel awoke to a terrifying sight: four black warships, barreling toward the nation's feudal capital, all under star-spangled banners and a cloud of black smoke.

The nation that hated immigrants was about to meet the nation made of immigrants.

Sakoku was over.

Despite two centuries of self-imposed isolation, elites in Japan knew a few things about that startling political invention called the United States of America. In 1841, a fourteen-year-old fisherman named Nakahama Manjiro had been shipwrecked in a storm on the uninhabited island of Tori-shima and rescued by an American whaling ship. When the whalers completed their mission in Hawaii, the Japanese teenager was offered the chance to leave and return home. Instead, he opted to continue to the ship's home port in Massachusetts, where he enrolled in school in Fairhaven, became fluent in English, and became known as John Mung. After a series of whaling trips — and months of lucrative work in the California 49er Gold Rush — he had saved enough money to buy his own whaling ship and return home to Japan. On February 2, 1851, he reached Okinawa, where he was promptly arrested, interrogated, and imprisoned in a series of jails for eighteen months. Though the death penalty was mandated for all Japanese who left the country, Manjiro won a reprieve from his captors by regaling them with incredible stories of the strange new land across the ocean.

Americans, Manjiro said, were "upright and generous, and do no evil." They had weird customs — such as kissing in public, reading books on the toilet, and cluttering homes with furniture — but their different way of thinking had produced some fantastic results. In war, they had defeated the

British, French, and Mexicans. In peace, they had produced a delicious food called bread, and transformed their clothes with handy things called pockets and buttons. Even more oddly, the Americans elected their leaders. And, of course, they also produced awe-inspiring coal-fired machines that powered locomotives across a vast landscape — and ships across oceans.

When those four black American ships churned into Uraga Channel near Edo (Tokyo) in 1853, some panicked Japanese thought they were being attacked by giant puffing dragons. Others called them "burning ships," though the official term came to be "black ships of evil mien." When the squadron approached, the Japanese immediately surrounded the warships with guard boats and hoisted a large sign in French: "Depart Immediately and Dare Not Anchor!" The Americans anchored anyway. Japanese sailors tried to scramble aboard up the anchor chains, but the American sailors pushed them backward with cutlasses and spikes. Worse, the Japanese saw what pointed behind the American spears — cannons larger and more numerous than had ever been seen in local waters. The Japanese city at the head of the bay bustled with a population of more than one million, but the nation itself had no navy. Realizing they could not repel the Americans with force, the Japanese desperately tried to sidetrack the invaders with the lure of local women. As historian Ian Buruma explained, "The Americans had guns, the Japanese lifted their skirts."

But the commander of the American squadron, Matthew Perry, would not be distracted. A veteran of the War of 1812, a fighter of pirates in the Caribbean, and a commodore during the Mexican-American War, Perry was a stern and imposing man whose crews called him Old Bruin. Buffeted by the winds of Manifest Destiny, Perry was dispatched across the Pacific Ocean with a brief letter from President Millard Fillmore to the emperor of Japan.

"Great and Good Friend," the letter began, "I have directed Commodore Perry to assure your imperial majesty that I entertain the kindest feelings toward your majesty's person and government, and that I have no other object in sending him to Japan but to propose to your imperial majesty that the United States and Japan should live in friendship and have commercial intercourse with each other."

What America proposed were three specific things: a new era of business trade;

permission for U.S. steamships to refuel with coal in a local port; and protection for shipwrecked American whalers. None of these wishes were immediately granted. After three days of talks and meetings, Commodore Perry and his squadron departed. He vowed to return shortly for an answer from Japan.

As soon as the foreigners steamed away, the shogunate was desperate to learn anything about these frightening intruders. They summoned Manjiro, the former teenage castaway, who was abruptly transformed from crackpot traitor to sage traveler with unique wisdom. Manjiro was, after all, about the only man in Japan who had experience with America. He warned the shogunate that America was content in peace, but ferocious in war. He advised Japan to cooperate.

Seven months later, Commodore Perry returned with American reinforcements. This time he filled the bay with ten ships, or one-fourth of the U.S. Navy, including more than 100 mounted guns and 1,600 men. Yet he also wanted to do more than scare the Japanese. He wanted to impress them with gifts carefully selected to show the superiority of American society. The presents included a quarter-sized steam locomotive, with 370 yards of track; two sets of the communications device recently perfected by Samuel Morse, the telegraph; the nation's first telescope and camera; a complete Double-Elephant Portfolio of John James Audubon's *Birds of North America;* more than a hundred gallons of whiskey; and "8 baskets of Irish potatoes."

Whether it was the display of military might or just the exotic spuds, the Japanese realized they were outmatched. On March 31, 1854, they boarded the sidewheel steam frigate USS *Powhatan* and agreed to the Convention of Kanagawa, which opened two Japanese ports to U.S. trade and guaranteed the safety of shipwrecked U.S. sailors. It was the first time Japan had been forced to submit to the same ignominious fate as other Asian countries — an "unequal treaty" with the West. Four years later, the *Powhatan* returned with an even more unequal deal, the Treaty of Amity and Commerce, which opened four more Japanese ports to trade and allowed the reestablishment of Christian churches in the country.

Japan recoiled. The unequal treaties may have opened the nation to new thinking and advancement, but they also deeply ingrained the belief among Japanese that an arrogant United States wanted to destroy their way of life. Soon after Commodore Perry sailed away, a backlash against the West swept Japan, and the dominant political saying became *Sonno joi,* or "Revere the emperor, expel the barbarians."

Only half of that slogan came true. Humiliated in front of the world, Japan girded itself internally with a powerful wave of nationalism. Though the country had been organized for centuries along feudal lines — the shoguns ruled the daimyo, who in turn ruled the tenant farmers, or serfs — the post-Perry Japan became far more centralized. Political power consolidated in the hands of the emperor, who became the embodiment of all things good, noble, and sacred. A new emperor, Meiji, was installed on February 3, 1867. He was fourteen years old.

To make sure all Japanese understood the new order, even if it was lorded over by a teenager, rulers issued a general proclamation:

Our country is known as the land of the gods, and of all the nations in the world, none is superior to our nation in morals and customs. . . . [Japanese] must be grateful for having been born in the land of the gods, and repay the national obligation. . . . In antiquity the heavenly descendants opened up the land and established the moral order. Since then the imperial line has remained unchanged. Succeeding generations of the honorable personages profoundly loved the people, and the people reverently served every honorable personage. . . . All things in this land belong to the Emperor. When a person is born he is bathed in the Emperor's water, when he dies he is buried in the Emperor's land. . . . However, during the past 300 years the imperial way had not prevailed. . . . Corruption was rampant, virtuous persons were punished, evil men enjoyed good fortune. . . . Now finally imperial rule has been restored, and fairness and justice prevail in all things. . . . If we repay even a smidgen of the honorable benevolence we will be doing our duty as the subject of the land of the gods.

Though the emperor was a living icon to venerate and rally behind, he did not possess the power to "expel the barbarians." In fact, the barbarians prospered, flooding the Japanese market with foreign goods that were cheaper and often better. Most other countries with fledgling industries would have reacted with a wave of economic protectionism, but Japan was banned by the unequal treaties from slapping tariffs of more than 5 percent on foreign goods. Local business suffered. Resentment built against the West in general and the United States in particular.

If the barbarians could not be defeated, they could be mimicked. Japanese leaders came to embrace the promise of capitalism and wealth. By the 1870s, Japan had agreed on a more practical and attainable national motto: *fukoku kyohei,* or "enrich the country, strengthen the military."

Enriching the country, Japanese-style, meant mixing the government with business in the hope of catching up with the West. The government launched the chemical, glass, and cement industries, and then turned everything over to private business when they became profitable. There were government banks, iron foundries, mines, factories, cotton mills, and telegraph services. Several other private industries, such as shipbuilding and munitions, were heavily subsidized. It was the birth of the public and private partnership that, a century later, turned into the industrial juggernaut known as Japan Inc.

As business burgeoned, the Japanese

military surged, too. One of the biggest government mandates was to develop the country's first navy. For this monumental task the leadership turned to the old whaling castaway Manjiro, who completed the first Japanese translation of the age's key maritime reference text, *Bowditch's American Practical Navigator.* He also taught naval tactics at a government academy; helped launch the modern Japanese whaling industry; and served as translator for the first Japanese ship to cross the Pacific Ocean and visit the United States. By the 1920s, the Imperial Japanese Navy was the third-largest in the world. By the 1930s, it was the most powerful in the region and among the most modern in the world.

The most far-reaching military change, however, came on land. In 1873, Japan enacted universal conscription. Most men age seventeen to forty were generally required to serve three years. Based on the model of the Prussian Army, which had just won the Franco-Prussian War, the Imperial Army became a unifying force in a Japanese culture that had been riven with feudal rivalries. Mandatory military service helped erase the distinctions between the old samurai class and peasant class; for the first time in centuries the poor were allowed to bear firearms. Three years in the Imperial Army left conscripts brimming with nationalism, patriotism, and undying loyalty to the emperor, all concepts that spilled over into everyday civilian life. Insular Japan transformed into a muscular Japan.

But an unused war machine grows restless. As the Imperial Army and Navy swelled with power, Japan scanned the seas and saw vulnerable neighbors. The new military was anxious to test itself, and so it did. In one stunning victory after another, Japan booted China from Korea and Taiwan, then crushed the Russian army and fleet in Manchuria and the Yellow Sea. It all took less than ten years. (In a prescient warning of what was to come years later at Pearl Harbor, the Japanese had won the Russo-Japanese War with a sneak attack on the Russian fleet at Port Arthur, Manchuria. It marked the first time an Asian power had taken on Europeans in modern war and won, convincingly.) Japan's conquests were significant: Manchuria alone was the size of Germany, France, and Italy combined. By the turn of the twentieth century, Japan had established itself as the preeminent Asian military power. The nation that denounced the foreign interloper had become one.

The easy conquests proved seductive.

When the colonial powers of Europe plunged into World War I, Japan seized the opportunity to expand its own reach across the Far East. In the first week of war, Japan cut a deal with the United Kingdom to side with the British, but only if Japan were allowed to take control of Germany's colonial territory in the Pacific. The Japanese easily won the German possessions of the Marshall, Mariana, and Caroline Islands. They also launched the world's first naval-based air raids to help take the German port of Tsingtao in China. At the same time, Japanese industry profited handsomely, both in money and know-how, by selling war goods to combatants.

Japan emerged from World War I with new territories, fewer than 1,500 casualties, and even more self-confidence. Most importantly, though, it won a seat at the Paris Peace Conference. For the first time in an international negotiation, the major powers of the world included Japan.

However, with the new recognition also came humiliation. To prevent another world war, the United States and the United Kingdom advanced the idea of a League of Nations, which would resolve international disputes through negotiation instead of militarization. During the drafting of the organizing principles of the League of Nations, Japan advanced a racial equality proposal, calling for the new organization to grant "equal and just treatment in every respect, making no distinction, either in law or in fact, on account of their race or nationality." Japan's racial equality clause was either amazingly shrewd or fantastically naive. In the United States, Congress had just passed the Asiatic Barred Zone Act, which banned most Japanese immigration at the same time the gates at Ellis Island were being thrown open to white Europeans. Japan's equality clause also was political poison for the racist Southern Democrats whom President Woodrow Wilson would ultimately ask to approve the League of Nations. On top of that, racial equality was anathema to the fledgling British federation that had just embraced the anti-Asian immigration policy called White Australia.

Ultimately the United States rejected the racial equality clause (as well as, eventually, the whole idea of the League of Nations). Japan seethed. After being subjected to the gunboat diplomacy of Commodore Perry, and the enactment of a series of unequal treaties, the Japanese had plenty of reason to feel alienated from the United States. Did even the modern descendants of the white barbarians believe they were racially superior to the Japanese?

By the time Paul and Taeko Tatsuguchi had returned to Tokyo in 1939, Japan had spent decades feeling as though the world was aligned against it. Japan was clearly the region's preeminent power, both in military and business, but it still had something to prove.

5
CONSCRIPTED

She was small, and she fussed and cried and blurted through the night. Paul and Taeko could not be more thrilled.

In September 1940, the Tatsuguchis' new baby daughter changed the world for them. They felt so blessed. They named her Misako, but, to commemorate the couple's love for America, they added a Western name, Joy, which fit perfectly with the ebullient mood of the new family. The Tatsuguchis reveled in the Japanese parenthood traditions — the first kimono, the first slippers, the first chopsticks. In their neighborhood, Taeko gravitated toward other mothers with new babies. As the family provider, Paul labored at the sanitarium with new purpose and direction. The couple's regular nature walks turned into regular baby walks. They could imagine no happier existence.

And then came the letter from the Imperial Army.

Paul had always known he might be drafted. Military service had been compulsory for Japanese men since 1873. Exemptions could be negotiated for students and the sons of the rich, but the changed circumstances of Paul's family meant he had no possibility for a release from serving. He had told his medical school classmates back in California that his return home to Japan could result in his conscription. He dreaded the idea. As a devout Seventh-day Adventist, he was a pacifist who opposed war on religious grounds. As a former California college student who had seen firsthand the economic might of the United States, he also was a realist who believed Japan would be doomed in a war against America.

Now the day had arrived. On January 10, 1941, Paul Tatsuguchi was inducted into the Imperial Army of Japan.

No longer would he be called Paul. In the eyes of the Japanese government, his name from this day on was Nobuo Tatsuguchi.

The military enlistment split his heart with a twisted mix of pain and pride. He felt terrible leaving behind his wife and baby girl, especially when the family had not yet fully settled into their new home. How could Taeko and Joy survive on Nobuo's meager Army salary? Taeko longed for the life of a surgeon's wife, not someone who scrimped on checks from an absentee Army man.

Yet Nobuo could not turn his back on patriotism. His country had called, and he had answered. Japan needed him and wanted him. He did not want his loyalty to ever be in doubt.

Alas, he learned, it could. As far as Nobuo knew, he was the only physician in the Imperial Army who was not awarded the rank, and, especially, the extra pay, of an officer. He had asked time and again for officer training, and even spent the extra 400 yen to buy his own officer's uniform. No matter how hard he tried, he remained stuck as an enlisted man. He was never given a firm reason why, but he didn't have to ask. He was seen as an outsider. Almost everyone else in the Imperial Army had had some form of military training over the years. Nobuo didn't know the Imperial Army routine, and it showed.

What set him apart even further from his peers was his time abroad in the United States. Even by the early 1940s, relatively few Japanese had ever traveled past the shores of the homeland. Tatsuguchi, however, had lived for a decade among the white barbarians across the sea. In a place that stressed conformity and obedience, he had a different manner and sensibilities. He wasn't viewed as being fully Japanese.

Though the military would not change its opinion of him, Tatsuguchi began to change his view of the Imperial Army. He began to feel a part of it. It would have been difficult not to. The Army was devoted to shaping every recruit's body and mind. Physical training was much the same as in every elite military unit around the world. There were twenty-five-mile marches, multiday maneuvers, and challenging treks through the dark and cold.

What set the Japanese Army apart, though, was the intensive campaign to mold every recruit's thinking.

The centerpiece of military indoctrination was the Imperial Rescript to Soldiers and Sailors. Tatsuguchi and all other recruits were required to meditate on the rescript at least ten minutes each morning, and recite parts of it by memory each evening before dinner. The rescript was so important to the core identity of soldiers that, when one officer bungled the words in front of his troops, the humiliation led him to commit suicide. "This Rescript, and the one on Education, are the true Holy Writ of Japan," explained anthropologist Ruth Benedict in her landmark cultural history, *The Chrysanthemum and the Sword.*

Issued in 1882 by the emperor — the ruler deemed "coeval with heaven" in the schoolchildren's daily pledge — the Imperial Rescript to Soldiers and Sailors ran several pages. "We [the Emperor] are the head and you are the body," the rescript states. "We depend on you as Our arms and legs. Whether We shall be able to guard the Empire, and repay the benevolence of Our Ancestors, depends upon the faithful discharge of your duties as soldiers and sailors."

Again and again the message was hammered into conscripts: More than your wife, more than your children, more than your government, you must dedicate yourselves, no matter the cost, to the heavenly emperor.

"Neither be led astray by current opinions, nor meddle in politics, but with single heart fulfill your essential duty of loyalty, and bear in mind that duty is weightier than a mountain, while death is lighter than a feather," the rescript stated. "Never by failing in moral principle fall into disgrace and bring dishonor upon your name."

War was noble and purifying, death a duty. Defeat equaled disgrace. Soldiers were obligated to fight to the end. When confronted with the chance of surrender, an honorable Imperial Army man instead must always choose suicide. In the service of the emperor, death was lighter than a feather.

The indoctrination was daily, and relentless. It created a military culture that, in coming years, would launch a thousand banzai attacks.

It also was a culture completely at odds with Nobuo's religious faith. Seventh-day Adventists saw no honor in suicide. They put the highest possible priority on preserving the blessed life that God gave them. In the United States, these beliefs allowed Adventists to seek and receive conscientious objector status that allowed them to avoid going into battle. In Japan, there was no conscientious objection, only fealty to an emperor who demanded the ultimate sacrifice in his behalf.

Fortunately, Nobuo was able to sidestep the whole faith vs. service conflict. The Imperial Army needed him as a physician, not a marksman. He could honor his religious beliefs by working to heal others. He became a military doctor. His first assignment, remarkably, was the First Imperial Guard Infantry Regiment, which protected the emperor, his family, and their network of palaces and properties. Though his exact duties remained shrouded in secrecy, Nobuo practiced medicine and was stationed in Tokyo, where he remained close enough to home to visit his family occasionally. Taeko was always grateful to see him, though she remained concerned over his failure to win the higher paycheck enjoyed by his peers in the officer ranks. At home, Nobuo loved to play hide-and-seek with Joy, who was starting to walk. He relaxed by playing classical music on any piano he could find.

By the summer of 1941, relaxation and free time became scarce for Nobuo. Japan was plunging deeper into world crisis.

While the United States and the West were preoccupied with Hitler's drive through Europe, the reality was that Japan had been at war far longer. More than two years before Nazi boots marched through Poland, the Imperial Army of Japan had invaded China.

For the prior decade, China was locked in a ferocious civil war between the Nationalists, led by Chiang Kai-shek, and the Communists of Mao Zedong. By 1937, the civil war had killed five million Chinese, but neither side held a clear advantage. Japan saw an opportunity.

On July 7, 1937, Japanese troops on training exercises in China skirmished with Chiang Kai-shek's Nationalist soldiers at the Marco Polo Bridge near Beijing. The Japanese were spoiling for a fight. Six years earlier, in its voracious quest for coal, timber, and manpower, Japan had invaded Manchuria to the north, dominated its economy, and installed a puppet government. When Chinese troops were surprised by military maneuvers in the night across the Marco Polo Bridge, they fired. Japan had all the excuse it needed to turn a flare-up into all-out war.

The confidence of Japanese military leaders bordered on arrogance. In a memo to the emperor, War Minister Hajime Sugiyama predicted that Japanese troops would vanquish China within a month or so. A prior war minister, Araki Sadao, had even boasted that "three million Japanese armed with bamboo spears can defend Japan against any enemy."

The military leaders were delusional. By the end of the year, Japan had been forced to dispatch 600,000 troops to China, a transport that turned out to be just a start. With a clear technological edge, Japan's military controlled the sky and the sea, but China had men — waves and waves of men. The Battle of Shanghai spanned four months and resulted in 300,000 soldiers and civilians killed. That bloodshed was followed by the six-week Nanjing Massacre, which saw the deaths of as many as 300,000 Chinese, including the slaughter of 60,000 prisoners of war. Japanese troops gang-raped at least 20,000 and possibly 80,000 Chinese women.

One infamous symbol of Japanese brutality was the two officers who held a contest to kill at least 100 Chinese with a sword. According to the *Tokyo Nichi-Nichi Shimbun* newspaper, which promoted the killing contest with a series of breezy stories, the winner could not ultimately be determined because both men surpassed the milestone of 100 sword kills during the same battle. One officer complained that, as the contest progressed, his speed was handicapped by nicks and dents in his sword.

Even deeper depravity curdled behind battle lines. In Manchuria, a physician named Shiro Ishii, trained at the prestigious Imperial University, was on track to become the Japanese match of the Nazis' Josef Mengele. At his Unit 731 prison complex, euphemistically called the Anti-Epidemic Water Supply and Purification Bureau, Ishii and his cohorts turned thousands of Chinese adults and infants into human guinea pigs, infecting them with the plague, anthrax, and smallpox, then cutting them open alive, without anesthesia, to judge the results. Other prisoners, which Unit 731 referred to derisively as "maruta," or logs, were subjected to excruciating experiments with frostbite and chemical weapons. Biological warfare armaments developed at Unit 731 and released in the field eventually killed tens of thousands of Chinese, with some estimates as high as 500,000. Years before the attack on Pearl Harbor, the Japanese military had proved that it could be a ruthless and depraved enemy.

The Japanese invasion was so powerful, and so horrific, that the Chinese Nationalists and Communists declared a truce in their civil war to unite against the eastern invaders. The result was a war the Japanese could not win, and could not end. The Sino-Japanese War, the true beginning of World War II, eventually resulted in the death or wounding of 3 million Chinese troops and 17 million Chinese civilians. About 500,000 Japanese were killed, with another 1.5 million wounded or felled by disease. Deaths in the Sino-Japanese War exceeded the combined death toll of every nation during World War I. In the history of the world, the number of deaths in the Sino-Japanese War was exceeded only by the Mongol conquests launched by Genghis Khan in the thirteenth century, and the civil wars in China in the third, eighth, and nineteenth centuries.

The mounting death toll in China worried Nobuo and Taeko Tatsuguchi, who pored over local newspapers for details. On the battlefield, doctors were in high demand. Nobuo did not want to be sent away. Being shipped to a hostile land overseas, far from his wife and daughter — that was not why they had returned home from California.

If the military quagmire in China made Japan increasingly desperate, it alarmed the United States. With its first push into Manchuria, and now an all-out war in China, Japan was upending the balance of power in the Far East. Foreign Minister Hachiro Arita justified his country's imperialist push by claiming creation of the Greater East Asia Co-Prosperity Sphere, which was described as a "bloc of Asian nations led by the Japanese and free of Western powers." For the Japanese, the Co-Prosperity Sphere was a Monroe Doctrine for their own backyard, a policy that would, in the words of the official government slogan, keep Asia for the Asians. Japanese imperialism increasingly was described as a spiritual quest. The battle in China amounted to a holy war, and Japan was destined under its divine origin to achieve *hakko ichiu,* a phrase that came to mean "all the world under one roof."

In the United States, President Franklin Roosevelt and others began to consider a very troubling question: Were the Japanese launching a kind of Third Reich in the Far East?

In September 1940, the Japanese only confirmed those fears by uniting with Hitler and Mussolini to sign the Tri-Partite Pact. (Four years earlier, when Japan had signed an anti-Marxist agreement with Germany, Hitler had proclaimed the Japanese to be "honorary Aryans.") The Tri-Partite Pact required Japan, Germany, and Italy to join in a mutual military defense if they came under attack by any nation not already involved in the war. The alliance was aimed directly at the United States, which had remained neutral in World War II even as the Nazis marched across Czechoslovakia, Poland, Denmark, Norway, France, Luxembourg, Belgium, and the Netherlands.

Like most Americans, Roosevelt remained more concerned about Hitler in Europe than Japan in Asia. He believed the United States Navy was already short of ships in the Atlantic, and had none to spare for a confrontation with Japan in the Pacific. Nevertheless, in 1940, Roosevelt tried to show the Japanese what power he did have by transferring the Pacific Fleet 3,000 miles from San Diego to Pearl Harbor. When asked to describe his policy with Tokyo, President Roosevelt said he would "slip the noose around Japan's neck, and give it a jerk from time to time."

The Japanese were willing to hold their breath. Hitler's quick and easy victories across Europe inspired them. With colonial European powers gripped in a battle for survival thousands of miles away, the Japanese pounced on their weakness in the Pacific by dispatching troops to French Indochina (Vietnam, Cambodia, Laos). Japan's publicly stated goal was to cut off military supplies from the Chinese, but invasion of Indochina also bolstered *hakko ichiu* and the Co-Prosperity Sphere, ideas made even easier to achieve now that France had been vanquished by Japan's new friend, Nazi Germany. Japan swept into Hanoi and Saigon, taking control of roads, rails, and ports, while converting Indochina into a client state that was forced to grant the best business deals to Tokyo.

Roosevelt was furious over the invasion.

89

Almost half the raw rubber imported to the United States came from Indochina. With battles intensifying in both Europe and China, the United States could ill-afford to run short of a commodity so crucial to its economy and military. The White House also grew concerned that Japan's expansionist military would cast an eye toward the Philippines, where the United States had spent considerable sums on military bases, harbors, and airstrips.

With Japan unwilling to back down, the Roosevelt administration jerked the noose. After the Battle of Shanghai and the Nanjing Massacre, the White House announced a "moral embargo," which put U.S. companies on notice that the president strongly opposed the sale of aircraft to Japan. As Japanese attacks on China intensified, Roosevelt extended the moral embargo to airplane parts and aviation fuel technology. When Japan invaded Indochina, Congress approved the Export Control Act, which converted the moral embargo into an enforceable embargo, banning the sale of U.S. aircraft, parts, chemicals, and minerals to Japan. Japan's refusal to withdraw troops from Indochina was greeted with an extended ban on the sale of iron and steel scrap. Meanwhile, the U.S. adopted a Lend-

Lease policy that, among other things, contributed $1.6 billion of wartime supplies to China. Roosevelt was trying to do everything he could short of military action, which had little public support. A Gallup poll found 88 percent of Americans opposed joining the rest of the world in war.

In Japan, military and political leaders increasingly blamed their costly stalemate in China on meddling outside forces. The best scapegoat was the United States, which, in addition to the embargoes, refused to grant diplomatic recognition to Japan's new dominion over Manchuria and Indochina.

The United States and Japan were at loggerheads. The one crucial material held back from embargo by the United States was oil. About 80 percent of the petroleum consumed by Japan and its war machine came from the United States. Tokyo needed American oil to power both its war and peace, and the two nations knew it. Extending the embargo to oil would be tantamount to a declaration of war.

By June 1941, Japanese companies had amassed licenses to import a nearly three-year supply of crude oil from U.S. companies. With Japan wreaking havoc in China — and dispatching 125,000 troops to Indochina — the Roosevelt administration knew the Japanese oil contracts amounted to, essentially, a license to kill. He could jerk the noose only so many times. On July 26, 1941, President Roosevelt issued Executive Order 8832, which froze all Japanese assets in the United States and effectively canceled the oil contracts. The net effect: The oil embargo of Japan was on.

The two countries launched intensive negotiations. The U.S. demanded a full Japanese pullout from China and Indochina. Japan called for a six-month cooling-off period and promised to halt its expansions if the United States would restore the flow of oil. Cut off from all U.S. supplies, Japan now had oil reserves that would last perhaps a few months. The clock ticked. In Tokyo, the press described the nation as "a fish in a pond from which the water was gradually drained away."

While diplomats talked, Japanese leaders secretly pursued an alternative solution. To the south of the new Japanese client state of French Indochina stretched the world's fourth-richest petroleum field. The Southern Resource Area of the Dutch East Indies (Indonesia) was controlled by the Netherlands, but the Dutch had been vanquished the prior year in Europe by the Nazis. A military strike on the Southern Resource Area could provide all the oil Japan needed for both its homeland and its war machine. The biggest complicating factor, once again, was the United States. Its Philippines military bases could thwart naval and troop movements from Japan to the oil fields of the Dutch East Indies.

In Tokyo, Nobuo and Taeko Tatsuguchi watched with dread as political and public opinion turned against the United States. More than almost all their countrymen, the Tatsuguchis had seen the great skyscrapers and factories that rose on the other side of the sea. Compared with Japan, the United States had nearly double the population, five times the steel production, seven times the coal, five times the ship-making capacity, six times the airplane-making capacity, and nearly ten times the gross domestic product. Japan's mighty military was barely holding its own in the war against China. How could it expect to defeat the Chinese while battling the United States as well?

For months, Nobuo Tatsuguchi had worried that he would be redeployed from his duty at the Imperial Guard to the war in China. Now Tatsuguchi feared he could be assigned to something worse — a war against his classmates from the United States.

■ ■ ■ ■

PART TWO:
LAIRD

■ ■ ■ ■

6
TRAPPED

Dick Laird was stuck. A half mile from daylight, in a crumbling crook of the Powhatan Coal Mine of southeastern Ohio, Laird had jammed his arm into a rock seam. The seam didn't give back. He tugged and pulled and jerked. No luck.

The air was dank and thick with dust. With every breath the beam from his headlamp bobbed on the mine wall. He tried to stop panting. He tried not to panic.

In the dark behind him a work crew waited. Laird did not want to let them down. Before dawn he had gathered with dozens of these men — his neighbors, his buddies, his uncles — to begin the long trek underground. At the mine entrance, he could stand upright, but by the time he had snaked through a confusing maze of tunnels to the day's work site, he was hunched on all-fours. His back throbbed. His mucus ran black. His knees were skinned raw.

Laird was only sixteen years old. It was his second year working for the Powhatan mine.

He was supposed to feel grateful for the work. It was November 1932, the depths of the Great Depression, and the unemployment rate for Ohio was 37 percent, or double the national average. In Laird's neighborhood it felt even worse. Desperate families were fleeing the shuttered factories of Cleveland, Akron, and Pittsburgh for his Appalachian hills of Belmont County, Ohio. Jobs were scarce here, but a newcomer could still shoot rabbits and grow cabbage to survive. Old-timers and newcomers eyed each other warily. If Laird made one serious mistake in his mine job, there were dozens of men hungry for the chance to do it right.

All the rock on Laird's arm was becoming unbearable. Four fingers had gone numb, and his thumb barely tingled. He had been trying to retrieve his mining pick from a partially collapsed coal seam when even more coal dropped on him. His hand was trapped alongside the wooden shaft of his pick, and it poked awkwardly in his face. He scraped the mine floor with his boots to find something, anything, to help extract himself from this mess, all without drawing attention from other miners. If he became known as a screw-up, he would surely lose his job.

On the floor his boot found a steel wedge. Ordinarily, the tool was used to widen a crack in the mine headwall before setting an explosive. Now Laird needed it to save his arm. He swept the steel closer with his foot, and, with a painful reach to the ground, scrounged up the wedge with his free hand. He hacked out mucus. He fought to catch his breath. This was it.

With all the might in his left arm, Laird rammed the wedge into the mess of rubble. Through the collapsed rock his trapped arm felt the thud. Laird slammed the wedge again, and again, and again, until the handle of his pick budged. Laird saw the movement, and thrust his shoulder hard into the handle to leverage out another inch of rock. Now his wrist could wriggle. Could he take back his hand without toppling the whole wall? The longer he waited, the more he feared his chances. Laird gathered his strength, braced himself, and pulled for dear life.

It worked. His right arm rocketed loose, free at last, but the sudden release sent Laird flying backward onto his butt. His fingers throbbed. For this he was grateful.

Pain meant they were still attached to his hand.

"You all right?" someone called from behind.

"I'm all right," Laird told him. It was an automatic response, one offered without thinking. When so many other men wanted to take his job, he'd damn well better say that he was all right. Yes, the mine had given back his arm, and the whole ordeal might cost him a fingernail or two, but the truth was that he wasn't all right. His hand was free. His life wasn't. Six more hours until his shift ended, and he was still trapped.

Laird returned that night to a house that was hard to call a home. His mother, Bertha, lived there only occasionally. She disappeared for months and then returned without warning. No one was quite sure where she went, but Laird was pretty sure he knew why she went.

Mainly, it was to get away from his father, who was also a coal miner. Frank Laird had started out with some family money — a farm in Kansas, and there were even rumors of some oil wells — but he had gambled and drunk it all away. One of Laird's earliest childhood memories was of his father stinking of booze and passed out in front of the fireplace. When his father finally came to, he complained of the heat and issued an order: "Bertha, move the fire back." She moved herself back.

Everyone in the family knew the one good thing about a father who was too drunk to stand: From the floor, he couldn't hit anyone. There came to be a magic time in the family's night when the father had guzzled enough to hit the floor, or to just swing at someone wildly and miss. That was a good night. The danger came during the father's start-up, when his temper went bad but his aim was still good. Those were the times to be out of the house.

In all his years, Laird could not remember his father giving him a single hug, or a pat on the head, or even saying, I love you. Laird thought this was how all fathers acted. Then he compared notes with other buddies. And he wondered.

He wondered, for example, about the issue of his own name. It wasn't really Dick. The official birth certificate said "Charles Laird," but his father called him Dick Warder Laird. Turns out that Dick Warder was name of the local sheriff. The father had had enough encounters with the law to realize that he needed to do something, anything, to win a soft spot in the heart of the man who could lock him up for the night.

Laird was the youngest of five children, and the oldest three, Cliff, Oak, and Earl, were hellions. For laughs, they sneaked snakes into beds at home and picked fights in the schoolyard. When the fighting slowed, Cliff took his traditional black tin lunchbox and painted it pink, with flowers. Want to make fun of his girly lunch box? Cliff was looking for any excuse for some kid to start an argument that might lead to a brawl.

The parents seemed to look for any excuse to deliver a whupping, too. The oldest son, Cliff, once offered to pay fifty cents to Dick to take over his chore of hauling in kindling and coal for the fire. Cliff failed to pay up, so Dick lifted the coins off his brother's dresser. To Laird's mother, this was theft. She ordered Dick to return the fifty cents — and to bring her two willow switches from the creek. Laird knew those branches were intended for his backside, so he secretly used his pocketknife to slice a weakening ring around them. Sure enough, during the first lash, both switches snapped. When his mother sent him back to the creek for two sturdier switches, Laird repeated his trick, and got the same result. Fed up, his mother snatched the father's razor strop, and, according to Laird, "She damned near killed me."

His sister was not spared, either. Laird returned home one day to find his mother and a young Alice in the throes of some indecipherable argument. The back-and-forth continued until the mother hoisted the little girl by the legs and dunked her headfirst into the backyard rain barrel. The mother pulled the girl out, pigtails dripping, and demanded: "Are you going to do it again?" The girl didn't answer. Back into the barrel went the girl's head, but again there was no answer. The mother delivered another dunking, and another, until finally Alice, still hanging upside down and sopping wet, replied, "No, Mother."

For long stretches during the Great Depression, Laird's family of seven lived on $1 a day. On his walks from school, Laird picked up spilled coal along the train tracks for the night's heat. The one boyhood Christmas present Laird could remember, a red Radio Flyer wagon, was given to Dick mainly to increase the amount of coal he could lug home. Years later, at age twelve, Laird had improved on his red wagon by converting an old mine dynamite box into a coal-hauling wheelbarrow. His invention was soon copied by dozens of neighborhood buddies. Their fathers couldn't fully support a family on a coal-mining paycheck, so the kids scrambled to help out with coal-mining scraps.

Hard times also forced Laird to scrounge food. In the summer, he topped off his coal wagon or wheelbarrow with dandelion greens for that night's dinner. He caught squirrels and rabbits with boxes, snares, and pit traps. When the family was especially hungry, Laird had tied a kernel of corn to a kite string and cast it out like a fishing line toward the property next door. More than once he had reeled in that night's dinner — the neighbor's chicken.

Nothing went to waste. When a mule at the coal mine broke its leg, Laird's father was ordered by the bosses to shoot and kill it. Instead, Laird's father tried the impossible. He started nursing it back to health. After several weeks, the leg healed enough for the mule to try kicking down a fence. That broke the leg all over again. The mule became stew.

Laird's boyhood passed without joy or roots. On his downward spiral of poker and alcohol, his father had moved the family at least ten times through the coal towns of Pennsylvania, West Virginia, and Ohio before Dick Laird was even six years old.

Laird couldn't remember much about each stop except the names: Harrisville, Dog Run, Basil Stop, Clarksburg, Fredericktown, Clarington, Vestaburg, Bellaire. They were ramshackle places within about a hundred miles of each other, and all rife with the feeling of desperation. Most Laird family moves came because the work had run out. Sometimes, however, the family was run out. Oak and Cliff had learned to sneak into the hills to make moonshine, which made them popular with some neighbors but not with the law. With all the moves and all the run-ins with law enforcement, the Laird family had built up a deep distrust of outsiders.

The one stable thing in Dick Laird's life was school. He loved it. The classroom was his refuge, the one safe spot where no one beat him or ridiculed him or screamed at him. It also was the only place in his life that offered him a routine: the bell clanging to start the day; the hallway scramble to separate rooms for history, geography, math, and English; the recess games of marbles, baseball, and, with the arrival of new European immigrants, soccer. Laird's favorite, music class, was held in the room called the Chapel. His voice was clear and strong. He had a knack for memorizing songs, but stood out among classmates for another reason. Laird was a fainter. All students in choir were required to stand, and by the time the choir assembled every Friday, Laird had run out of food and energy. "There he goes again," called the kids in the choir when Laird plopped over. After a few weeks, his teacher had learned to put Laird in the front row, where he was easier to catch on his way down. Even better, the choir teacher began making sure Laird had something for lunch that day. With a stale old bun or biscuit in Laird's belly, the fainting stopped.

His teachers showed him how to be meticulous. He stood up straight, kept his shirt tucked in, and looked adults in the eye. He made sure his desk was in order. He took pains to use precise handwriting. He wasn't the greatest reader, but he did enjoy math, with all its order and logic and certain answers. He got Bs but pushed for As. When his father was drinking, and his mother was disappearing, and his brothers were moonshining, and the whole family was pulling up roots again and again and again, school just made sense to Dick Laird.

At age fourteen, Laird was forced by his father to quit.

Laird was crestfallen. Education was the

ticket to a better life, the teachers always said, and Laird really wanted to believe the claim, even though he had never once met anyone who had actually used school as a way to break out of Appalachia. At the very least, every day he was in the classroom was a day he was not in the coal mine.

To his father, however, that was exactly the problem. The family needed money. School didn't pay. The mine did. It was time for the boy to start earning his keep.

Besides, the father had put in enough years so that he personally didn't have to dig anymore. He worked above ground, managing all the mining livestock. There were mules and ponies that hauled coal cars from seam to surface, and horses and oxen that moved even heavier loads to rail depots. Frank Laird knew he was lucky to breathe fresh air all day. The sooner his son got started underground, the better his chances to win promotion to work in the meadows above.

First, however, Dick Laird had to start with the most grueling grunt work. That meant hiring on as a picker. These were the boys — and every picker was indeed a boy — who stooped over vast troughs of coal destined for market and stripped out the worthless chunks of slate. In town it was easy to figure out who was working as a picker. That boy had raw hands, a hunched neck, and eyes that gravitated toward the ground instead of the sky. Laird was grateful when, after a few months, he was bumped up to a better job.

At least it was supposed to be a better job. His new assignment was working as a trapper, the kid who opened and closed underground doors for load-hauling miners. The good news was that he was upright, and, for the first time in months, his neck stopped hurting. The bad news was that standing around all day to operate doors was boring and lonely work.

Laird was angling for his next bump up as a mule driver, which at least would have allowed his legs to move, when he caught the eye again of the mine bosses.

Among his peers, Laird stood out. He was six feet tall, at least a forehead higher than most others who labored underground. Even more importantly, Laird had wingspan. In a coal mine, long arms were wasted on a mule driver.

So at age sixteen, Laird started on the real deal. Like many of the better young coal miners, Laird had strength and stamina, toughness and drive, the heart to push a little harder when others slumped exhausted over their picks. But there were also traits that set him apart. He showed up clean to work and kept his tools scrubbed and organized. He listened to his foreman. He made a work plan and kept to it. In some ways, figuring out coal extraction problems deep below the surface of the earth was like figuring out fraction and decimal problems in the classroom with seventh grade math teachers. If he kept plugging away, he figured out the answer.

At about this time, people outside the house stopped referring to him by his first name or nickname. From now on, it was Laird, just straight up Laird. Being known almost always by only his last name was one more proof that he had grown up early.

After a few more months, the Powhatan Coal Mine turned Laird into an explosives man.

The promotion played to Laird's strengths, allowing him to come up with a specific routine and insisting that everyone follow it. First he ordered the shorter men on his crew to scrape out, with mining picks, a three-foot wedge at the bottom of a coal seam. Then he had the crew drill the face with a series of holes, which Laird filled with black powder charges. If Laird placed and angled each bore correctly, then his simple blast would shower tons of material onto the mine floor.

It was rarely that easy. For starters, everyone in the mine wanted something different from him. Bosses wanted him to use less black powder, because that saved the company money. Miners, however, wanted bigger blasts, because that freed up more coal for extraction. Everyone wanted to cut the amount of time spent setting up for new detonations, but extra time to Laird meant extra safety. If there was just one unseen weakness in the wall, or too much explosive in the wrong spot, or one faulty bore angle, then everything could come crashing down on Laird's head. Or, as he already had learned the hard way, onto his hand.

In his two years working underground, Laird had seen plenty that went wrong — mangled fingers, crushed pelvises, smashed feet. (By the time he was sixteen, Laird himself had already broken one leg, two ribs, and four fingers, plus his nose and left foot twice.) And then there were the accidents that were much worse.

Though it was bad luck to talk about fatal accidents while still working underground, miners couldn't avoid the headlines they saw in town. The bad news was steady and frequent. In just the past four years, there were 195 men lost in an explosion at the Mather No. 1 in Pennsylvania; 17 at the No. 1 at Yukon, West Virginia; 10 at the Baltimore No. 5 in Parsons, Pennsylvania; 13 at the Irvons No. 3 at Coalport, Pennsylvania; 14 at the Kingston No. 5 in Kingston, West Virginia; 46 at the Kinloch in Parnassus, Pennsylvania; 12 at Yukon in Arnettsville, West Virginia; 16 at the Pioneer in Kettle Island, Kentucky; 82 at the No. 6 in Millfield, Ohio; 38 at the Boissevain in Boissevain, Virginia; 10 at the Splashdam No. 6 in Splashdam, Virginia; 23 at the Zero in Yancey, Kentucky; 54 at the Moweaqua in Moweaqua, Illinois. To most people the mine names and numbers of deaths were a blur, but Laird was acutely aware of every accident. He felt like he was living on borrowed time.

Coal mining remained one of the world's most dangerous professions. In Laird's first year of work, a total of 2,063 coal miners were reported killed on the job in the United States.

In other words, about one of every 340 miners who started work on January 1 would be killed by the end of the year. Laird looked around the crowds of men gathering inside Powhatan every shift change and wondered which ones wouldn't make it back out. Would it be that father? Or that buddy from school? Or would his own neck be snapped? Every trip down that long, dark, dusty shaft just increased his chances of becoming one of the 340.

On his long walks home from the mine, Laird doubted he would even have the chance to grow up and make a living from coal. The Great Depression was ravaging business across the world, but few businesses had suffered like the U.S. coal industry. In just three years, annual production had plummeted 40 percent, from 608 million tons in 1929 to just 359 million tons in 1932. Prices plunged. Mines shuttered. In many Appalachian towns, nine out of ten coal miners were out of work. The men lucky enough to still have jobs faced pay cuts and fewer hours.

Grasping for survival, mine owners scrambled to attack costs. That meant mechanization. The mules and oxen that used to haul coal were replaced by conveyers, trolleys, and trains. More jobs lost. Three hundred miles away, in Detroit, Henry Ford was declaring that machinery was the new messiah, but in Appalachia, swapping men for machines spawned anger, resentment, and mobs. Unions, weak from unemployment and fractured from political radicalization, could not mount effective opposition, and lawlessness rose. In parts of West Virginia, superintendents hired armed guards to deliver new equipment to mines.

In the rush to dig up more coal more cheaply than ever, safety standards slipped. Laird narrowly escaped another wall collapse. Converting the coal trolley to electrical power meant that charged wires dangled from mine ceilings. Sometimes those wires fell. In air thick with coal dust, an electrified mine was one spark from catastrophe. (In fact, years later, on July 5, 1944, the Powhatan suffered one of the worst accidents in U.S. mining history. Sixty-six men were trapped underground and killed when a miner accidentally knocked a wire onto a trolley rail and ignited a flash fire. Rescuers needed 644 days to recover the bodies.)

By his seventeenth birthday, Laird had concluded that coal mining was a dead end. He tried to punch his way out of it.

The one tool his older brothers had shown him how to use was his fists, and Laird turned out to be a tough boxer. His reach was long, and he was skilled at withstanding punishment. He was patient. He threw few wild punches. After a full shift underground at the mine, he trained by running home. Sometimes between rounds he hacked up a wad of black mucus, but many of his opponents did the same. Within a few months, Laird had won enough matches to advance beyond the local Golden Gloves. At the regional tournament in Pittsburgh, though, trouble struck. In a pre-fight health checkup, the ring doctor discovered that Laird suffered from a heart murmur. That disqualified him from any more boxing. Boxing was yet another path that would not lead out.

By 1933, life beyond the Powhatan mine looked as grim as life inside. Across the country, 100,000 people a week were losing their jobs, and one of every four Americans lived in a house with no regular wage earner. As many as two million Americans wandered the country homeless. Tens of thousands of people settled in cardboard shantytowns in New York's Central Park, in Chicago, St. Louis, Los Angeles, and Seattle. Almost half of the nation's 25,000 banks had failed, wiping out savings accounts of nine million people. Food riots erupted in Minneapolis, Oklahoma City, San Francisco, and central Arkansas.

And that was just the man-made depression. On the Great Plains, where Laird's father had grown up, Mother Nature had vanquished any thoughts of the family returning. Drought and wind had conspired to turn more than 100 million acres of farmland into a Dust Bowl of despair. The natural disaster left a half million Americans both homeless and jobless. Billowing mile-high walls of black dirt clouds had blotted out the sun half a continent away in the Ohio River Valley. As if Appalachia needed the world any darker.

At home, Laird expected more cuts at the mine and more bottles from his father. He needed a new direction.

In September 1935, Laird joined a buddy for a weekend trip twenty miles up the Ohio River, to Wheeling, West Virginia. The plan was to cut loose, drink whiskey, and meet girls. Then the buddy persuaded him to stop inside a military recruiting office.

The more Laird heard about the U.S. Army, the more he liked. Being a soldier was a job, a steady job, and it was above ground where you could breathe deep and see the sun. Sure, the military was all about confronting danger, but this was peacetime. America was still weary from the last world war, and Laird knew no one who had the appetite for another. Could his odds of being killed in the peacetime Army really be any worse than his 1-in-340 chance at the

Powhatan mine?

Best of all, the Army was his gateway out of Appalachia, a fresh start in a new place. He could serve his country, and, with a dependable salary, his family, too. He knew his parents would approve. This was the break he was looking for.

But there were a few big hitches. For starters, to be accepted into the Army, Laird had to pass a written exam. Recruiters assured him the test was no big deal, but it struck at the heart of Laird's worst insecurity. He had no book smarts. He could drop a squirrel with a headshot from three trees away, but he didn't know anything about algebra, geometry, chemistry, or physics. His knowledge of U.S. history was sketchy, and he knew even less about the world beyond. He didn't read books. In the how-to manuals that explained the practical, such as car repairs and home electrical wiring, Laird usually skipped the text and went straight for the pictures. How could he ever pass a written Army test?

Luckily, in the few years that Laird had gone to school, he had paid attention. He remembered multiplication and long division. He could name the president (Franklin Delano Roosevelt, elected after pledging "a New Deal" for the American people);

vice president (a Texan, Cactus Jack Garner, who famously described the nation's No. 2 job as "not worth a bucket of warm piss"); and the number of stars on the U.S. flag (forty-eight, with the admittance of New Mexico and Arizona). Recruiters told him he scored an 85 on his test. He was in.

Or so he thought. Laird soon learned that he faced another obstacle. He had to pass a physical exam. The recruiters hadn't given this test a second thought — Laird was six feet tall and 160 pounds, with the sculpted shoulders and arms that came from working coal all day — but Laird sank into a panic. He had been forced out of Golden Gloves boxing by a heart murmur. Would the same ailment end his Army enlistment?

Laird mentioned his fear to his buddy, who mentioned it to another guy, who told somebody else. Next thing he knew, Laird was drinking some mysterious liquid that, the stranger claimed, would suppress the heart murmur in time for the physical a few days later.

Did the elixir work? Was the Army doctor incompetent? Or was the military so hard up for peacetime recruits that it turned a deaf ear onto a teenage recruit's bum ticker? Laird never figured out the true answer, but the Army gave his heart a passing grade.

Two hurdles down, one big one to go. Laird was to report for duty in September, or three months before his eighteenth birthday. There was no wiggle room in the military age requirement — a seventeen-year-old could not join the U.S. Army.

He had no way around the age problem. His birth certificate couldn't lie. His birthday was December 18, and there was no changing that. After coming home from the Army recruiting office, though, Laird had felt like he was in a different place. He'd told his parents about his sign-up, and, as expected, they approved of it. He'd quit the mine and said his goodbyes to all his family and friends. In his heart and his mind, Laird was already in the Army. If only the Army would take an underage soldier.

Laird decided to chance it. He boarded an eastbound train in Bellaire, Ohio, and rode 130 miles west to Columbus, home of the Fort Hayes Army base. It was the furthest from home Laird had ever traveled, and also the furthest west. Columbus was hot, flat, and, with a population of 300,000, extremely crowded. It smelled better than Pittsburgh, though.

At Fort Hayes, Laird fell in line behind other recruits. He filled out his paperwork, but had the feeling no one was examining it very carefully. When an Army admissions worker asked for his year of birth, Laird responded, truthfully, 1916.

That was it. Nobody asked him about the month or date of his birth. It was all spelled out on his forms, but no questions were asked. At the age of seventeen years and nine months, Charles Warder "Dick" Laird was accepted for training in the United States Army.

7
ESCAPE

She was out of his league, a real looker, the kind of woman who made serious men go mushy. She had eyes like Marlene Dietrich but a face that just wanted to smile. Her dimples proved it.

Her name was Rose Thompson. She was Dick Laird's blind date, set up by an Army buddy, and he couldn't believe his luck. He had been assured that his blind date had a "nice personality." As they walked the sidewalks of Columbus, Dick in his service uniform and Rose in a pretty dress, she was turning heads. Laird couldn't decide whether to feel proud or angry that so many men were eyeballing his date.

Laird was naturally shy and had little experience with girls. He couldn't think of what to say to Rose. He didn't want to mess this up. He could tell that she felt a little nervous, too. She compensated by talking, not quite a babble, but enough to carry much of the conversation by herself.

There was the weather, and life in Columbus, and how Laird had survived his six-week Army recruit training. Most of all, though, were the stories from the heart. On their first date, and then the second, and the third and beyond, Laird was struck by how much they had in common.

Like Laird, Rose Thompson had grown up in the Ohio River Valley, but about 160 miles farther south, in Huntington, West Virginia. She had lived in houses with no running water or electricity, and had to use cardboard to patch holes in her shoes. She'd also had a miserable family life.

Rose's parents divorced when she was four. Her mother died soon after, and Rose moved in with her grandmother until she died, too. Rose then spent years being bounced between aunts, grandparents, stepmothers, and other relatives who didn't want her. On many nights, all that stood between Rose and another merciless whupping was her older brother, Hen. When he married at age fifteen, Rose lost her main source of love and protection.

On their date night walks around town, Rose confided to Dick that she was treated as a "slave girl" who labored mainly to raise two daughters of another aunt. Rose called them "society girls," though they never wore white gloves or sipped tea. To Rose, a society girl was someone who didn't have workdays that started before dawn to fetch water, make everyone breakfast, clean the house, do the laundry, make dinner, and help the girls with their homework. Around all this, Rose tried to fit in time for school.

Like Laird, she found refuge in the classroom. She idolized her teachers and dreamed of leading her own students one day. She worked hard enough to finish at the top of her high school class, but panicked at the idea of delivering a valedictorian or salutatorian speech on graduation day. Rose did not want to be the center of attention, so a classmate delivered the commencement speech instead. She couldn't afford college tuition, and enrolled at a secretarial school.

Hoping for a break from raising someone else's children, Rose moved in with yet another aunt, Ora. She was fine, but had a husband, Adam, who drank all day, every day, and a brother who sometimes joined him.

Something had happened to Rose at Aunt Ora's house. Rose wouldn't tell Laird what — she was private like that — and Laird didn't feel that he had any business pressing her on it. All he knew is that Rose left home in a hurry to seek a fresh start in Columbus. She kept in touch with her family in West Virginia about as often as Laird did — hardly ever.

With the shared experience of an awful childhood and broken family life, Laird really felt something for Rose. Sometimes it felt like lust, and sometimes it was love. Either way, she was on his mind a lot. He thought about her during Company D's fifty-mile marches along Highway 23 from Fort Hayes to Chillicothe. She was on his mind between blasts of mortar fire at the training range, and during his hours-long marathons of painstaking work copying maps.

When Laird had won expert marksmanship scores on the .45 caliber pistol, and the .30 caliber machine gun, and the .30-06 rifle and bayonet, he was proud to tell Rose. When he was among the select few chosen for security duty at the Kentucky Derby, he told Rose all about it. Rose was also the first to know when Laird gained promotion to private first class.

"The Army must have been my calling because I took to it like a duck to water," Laird wrote in his journal. The military gave him everything that his life in Appalachia did not. He had structure, rigor, rules, routine, and camaraderie. On top of that, he got a daily breakfast, lunch, and dinner. Army life was boosting Laird's strength and confidence. The regular meals also boosted his weight.

His wallet, however, still needed help. The problem central to most of Laird's dates was figuring ways to stretch his meager military salary. A typical night out for Laird and Rose was seeing a 15-cent movie, then walking arm in arm across East State Street for a bowl of 10-cent chili at the diner. Laird and Rose repeated the ritual often enough to become friends with a waitress, who occasionally favored them with free refills of chili and extra handfuls of crackers. The one free entertainment Laird and Rose enjoyed on date night was playing Let's-Sneak-Past-Rose's-Landlady. She had banned men from visiting the apartment of any female tenant. Laird learned how to shinny up the apartment building's rain spout.

When Laird won his second Army promotion, to corporal, he beamed and told Rose how his pay was rising from $21 a month to $45. That night at the diner, they ordered steak.

Not all was bliss. Every time Rose felt that Laird was settling down, and thinking about making a life with her, he did something wild and reckless. His Company D had a reputation for debauchery, and Laird decided he was honor-bound to meet it. Residents of Chillicothe had learned to fear visits from Laird's unit. "When Company B comes down from Fort Hayes," the Chillicothe locals warned, "bring in all the girls. But when Company D comes down, bring in all the girls — and the dogs." With the rest of Company D, Laird drank and brawled in bars and raised hell on the streets. His father would have been proud.

At one point, while on a training mission in Fort Knox, Kentucky, Laird met a fellow soldier who also was from West Virginia. In the minds of Laird and Private Russell Hull, the states of West Virginia and Kentucky held in common one great thing: moonshine. They believed that West Virginia's must be better, but just to make sure they forked over $3 for a gallon of hooch that, true to stereotype, came in a jug with a finger hole.

Several hours later, Laird and Hull were sprawled beneath an oak tree and swapping slurred stories about their West Virginia fathers, Laird's the menacing coal miner and Hull's the Appalachian preacher. Laird grew so drunk that, when he stood up to relieve himself, he misfired. When the drinking buddy finally stopped laughing, he managed to direct the wobbly Laird back to the Company D barracks and into the shower, where the young soldiers had the misfortune of being seen by their squad sergeant.

If he were back home in West Virginia, Laird would have used a simple left jab and right hook to dispatch Sergeant Taczanowski, who stood just five-foot-two and carried the nickname Squeaky, for a voice that reminded troops of a barking squirrel. But Laird was in the Army now, and Laird had to respect rank. Even drunk, Laird knew he should not fight his Army superiors, though he seriously considered it.

The next morning, as punishment, Sergeant Squeaky assigned an extremely hung-over Laird to garbage detail. The first whiff of cafeteria garbage, combined with the smell of coffee grounds, made Laird keel over with nausea.

"I'm too sick to be doing this today," Laird told his sergeant.

"No, you're too young to be getting that drunk," the sergeant replied.

Rose agreed. There were things about Laird that she just didn't understand. Laird kept telling Rose that he loved her. If he really did love her, though, then why was he going on those big weekend benders? Couldn't he control himself? He'd always seemed so honest and sincere. Why couldn't he just grow up? She knew Laird had a strong inner compass, if only he would heed it. Was it possible to turn him around? Did she even want to try?

And then, one day, these questions were no longer just abstractions.

Rose was pregnant.

It's hard to say who was more flabbergasted by the news.

Laird felt like he had been run over by a train. In his last few months in the Army, he was finally making way in the new direction in his life. The coal mines were behind him, and he was a world away from the misery at home. He enjoyed regular meals, a warm bed, friends, and, for the first time in his life, some sense of security. On weekends off, he largely had the freedom to do as he pleased. He was making something of himself. A baby? Marriage? Fatherhood and family? He wasn't ready for that.

Rose, however, had no choice. In the 1930s, motherhood without marriage was shameful. It would make her a social outcast. She was barely making ends meet now on a typist's salary — she'd had to hold off the landlord a few times while she scraped together enough for the rent. How could she support herself and a baby, too? She had no family, no money, and no prospects for help. For Rose, marriage with Dick Laird wasn't just the right thing to do. It was the only thing to do.

On top of this, there was the issue of Rose's secret, the whole reason why she had moved to Columbus in the first place. Two years earlier, long before she had even met Laird, Rose was living with an aunt and uncle when she was raped by another relative, though Rose was reluctant to use the word "rape." As she wrote in her diary, "It wasn't really that. It was just that he was older and held me down and I really didn't know what was going on."

The result, though, was devastating. Wrote Rose: "I got pregnant in just one time."

Aunt Ora and Uncle Adam threatened to kill the relative, who responded by running away, never to be seen or heard from again. This left Rose alone and sixteen years old, with a baby on the way.

Rose couldn't tell if her father and brother were disgusted or just ashamed. Either way, they did not want an unwed teenage mother in the family. They gave Rose a grand total of $4 and put her on the bus to Columbus to "deal" with the baby. Unfortunately, that

$4 could buy only half the bus fare. Short of cash, the pregnant Rose was forced off the bus in Chillicothe, where she stood by the side of the road to hitchhike the remaining fifty miles.

Fortunately, she was picked up along the way by a sympathetic farmer and his wife, who offered Rose a room to sleep in, plus $5 a week, if she helped them with vegetable canning. Rose worked until her pregnancy's eighth month. Just before Christmas, she moved out of the farmer's home and into the Florence Crittenton Home for unwed mothers in Columbus.

On the night of December 31, 1934, Rose gave birth to a girl. It was late enough on New Year's Eve that the doctor wondered aloud whether he should try to hold off on the delivery until after midnight. The first baby of the New Year always received a story in the local newspaper and a cascade of gifts and prizes from local businesses.

The Crittenton manager, however, set the doctor straight. Her pregnant residents were considered bad girls, and a bastard child put up for immediate adoption was definitely not something to be hailed by the Columbus business community. Even if Rose's baby was the first of the New Year, nobody was going to celebrate it. Rose put her baby girl up for adoption. She never met the couple who accepted the baby.

After childbirth, Rose did not return to West Virginia. No one back home wanted to see her, and, considering the way she had been treated, she had no one back home she wanted to see. She stayed in the Crittenton home, patching together odd job after odd job in town, until she had saved enough money to move into a room, with a roommate, at a nearby boardinghouse.

That's when she met Dick Laird. She liked him a lot. He was tall and handsome, strong enough to go jaw-to-jaw with an Army rowdy in a bar, but with a gentle streak that led him to bring a handful of flowers, sometimes picked from a stranger's garden, on some of their dates. He wasn't a smooth talker. He fidgeted when he ran out of words, which was often. Still, he was honest and sincere. He looked her right in the eye. Rose wanted to tell Laird about her past — the rape, the pregnancy, and the baby — but she was afraid the story would scare him off. She really didn't want to scare him off.

Now Rose Thompson was eighteen years old, single, and pregnant for the second time. Dick Laird was the best thing she had going. In fact, he was about the only thing she had going.

But the more her pregnant belly grew, the less Laird saw of her. At first he blamed his absences on increased training at faraway Fort Knox. Then he claimed other weekend obligations. Finally, when Rose pressed hard for marriage, Laird responded bluntly: He couldn't marry her because he didn't rank high enough in the Army.

It's not clear whether Laird truly believed he had to become an officer to be allowed to marry, or if he was just using the murky rules of the U.S. Army as a convenient excuse to duck responsibility for his girl-friend's pregnancy. Either way, Rose was crushed. She would have her baby out of wedlock.

This time, though, she was determined to stay out of the Crittenton home. Giving up her baby for adoption last time had scarred her heart with guilt, anger, and despair. She didn't think she could survive another adoption. Whether Laird wanted to help or not, Rose was determined to keep this baby. But how?

Rose had no family to help work over her dilemma, but she did have the next best thing: Her boardinghouse roommate, Peg, had married and moved forty miles east, to Springfield, Ohio. The roommate and her husband, Don, invited Rose to live with them. On September 18, 1937, Rose gave birth in Don and Peg's house. She named the baby Peggy Laird, though she would call her baby P.J., to avoid the confusion of having two Peggys in the house.

There was no confusion of having two fathers in the house. Don was a great help with the baby, but Laird was mostly absent. He visited occasionally, and seemed more interested in the baby than the mother. As the weeks passed by, Laird visited less and less, until one week he did not visit at all. He abandoned Rose, and he abandoned their daughter.

In her diary, Rose described this period as "a very black point in my life." As for Laird, he didn't really describe it at all. On the baby's first birthday, September 18, 1938, Laird received his honorable discharge from the Army.

After two years in the Army, Dick Laird had his new life. He still hadn't come to terms with it. He returned to Bellaire, Ohio, where he pooled his life savings, $84.68, with his brother Cliff, and bought a Chevy dump truck. The plan was to start a coal-hauling business, but many of his customers were broke and didn't pay. At one point, while trying to pry off a flat tire on a winter day, Laird accidentally whacked himself in the mouth with a sledgehammer handle, splitting his lip and knocking out his two front teeth. The accident led Laird to tally up the bodily damage toll of his first twenty-one years of life — one broken leg, two broken ribs, four broken fingers, a left foot broken twice, and a nose broken twice. His list omitted Rose's broken heart.

A few months of life back in Bellaire had convinced him, once again, that he didn't want to live there. The military remained his best chance for a ticket out. Why not try again? Joined by a buddy, Laird reenlisted in the Army on August 1, 1939. The Army fixed his busted teeth. He was assigned to the Brooklyn Army base, then shipped out via the Panama Canal to San Francisco and, ultimately, the Fort Shafter Army Base in Honolulu, Hawaii.

He was 4,600 miles from Rose and his toddler daughter. Rose figured he wasn't coming back. She was broke, lonely, and scared. Hoping for something better, she met and married a poker-playing cab driver named George Breckenridge. "I was looking for a family who would love me," Rose wrote, "and he was looking for a doormat. I became one for a time." Rose quickly became pregnant again. Soon after, her new husband started beating her hard enough and often enough for their landlords to take notice. When their daughter, Nancy Lou, was born, Rose realized that her husband was losing so much money on the gambling tables that he couldn't pay the bills. Rose went back to work. She felt her life falling apart again. Her daughter with Laird was being raised by friends. Her daughter with Breckenridge was being raised by her mother-in-law. Rose was being beaten time and again. She could not imagine any way out.

And then, one day, out of the blue, in 1941, Laird returned home on leave from Hawaii. He came to see his daughter, Peggy, but spent the most time with Rose. He felt ashamed for abandoning them. Laird told her he had grown up during his second Army enlistment and that he was a new man. He fell in love again with Rose. The feeling was mutual. "I knew I could never live without him," Rose confided to her diary.

Laird returned to California for Army duty, but Rose made up her mind. She wanted a life with him. Aided by landlords who testified to the savagery of her beatings, Rose went to court to divorce her husband. A judge ended the marriage and ordered $20 a week in child support, but Rose never saw a penny. Reality set in. She had two daughters, an iffy bookkeeping job, and an exhausting struggle each month just to make the rent. She couldn't take it anymore. She dropped off Peggy with friends, packed up her other daughter, Nancy Lou, and left on a train for California to take Laird at his word.

When Rose arrived in Los Angeles, however, Laird was nowhere to be found. Rose panicked. She had spent nearly all her money to travel 2,300 miles to see Laird. Was he abandoning her again? Rose had no idea how to contact Laird other than writing him a letter. That would take days. With a toddler in a train station and no place to stay, Rose had little time to spare.

Desperate, she hurried to a Red Cross office and begged for help. Workers there were able to figure out that Laird was in the Mojave Desert on Army maneuvers run by General George Patton. For ten days, Rose waited in a $2-a-day hotel.

When his military maneuvers finally ended, Laird knew what he wanted to do. For the first time, he could envision a life, a good life, beyond work and Appalachia. He had no engagement ring. Rose didn't care. Outside his Army base in San Luis Obispo,

Laird and Rose found a justice of the peace and married. They were together at last, and they couldn't be happier.

■ ■ ■ ■

PART THREE:
WAR

■ ■ ■ ■

8

PEARL

In the span of two hours, the world changed. Starting at 7:48 a.m. on December 7, 1941, the Japanese killed more than 2,400 Americans; sank or damaged 21 ships; and damaged nearly 90 percent of the U.S. aircraft in Hawaii. In the process, they rocked the United States out of its isolationism and into World War II.

Dick Laird and Nobuo Tatsuguchi were stationed thousands of miles from the carnage, but Pearl Harbor was the boulder that triggered the landslide that would certainly, inevitably, force them together.

At the time of the sneak attack, Laird was training with his 7th Infantry Division in Northern California. In the days following the attack, he and his unit were deployed as emergency defense troops across the Pacific Coast. They girded for battle when patrols reported that the Japanese fleet was assembling just ten miles off Monterey, then

164 miles from San Francisco. They braced when another report held that enemy paratroopers had landed just east of California State Route 1. All these alerts turned out to be false, but Laird and his fellow soldiers were on edge.

After three months of chasing rumors, Army commanders concluded that the Japanese weren't invading California, at least for now. They reassembled troops and began training for a counterattack. Laird practiced loading boats at the Monterey Pier and he repeated amphibious landings at the mouth of the Salinas River. By April 1942, Laird and his fellow soldiers were moved to the Mojave Desert, where, they assumed, they were preparing to take on the Desert Fox, Nazi Field Marshal Erwin Rommel, in the sands of North Africa. After all, they were a motorized division that specialized in tanks and trucks. Laird learned how to withstand the heat and to make water last in the aridity. He took salt pills to prevent heat stress. Guns, mortars, and transports were all broken down and adapted to work in the wind and grit of the desert. He was issued desert boots, desert clothes, and desert canteens. Dick Laird was ready to fight Nazis in the desert.

Then plans changed.

Because Japan recorded time on the opposite side of the International Date Line, Pearl Harbor day in Tokyo was December 8, 1941. To the Japanese, it was not a Day of Infamy. It wasn't much of a day of anything. Their country had already been at war for four years and suffered hundreds of thousands of deaths and casualties in China and Indochina. Yes, the sneak attack at Pearl Harbor had been an outstanding military success, but it was also just another front in a fight thousands of miles from the homeland.

Nobuo Tatsuguchi knew it was much worse.

The new war broke his heart. He loved Japan, but he also loved America. He could not understand how his countrymen believed they could defeat a nation so vast and mighty. Even the military mastermind of the Pearl Harbor attack, Admiral Isoroku Yamamoto, doubted the path his country had chosen. "Should hostilities once break out between Japan and the United States," Yamamoto wrote to a wealthy Japanese businessman and politician, "it would not be enough that we take Guam and the

Philippines, nor even Hawaii and San Francisco. To make victory certain, we would have to march into Washington and dictate the terms of peace in the White House. I wonder if our politicians have confidence as to the final outcome and are prepared to make the necessary sacrifices."

More than any other top Japanese leader, Yamamoto knew the United States. He had traveled across the country and even studied at Harvard for a semester to learn English. He believed Japanese generals had arrogantly overestimated their own power and downplayed the strength of the U.S. "It is a mistake to regard Americans as luxury-loving and weak," he told former classmates from Nagaoka in September 1941, just three months before Pearl Harbor. "I can tell you that they are full of spirit, adventure, fight, and justice. Their thinking is scientific and well-advanced. Lindbergh's solo flight across the Atlantic was an act characteristic of Americans, adventuresome but scientifically based. Remember that American industry is much more developed than ours, and, unlike us, they have all the oil they want. Japan cannot vanquish the United States. Therefore we should not fight the U.S."

Despite Yamamoto's opposition, Japanese

generals and politicians were convinced more of their greatness than their limitations. Just ten hours after their stunning attack at Pearl Harbor, the Japanese launched another front to the south and invaded the Philippines. They decimated U.S. planes on the ground, forcing the remaining U.S. Navy fleet in the Philippines to flee to Java. Five months later, the Imperial Army had vanquished General Douglas MacArthur and his ground troops, too. More than 60,000 American and Filipino servicemen were taken as prisoners of war; as many as 10,000 died or were killed by Japanese brutality during the sixty-mile Bataan Death March.

Every new battle, every escalation in war — it all rocked the Tatsuguchis. Because of Pearl Harbor, the loyalty of Nobuo Tatsuguchi was questioned every day. He assured any and all who listened that he was faithful to Japan, but he could not escape the whispers. Why had he lived so long in the United States? Why did he keep some American customs? Could Nobuo Tatsuguchi be a spy? He knew the questions were ridiculous, but, as far as he knew, he was still the only surgeon in the Imperial Army who hadn't been rewarded with the status and pay of an officer. He was an honorable

Japanese military man. His doubters could not be sated.

The suspicions spanned the Pacific. On February 19, 1942, President Roosevelt signed an executive order that forced the relocation and incarceration of 110,000 Americans of Japanese ancestry. Deepening the racial wounds of the war, Roosevelt's order meant that internment camps were for people who looked like the war enemy in the Pacific, not the white German or white Italian war enemies across the Atlantic. If the Tatsuguchis had remained in California and applied for citizenship in the United States, they would have lost all assets and been imprisoned throughout the war. Internment camp in the United States or forced military service in Japan — the Tatsuguchis faced only bad options.

In Japan, Nobuo Tatsuguchi's loyalties were questioned, but his medical skills were needed. His native country could no longer afford to allow a talented doctor to stay home in Tokyo.

Tatsuguchi soon received two pieces of life-changing news: His wife was pregnant. And he was being reassigned to serve overseas.

He and his wife were crushed. Taeko had a toddler at home, with another baby on the way, and the whole family was scraping by on the meager salary of an enlisted man. Now her husband was being sent away in wartime for an indefinite period. How was she going to do this?

All Tatsuguchi could do was offer calm reassurance. Remember — he was a surgeon, not a warrior. He would fulfill his duty to his faith and his country by healing, not killing. Besides, doctors were supposed to remain out of the line of fire, weren't they?

His deployment did offer one possible advantage. Serving his country overseas should remove all doubt about his dedication to his homeland. In his heart, Tatsuguchi was an optimist. He did not want to fight, but he did not want to be doubted, either. This was his chance to prove his fidelity to his homeland.

And so Tatsuguchi was dispatched 3,000 miles from home, to the real prize of Japan's war in the Pacific — the oil fields and rubber plantations of the Dutch East Indies. The Japanese Southern Force had launched the assault against Borneo ten days after Pearl Harbor. Within two months, fifty Japanese warships and 50,000 troops had claimed the entire region, from Singapore south and east in a three-thousand-mile swath to Sumatra, Java, and New Guinea.

Tatsuguchi arrived seven months after the fighting was over, in October 1942. He was assigned to Rabaul, New Guinea, the main military base of the Japanese in the South Pacific, and found comparatively little medical work. The entire military operation had claimed the lives of fewer than a thousand Japanese. However, the subsequent Japanese occupation of the Dutch East Indies was heartless and brutal, killing an estimated four million through famine, disease, lack of medical attention, forced labor, and executions of prisoners of war.

If Tatsuguchi witnessed war atrocities in the South Pacific, he didn't tell his wife about them. He was a proud Japanese soldier, but a proud Seventh-day Adventist, too, and he returned home to his pregnant wife in Tokyo later that same month without confiding any crisis in either his religious faith or his military oath.

Taeko could not help but wonder how Nobuo's military indoctrination was changing his outlook on life. The Japanese Infantry Manual pushed for the creation of fighting zealots. "A striking feature of the doctrine is its excessive emphasis on 'spirit,' " wrote Japanese military historian Saburo Ienaga. "The literature is full of phrases about 'the attack spirit,' 'confidence in certain victory,' 'loyalty to the emperor,' 'love of country,' 'absolute sincerity,' and 'sacrifice one's life to the country, absolute obedience to superiors.' "

Even more ominously, troops were taught that surrender in battle carried the ultimate shame. "A commander who allows his unit to surrender to the enemy without fighting to the last man or who concedes a strategic area to the enemy shall be punishable by death," the manual stated. "If a commander is leading troops in combat and they are captured by the enemy, even if the commander has performed his duty to the utmost, he shall be punishable by up to six months confinement." Once in war, Tatsuguchi knew his choice would be victory or death.

On temporary leave back home in Japan, Tatsuguchi began to display an unusual interest in the North Pacific. Like all soldiers, Tatsuguchi had been banned from discussing any future troop movements, even with his wife. Still, Taeko couldn't help but notice his newfound curiosity about islands to the north of Tokyo and beyond.

While her husband studied maps and books about flora and fauna of the North Pacific, Taeko had more pressing concerns at home. This second pregnancy was much more difficult. She suffered morning sickness when she woke up, and fought to keep down food the rest of the day. She felt frazzled. Were her nerves on edge because of her pregnancy, or her husband? Taeko worried about both.

She had good reason. On a rainy night shortly after returning from New Guinea, her husband came home and delivered the abrupt news: He was shipping out immediately to an undisclosed location.

There was no time to delay. The weather was bad. Taeko was not feeling well. Their young daughter, Misako Joy, was already asleep, so Taeko decided it would be better not to accompany her husband to the base to bid him farewell before his next deployment.

As the days passed, Taeko was filled with regret. Had she made the wrong decision to not send him off with a heartfelt goodbye at the base? He had returned home from Papua New Guinea after only a few weeks. Surely he would return home soon from this new but secret deployment. Still, this was war. Was the comfort of a sleeping child more important than a chance to spend the most time possible with a husband being shipped out to some mysterious new war assignment? Where was Nobuo? When would she see him again?

She knew the Imperial Army limited his communications home. Spies could scan love letters to wives and girlfriends looking for any mention, however inadvertent, of troop movements or likely attacks. This meant Nobuo was banned from mentioning a date or location in his letters. The easiest way for whole swaths of his letters to be blacked out by military censors was for him to hint at any future plan. Yet Taeko longed to hear any news.

Finally, after several weeks, she received a postcard from the northern Japanese island of Hokkaido. "You must have been wondering what happened to me since I didn't write for quite some time," Nobuo wrote. "The autumn flowers are blooming near the barracks and surrounding mountains." To win passage through military censors, Nobuo's letters had to be intentionally vague. Still, there was one sentence, wedged between his more mundane talk of the scenery and military food, that stood out: "I might see my classmates from med school."

Taeko began to suspect the worst. The attack on Pearl Harbor was almost a year ago. The United States had been driven out of the Philippines. At this point, Taeko knew the only way for her husband to meet his medical school classmates was on a battle-field.

One day she received a package in the mail from Nobuo. It contained the officer's uniform he had purchased for 400 yen. Taeko did not know what to make of it. She worried that the return of the uniform meant he had given up any expectation of being appointed as an officer. That would be devastating, both to him and to her. So many of their hopes had been pinned on his promotion, which would have meant more money for the family, but, more importantly, would have signaled that he had finally earned the trust and respect of the Imperial Army. Why was Nobuo the only surgeon who had been held back from being named an officer? The package from Nobuo contained no explanation. All Taeko could do was guess. None of her guesses were pleasant.

Not long after, in the new year of 1943, more mail arrived. This time it was not a package from her husband, but an impersonal military envelope. Taeko braced herself. The Japanese military custom was to send a personal item from a soldier before a battle that could prove fatal.

Taeko opened the envelope. It contained a lock of Nobuo's black hair.

Somewhere in the North Pacific, Nobuo had been informed by his commanders that his days were numbered. Under orders, he had taken a knife or a scalpel or scissors and sheared off a personal memento for his wife. She could not imagine his dread. She could hardly bear her own.

Taeko had a toddler at home and a new baby on the way. She struggled with her current pregnancy. She had no job or any independent means of support. Her husband was far away. He had been denied the officer rank and paycheck he clearly deserved. She didn't know when, or whether, he would return. Was she supposed to feel grateful that some military commander she did not know had ordered her husband to mail home a tuft of his hair?

Weeks of silence followed. No mail, no news — nothing. It was as if her husband had fallen off the face of the earth, which, in many ways, was exactly what he had done.

Nobuo Tatsuguchi was training for Attu.

Natives called it the Cradle of Storms, the place where weather was born. The births were almost always ugly. The westernmost island of the Aleutian chain of Alaska, Attu was home to some of the world's worst weather. It snowed eight months a year. The remaining four months of summer were thick with rain and snowmelt. In fact, Attu enjoyed, on average, only ten days a year of clear skies. A volcanic fortress at the intersection of warm Pacific Ocean currents from Japan and icy northern currents from the Bering Sea, Attu was almost always shrouded in fog. The rare exception came during williwaws, the unpredictable blasts of hurricane-force winds that rocketed down the island's 3,000-foot mountains to the rocky shores. Williwaws were the one natural force that could clear out the fog for a few minutes. When the 80 mph gusts subsided, though, the fog crept back. Some days it was so thick a man could stretch out his arms and fail to see his hands. The wind and fog and cold and rain and snow were so relentless, and so brutal, that not a single tree survived on Attu.

This was where Japan decided to launch its ground war against the United States.

To an Imperial Army general poring over maps in a comfortable office in Tokyo, invading Attu almost made sense. The island was closer to mainland Asia than mainland North America. It was the midpoint between Nobuo Tatsuguchi's Army barracks in Hokkaido, Japan, and Anchorage, Alaska. In theory, Japan could use Attu as a forward base to launch attacks against mainland Alaska before leapfrogging down the Pacific Coast to the Boeing bomber plant and Bremerton Navy Yard in Seattle, then on to San Francisco and Los Angeles.

Attu offered defensive benefits, too. A persistent Japanese worry was that Russia was about to join military forces with the United States, but Attu offered one way to split the Allies. Some Imperial Army commanders feared the United States could use the island as its own forward airbase to support and supply counterattacks on Tokyo. Those generals wanted to militarize Attu before the United States did.

These were all just theories, though. In reality, the harbors of Attu were too rocky and treacherous for regular military ship traffic. For fighter pilots, Attu was a nightmare of relentless fog, ferocious winds, and six feet of annual snowfall. The few places on Attu flat enough for an airstrip were comprised mainly of muskeg, a swampy and spongy earth that could hardly support the weight of a concrete runway, much less heavy planes full of troops and munitions. Attu had no full-time electricity or phone service, no paved road or vehicles, no water treatment or sanitary sewer. And then there was the remoteness. Attu was as far west as New Zealand, so far out that mapmakers actually curved the International Date Line around the island just to keep North America on the same calendar page. The island was three time zones from the Alaskan capital, Juneau, which was more than 2,000 miles away. It was hard to imagine a place with less strategic value for any conquering force.

However, the Japanese believed Attu did possess one distinct advantage. It could serve as a decoy.

Admiral Isoroku Yamamoto had concluded his country could not win a long war against the United States; America's factories and natural resources were simply too great for the emperor's forces to keep pace. The only chance for Japanese victory was to strike swiftly and prevent the United States from regrouping. Though Pearl Harbor was a crucial first step, Yamamoto knew the U.S. still had enough surviving warships to threaten the balance of naval power in the Pacific. Yamamoto hoped that if Japan could target and destroy the United States' four remaining aircraft carriers, then Washington would have little choice but to sign a peace agreement with Tokyo. Japanese resolve to wipe out the aircraft carriers was only strengthened four months after Pearl Harbor, on April 18, 1942, when Lieutenant Colonel Jimmy Doolittle launched his B-25B from the USS *Hornet* in the West Pacific and led fifteen other bombers on a daring air raid on Tokyo. Doolittle's bombs did little damage to any military target, but shocked the Japanese, who for the first time had reason to question the ability of their leaders to keep them safe. Yamamoto knew that Japan needed a second, decisive strike, and soon.

Yamamoto launched an elaborate plan to lure the remaining U.S. aircraft carriers into the Central Pacific, near Midway Atoll, where Japanese forces would surprise, cut off, and destroy them. The Battle of Midway was supposed to deal a death blow to the U.S. naval threat in the Pacific. Yamamoto knew victory was not assured. He wanted to boost his chances with a feint, a surprise, a faraway sneak attack that would distract the Americans from the true Japanese plans.

The answer was Attu.

9
CONQUERED

The Imperial Army pushed up the hill with guns drawn and nerves on edge. It was June 7, 1942, and the Japanese were mounting another sneak attack on the United States. This time the assault came by land. Their target was Attu.

Nobuo Tatsuguchi remained in training in Hokkaido as a Japanese unit had landed a few hours earlier on the rocky northern shores of the Aleutian island. The attackers faced no gunfire and found no signs of U.S. defense. Surely, they thought, the Americans must be girding for battle just on the other side of the ridge. This was the first time in more than a century that anyone had seized U.S. soil, and the Japanese expected blood.

At the crest of the hill they braced for the enemy. Reports warned them to be prepared for fog and foul weather, but this was a rare sunny day on Attu. From the heights, the soldiers could see for miles.

What they spotted below was a settlement of nine wooden houses. All had red roofs and white walls. Scattered in between were a few barabaras, the traditional mud-and-sod homes of the Aleutians. On one end of the village was a Russian Orthodox church, with a cross atop a cupola, and on the other was a schoolhouse with a shortwave antenna rising above.

It was a Sunday morning, and every resident of Attu was attending Divine Liturgy at the church along Chichagof Harbor. When they heard a strange roar, worshippers rushed the door to find a Japanese fighter plane buzzing their village. From the hill beyond the church, soldiers charged. Villagers marveled at all the commotion. Attu had only forty-seven residents, half of them children, and altogether the villagers owned more fox traps than guns. With 1,100 troops, the Japanese could have conquered Attu Island with a bullhorn.

On the hillside above him, six-year-old Nick Golodoff watched the soldiers slip and stumble down the ice and snow and spongy earth. He thought it was madcap comedy. Then he heard a loud series of pops. Mud splattered around him. The Japanese were shooting at him. He ran for his life.

As soldiers tripped, their guns discharged

accidentally. Bullets ricocheted all over the hillside. With nerves already on edge, some troops mistakenly believed their comrades' misfires were coming from an unseen enemy, so they sprayed more gunfire down the mountain. The Japanese charge was so frantic, so disorganized, that one soldier was wounded by friendly fire and another was killed. The casualties only increased the frenzy, but for no good reason. Not a single Attu villager raised a weapon in defense. Most Attuans had never seen so many people at one time in their lives. Terrified, they ducked below tables, dived into storage cellars, or just stood paralyzed by fear. When one young villager asked the Attu chief, Mike Hodikoff, if he should shoot back at Japanese invaders, the chief waved him off. Surely, the chief told the Attu villagers, American troops would be on the way soon to defend them. A few minutes later, the chief's wife, Annie Hodikoff, was shot in the leg.

Five minutes passed, then ten, but there was still no sign of any American defenders. The Japanese launched a house-by-house search for villagers. They found Alex Prossoff and his wife, Elizabeth, hiding in the crawlspace beneath their home. At gunpoint, the Prosoffs were ordered out. Alex was handed a note in English saying the village would be destroyed by bombs and gunfire unless all residents surrendered immediately. Alex yelled to the barabara behind his house, and out walked six-year-old Nick Golodoff. He was terrified. He raised his hands in surrender. He was marched to the schoolhouse, where, after a time, he was reunited with his distraught mother and father. Six men fled to the hills, but they were rounded up and held at gunpoint in the schoolhouse, too.

At a house on the edge of the village the invasion turned frantic. For the prior ten months the only non-natives living on Attu were Foster and Etta Jones. Foster worked for the Bureau of Indian Affairs and forwarded four weather observations a day via shortwave radio to the U.S. Army and Navy bases at Dutch Harbor, Alaska, 850 miles to the east in the Aleutians. Etta was the island's schoolteacher.

At the moment, however, they were preoccupied with survival. Bullets pummeled their house. Windows shattered. The Japanese assault was so fierce that the chimney began to collapse, sending rocks tumbling down the flue and into the living room. At the start of the attack, Foster had been transmitting his regular 11 a.m. weather briefing. He sent out a few words about temperature and visibility, but concluded with ominous news: THE JAPS ARE HERE. They were the last four words Americans heard from any citizen of Attu for the remaining three years of World War II.

As the shouts of soldiers drew closer, Etta gathered all the weather reports and letters she could find and thrust them into the fire. Foster smashed his shortwave radio, then walked outside to surrender. A Japanese officer stormed the house and jabbed a bayonet at Etta's stomach. "Do not cry," he demanded, "do not cry."

Etta was ordered outside. She found her husband already there and surrounded by four soldiers with bayonets. They were forced into the schoolhouse with all the Attuans, including the chief's wife, whose gunshot wound in the leg was being treated by Japanese soldiers. Several officers spoke some English. They talked of their families and military time already served in China. They seemed civil.

Officers had confiscated the Joneses' house for themselves, which meant that Foster and Etta were ordered into an empty cabin. When Etta didn't walk fast enough to suit her guard, the soldier rammed her to

160

the ground with the butt of his rifle and then thrust his heel onto her stomach. During that short walk Foster was knocked down three times by soldiers. Eventually Etta and Foster stumbled into the dark house, where they huddled together in the dark but remained too stoic and scared to discuss their likely fate.

The next morning officers rounded up Foster and hustled him to another building for interrogations. After finding his smashed radio and a few unburned weather reports, the Japanese had concluded that Foster was a military man. Foster denied it. The Japanese pressed it. They demanded that Foster repair the smashed radio. Foster said he didn't know how.

Exactly what happened next remains lost to the fog of war.

Japanese interrogators and many villagers said a despondent Foster slit his own wrists. Etta and other villagers said the Japanese put a bullet into Foster's skull. Either way, a few hours later, Etta Jones was ushered into the interrogation building and shown her husband sprawled on the floor in a pool of his own blood. He was dead. She was devastated. (Decades later, Air Force historian John Haile Cloe found records from the 1948 disinterment of American bodies on Attu. They indicated that Foster's forehead was pierced with a bullet hole.)

Foster was sixty-three and Etta sixty-two. They had been counting the months until retirement together. They both earned it. A native of Vineland, New Jersey, Etta had devoted herself to the good of others and had labored for the past twenty years as a schoolteacher to the Eskimos and Aleuts of the Alaskan bush. She had learned to cook walrus and seal. She knew how to turn her dogsled team by yelling gee and haw. She grew accustomed to the remoteness of the wilderness. Her mother mailed letters to her at Thanksgiving that did not arrive until Easter.

And then there was the cold. Living in lonely outposts like Kaltag, Tatitlek, and Kipnuk, Jones learned how to collect drinking water by cutting ice blocks from the local river and stacking them in her backyard. In her cabin, tea water stayed fluid until the temperature outside dropped to minus 60. The painkiller in her medicine bottle didn't turn solid until minus 72. To go outside on a typical day in the winter, Etta wore: wool tights that reached to her ankles; two pairs of home-knitted, four-ply wool stockings; corduroy trousers; a wool jumper; ankle-high slippers of wolf skin with fur on the inside; boots with soles of moose hide; a reindeer parka with fur hood; fur cap with earflaps; and wool gloves covered with fur-lined moose-hide mittens. For a mere trip to the outhouse, she might wear less, but only if she moved with haste.

Luckily, she didn't bear all this hardship alone. In the Arctic Brotherhood Hall of Tanana, she had danced with a hardscrabble miner from Ohio who had snowshoed twenty-eight miles just to make the night's festivities. He regaled her with stories of the Klondike gold rush and fed her Alaskan blueberries the size of California strawberries. He was so flinty he had once shaved a dime to fill a fellow miner's tooth cavity. Etta and Foster Jones married at age forty-three. They were too old for children of their own, but too big-hearted to resist the children of others. Etta taught young natives how to speak English and mark time in increments more frequent than tide changes and whale migrations. Foster built and operated shortwave radios, which played music for villagers and relayed weather information to the government in Fairbanks and beyond. Together Etta and Foster formed a formidable team on the tundra.

For the past ten months Etta and Foster

Jones had lived with forty-five native Aleuts on Attu. It was a subsistence community. Villagers lived on seal, sea lion, seaweed, and, especially, salmon. In winter the men trapped blue fox, which they traded for flour, sugar, and tea. Extra pelts were sold to help support widows and the elderly. While Etta worked with the island's twelve school-age children, Foster forwarded four weather observations a day to the nearest inhabited island, Atka, 500 miles to the east, and Dutch Harbor, the larger town and military base. Several times Foster recorded wind speeds in excess of 100 mph; at least twice williwaws had lifted him several feet off the ground. For their work Etta and Foster Jones were paid $280 per month. Because Attu had no restaurants, bars, stores, or anything else to spend money on, the Joneses' savings for retirement grew steadily.

"We like Attu," Jones wrote her sister. "It grows on one, and the people are fine. There is no drinking, and that means much in a native village. Consequently, there is no fighting. All is peace and harmony."

Change lurked offshore. Twice in the winter of 1941–42, villagers trapping foxes on the uninhabited southern side of the island had spotted boats with Japanese flags.

The Japanese continued on without making contact. At that point, villagers knew that Japan was at war with the United States. Still, nobody thought much about the war with Japan. In fact, when a friend warned in a letter of the Japanese war threat, Etta was blunt. "We laughed at them," Etta said. "What would Japan want with Attu?"

On the day after Foster Jones was buried in a blanket in a seven-foot grave behind the Russian Orthodox church, soldiers ordered the Attuans to gather around the island flagpole to watch the raising of the Japanese flag. Even before the invasion, villagers had a long-standing contempt for the Japanese, mainly centered around old fox-trapping disputes. Now the death of Foster Jones, the shooting of the Attu chief's wife, and the ransacking of the village homes all combined to turn the contempt into hatred. Out of earshot of their captors, they mocked the Japanese flag, with its red rising sun over a white background, as a meatball, and as a target.

Villagers prayed for a rescue by American troops. None came. Three days after the red-and-white flag had been raised over Attu, the United States Navy denied the Japanese had even set foot in the Aleutians with this public statement: "None of our inhabited islands or rocks are troubled with uninvited visitors at this time." The lies continued another two weeks, until June 21, when the United States finally admitted, two weeks after the fact, that it had lost part of Alaska. For the United States War Department, Attu was too inconsequential to defend, but it was too embarrassing to admit having lost it.

To native Aleuts, Japanese commanders were surprisingly tolerable. When some soldiers stole food from Attuans, officers ordered it returned. Native homes were fenced off, but that was mainly to protect the prisoners from their captors. Neither Aleut women nor their husbands or fathers reported any sexual mistreatment. Some soldiers shared sake and beer with the villagers. A few even took Attu children on hikes and boat rides. Several photographs of Japanese soldiers playing with Aleut children were used in Tokyo for propaganda purposes. One picture reprinted in many Japanese newspapers showed Nick Golodoff, with a grin and some flowers, riding piggyback on a smiling Japanese soldier. The picture put a happier face on some ugly truths: At age six, Nick wasn't even the youngest prisoner of war taken by the Japanese — five other Attuans were younger.

At the same time, under Japanese control, a sixty-year-old former Attu chief, John Artumonoff, died of apparent natural causes.

Attu surprised many Japanese troops. Though they had been prepared for the harsh climate and topography, they were advised that Aleutian culture, so removed from civilization, would be simple and primitive. Instead, soldiers marveled at the Attuans' sturdy three-room houses with linoleum floors, two or three windows, and lace curtains. Most families had manual sewing machines and lamps fueled by gas or seal blubber. Racks outside barabaras sagged from the weight of so much drying salmon. Millions of gulls and seabirds nested in the Aleutians, and eggs made for an easy feast. Homes were so well-insulated that they heated in just fifteen minutes with stoves fueled by blubber or charcoal. "It looked more luxurious than the Japanese standard of living," wrote the Japanese battle photographer Kira Sugiyama.

Weeks passed. Villagers were allowed to take small boats to sea to harvest fish, but only if most of the catch was given to the guards. Japanese officers felt comfortable enough to bathe in 55-gallon drums in front of Attu children. The widow Etta Jones remained sullen and sick, but gradually her health improved. Some natives said they saw knife cuts on her wrist.

By the end of summer, the daily rains on Attu were turning into sleet in the village and snow atop the mountains. Bracing for a counterattack, the Japanese had been digging foxholes and trenches all over the island, but the skies and seas were free of Americans. Winter was coming. The Japanese had no desire to continue operating a tiny prisoner of war camp on a remote mountainous island with some of the worst weather on earth.

On September 14, 1942, the forty-one remaining prisoners of war of Attu were loaded onto a Japanese merchant ship, the *Yoko Maru*. They set sail for an Aleutian island to the east, Kiska, which had been conquered by the Japanese the day before they landed on Attu. In the ship's two-hundred-mile journey across the Bering Sea, an Attuan mother of two, Anecia Prokopioff, died on board and was buried at sea. At Kiska the surviving prisoners were transferred to a bigger ship, the *Nagata Maru,* and herded into a cargo hold that formerly transported coal. The uncleaned berth was the prisoners' home for the next two weeks and 1,600 miles across the North Pacific. On September 27, the prisoners, seasick and caked in coal dust, arrived at Otaru, Hokkaido, where the deprivations of war had already set in among the Japanese. There was little food for the guards in the prisoner of war camp and even less for the villagers, so the Attuans scavenged garbage for survival. They soon were beset with tuberculosis, beriberi, dysentery, and starvation. The Japanese transferred Etta Jones, the only Caucasian prisoner, to another POW facility in Yokohama and then to Totsuka, where she was housed with eighteen captured Australian nurses half her age. When she finally was freed at the end of the war, Etta Jones was one month short of her sixty-sixth birthday. She weighed eighty pounds, but at least she survived. Of the forty native Attu villagers shipped to the Otaru camp, only twenty-four got out alive. Twenty-one died, including four of the five babies born in Otaru. No villager, or Etta Jones, returned to live in Attu.

As a military feint, Attu accomplished little. Unknown to the Japanese at the time, the United States had cracked their diplomatic codes. The June 1942 attack at Midway was no surprise. Alerted to the general timing and location of the coming battle in the Central Pacific, the United States fleet commander, Admiral Chester Nimitz, deftly positioned three aircraft carriers to ambush the Imperial Navy. The Battle of Midway became the largest naval firefight of the war up to that time. The result was a mortally wounded Japanese fleet — four sunken aircraft carriers and one heavy cruiser, more than 200 aircraft destroyed, and over 3,000 men killed, including some of the nation's most experienced fighter pilots.

It was Japan's first major naval defeat in a century, and the country's military strategists bore heavy responsibility. The two aircraft carriers Japan had sent to battle in the Aleutians might have tipped the balance if they instead had joined the far more important fight at Midway. Yet there was no public acknowledgment of error. Prime Minister Hideki Tojo ordered that the whole debacle at Midway be kept secret from the public. The families of the more than 3,000 dead were falsely led to believe that their loved ones were fighting elsewhere in the Pacific. In fact, most Japanese did not even learn of the crushing failure at Midway until after the war was over. Instead, Tojo diverted public attention with his celebration of "the great Aleutian victory."

As for the Americans at Midway, Admiral Nimitz lost a carrier, a destroyer, and 307 men, but his nation, unlike Japan, had the industrial capacity to quickly replace the sunken ships. The Battle of Midway marked the turning point in the Pacific. For the remainder of the war, it would be the United States, not Japan, that set the terms of battle.

If Attu and the Aleutians had flopped as a decoy for Japanese battle plans, they fared even worse as a prize of war. Three days before the assault on Attu, a Japanese strike force launched an air and naval attack against the United States naval and army bases at Dutch Harbor. With two aircraft carriers, three cruisers, and five destroyers, the raid inflicted some minor damage on the radio station and barracks, but the Japanese were repelled after just two days of fighting. Some Japanese forces were redeployed a few hundred miles west to seize Kiska, which was guarded by only ten U.S. Navy weather technicians and their black-and-white shepherd dog named Explosion. Kiska was about one-third the size of Attu, with a taller volcano but a better harbor. Frustrated by the logistics of Attu, the Japanese decided to consolidate their Aleutian military operations at Kiska.

After shipping out the prisoners, the Japanese found little reason to remain on

Attu. The troops were cold, wet, and sick. With treacherous seas, the resupply from Japan was difficult. Engineers struggled to install any kind of roads or runways on the spongy tundra. Attu had become more trouble than it was worth. By the end of September 1942, the Japanese had pulled out. Foster Jones, John Artumonoff, and Anecia Prokopioff had died for a conquest that was no longer wanted.

Attu remained empty, or populated with a mere skeletal force, for several weeks. Then Japanese commanders began to second-guess their decision to withdraw. A reconnaissance plane had found the United States building an air base on Adak, an island in the Aleutian chain about halfway between Attu and Dutch Harbor — and within striking distance of Japan. That threat could not be tolerated. Besides, back home in Tokyo, the seizure of U.S. soil in Alaska had been a potent propaganda prize to counterbalance the country's naval disaster at Midway. Maybe there was something on Attu worth keeping. Maybe the weather would improve. Maybe better road builders could solve the puzzle of Attu's shifting soil. Maybe the Americans would come to fight after all.

As the ship with prisoners of war from Attu sailed west to Japan, it was soon replaced by another ship sailing east. On October 29, 1942, the Japanese Special Naval Landing Forces returned to Attu. At first the island was populated mainly by support personnel instructed to find some way to make Attu habitable. Soon after came the troops, hundreds and then thousands of them, trained and prepared for the cold — and ready for war.

In this second wave of soldiers came a surgeon named Paul Nobuo Tatsuguchi.

10
HEARTSICK

On an Imperial Navy ship far from anywhere, Nobuo Tatsuguchi felt queasy. Just a
few weeks before, he had been performing
surgeries on soldiers south of the equator in
the tropical steam of Papua New Guinea.
Now he was barreling across the North
Pacific to work on an abandoned island with
volcanoes encrusted in snow. At home his
wife was pregnant and sick. At sea his ship
was stalked by American submarines. His
journey from Japan to Attu would require
two more days, but upon arrival he would
be expected to win a war against the nation
he loved, perhaps fighting the very college
classmates he treasured. More than just his
stomach had turned upside down — his
world had, too.

He tried to stay optimistic. Even though
he had deployed to Attu in winter, the most
brutal season on the island, Tatsuguchi
found beauty in his natural surroundings.

In a letter to Taeko, he wrote, "Two weeks have passed since we arrived here. In spite of the bad weather I'm fine. It got colder today and it's hailing. I am writing this by candlelight, listening to the raindrops tapping the roof of the tent in the cave. We caught twelve trout in the river here yesterday. Tasty. Reminds me of Lake Chuzenji in Nikko [National Park.] The seaweeds here are dark and taste good. What a thrill to catch a three-foot cod."

At least that's what Taeko thought her husband wrote. Nobuo's handwriting was notoriously bad. After struggling to read notes from her husband and his former classmates in California, Taeko used to joke that American medical schools must offer a special class in poor penmanship.

In Tokyo, Taeko did her best to put up a brave front, but the truth was that she was heartsick. She missed him — his dry wit, his gentle teasing, his devotion to family and faith.

His military pay was only a fraction of what he made before the war as a doctor at the tuberculosis sanitarium. Now Taeko would be expected to support a second child on the same reduced Army pay. Others in Japan were making similar sacrifices, but they hadn't lived a good life overseas and seen what more was possible. Taeko and Nobuo were not political people. They wanted to raise a family and help their church and one day return to America. Taeko yearned for long walks again with Nobuo in Yosemite National Park, or Nikko National Park. Here or there, they belonged together. She wanted to be with him.

Nobuo's letters from Attu were infrequent and redacted by military censors. He was banned from writing about any dates or locations, though it appears from his letters home, as well as what is documented of Japanese troop movements, that Tatsuguchi had arrived on Attu sometime after November 1942. Knowing that all his writing was screened by strangers, Nobuo refrained from any emotional talk with his wife, though even in private times he wasn't sentimentally effusive. Mostly, he wrote in the matter-of-fact style of an observant surgeon. He was one of five men living in a space that should accommodate only three. Many soldiers spoke in dialects unfamiliar to him. He celebrated the New Year by eating a rice cake and building a snowman from drifts that stretched six feet high. The cod, trout, and salmon he caught were far better than any military food. Attu was so far north that in the winter it received as little as eight hours of light a day, though the fog and clouds were so persistent that it could only rarely be called sunlight. Supply ships carrying mail to and from Japan were infrequent, so Nobuo never knew when or if his notes were reaching home. "I haven't gotten any mail since I came here. I suspect this will reach you at the same time as the card previously written," he wrote to Taeko. "Some days I'm busy excessively because of my job and on others I'm not. For the first time since I came here I saw a beautiful starry sky last night. Dark, angry ocean is foggy every day. It snows constantly and the temperature is zero or thereabouts. We live in the damp cave. Sun doesn't come in and it's gloomy."

Ever the doctor, he passed along medical advice to his pregnant wife: Take vitamins and cod liver oil daily. Try to improve the appetite of their daughter, Misako, by letting her play longer outside. He voiced concern for his wife's pregnancy, but he could not hide his hope: "Waiting for good news from home," he wrote.

Finally it came. A military transport from Hokkaido carried a letter from Taeko to Attu with a joyful, life-changing paragraph: Their second daughter, Mutsuko Laura Tatsuguchi, had been born in February 1943.

The news buoyed him. The whole thought of having a new daughter to hold, to cuddle — to meet! — turned his spirits. His letters turned noticeably warmer. At home he had a new baby girl, and on Attu spring was arriving. "Four days ago, we moved to a new place surrounded by the open mountains," he wrote to Taeko one spring day. "Moving out of the damp cave feels good. Sometimes lying down in the sun to enjoy the warmth, then all of a sudden it starts to snow and gets cold. Washing my face with the cold water coming down from the waterfall, and exercise refreshes me. Rising sun reflecting on the ragged mountain covered in snow is such a beautiful sight."

He asked Taeko for more supplies — flashlight bulbs, batteries, a musical saw and bow, Ike-Jime fishing needles, and, especially books. Though he had brought along his *Gray's Anatomy* from medical school in California — it was a secondhand copy with the name of its prior owner, classmate Ed Lee, scrawled on the inside cover — Tatsuguchi asked his wife to also send along another American medical classic, *Lee McGregor's Synopsis of Surgical Anatomy.*

Wartime Japan was not the easiest place to round up any extra supplies, but Taeko did her best, even adding a tin of cookies and a photo of herself with Misako. Nobuo wrote that he was struck by how much his girl had grown in his months away from home. He teased that the daughter might even grow to become more beautiful than the mother.

Still, Taeko couldn't help but notice an increasing change in her husband's tone. The same months away from home that allowed his daughter to grow so much also seemed to sway Nobuo's beliefs. He had months of military indoctrination. He was surrounded by hundreds of soldiers who did not tolerate differing opinions. He had little contact with the outside world. He was removed from his church and minister. He was living in an echo chamber of pro-war anti-Americanism. For the first time in his letters home, he had begun to describe the United States as "the enemy." On shortwave radio, he heard a United States broadcast in Japanese from San Francisco, but he denounced it as "all propaganda." He even concluded one postcard by proclaiming, "The brave warrior guarding the North Sea is well." Taeko knew he was brave. She hoped he was joking about being a warrior.

Their marriage was five years old, but most of the past two years had been spent apart. Instead of worshipping at their

Seventh-day Adventist church every Saturday, he was being lectured daily about the glories of the Japanese Army, of the necessity to defend the emperor above all, of the soldier's code of death before dishonor. Taeko knew that war changed most men. She worried about the impact on her husband, and searched for hints in every note he wrote home.

Surviving a winter on Attu was character-building. Was it character-changing, too? The Japanese garrison on the island had gone from zero to more than 2,500 men, but these troops looked significantly different from the original invaders. Like Tatsuguchi, the latest Attu occupiers tended to be older and less seasoned. Many were farmers with little formal education beyond their military training. There were signs that they were considered expendable. If Attu were truly crucial to Japanese war goals, then the island wouldn't have been abandoned in the fall. Besides, the main Japanese fighting force in the Aleutians, more than 6,000 men, was now stationed on Kiska, the smaller island 200 miles to the east. The men of Attu spent their days digging trenches and foxholes. That made sense for defense, but troops struggled and mostly failed to build the runway and roads that would be crucial if Attu were to truly function as a forward base for offensive action against the United States.

The incessant wind, cold, fog, rain, and snow made life on Attu miserable, but increasingly Tatsuguchi and his fellow soldiers came to view the climate as their life insurance policy. "We call bad weather good here," he wrote to Taeko. The more ferocious the williwaw, the less likely the Japanese would face an American attack. Still, Tatsuguchi knew it was foolhardy to entrust his life to a plunging barometer. He could hardly help but wonder not only why he was on Attu, but also why Japan was there.

11
ATTU

Laird shivered. After weeks of Army training in the desert of Southern California, he wanted the soldiers around him to think his shakes came from the chill of the San Francisco fog. The reality was more embarrassing. Laird was scared.

With thousands of other soldiers from his 7th Infantry Division, Laird was boarding a transport ship for a destination unknown. Based on the clothes he had been issued, he suspected he was heading for someplace cool, or at least not the desert. This mission didn't look like training. It didn't feel like training. This time, Laird knew, it was the real thing — war.

At 1 p.m., on April 24, 1943, Laird's ship and four others set off from San Francisco Bay and turned north. His transport was so crowded that there was barely room to sit. They would be at sea for six days. Men would be forced to sleep in shifts.

Far off the coast, the soldiers finally learned the basic details of their mission: They were the muscle of what would become Operation Landcrab, the 15,000 men assigned to return Attu and the Aleutian Islands to American control.

Laird knew little about Alaska and even less about the Aleutians. Attu Island — he had never even heard of that place. The unknown worried him, as it did everyone else, but there was no room for fear on this ship. Laird was now a leader of men, the first sergeant of Company H of the 32nd Infantry, 7th Division, and he knew that any sign of uncertainty in such tight quarters would fly like a spark underground in his old Powhatan Coal Mine.

His heart already burned with one regret. He wished he had done a better job of saying goodbye to his wife, Rose. Because of his recent promotion, Laird was responsible for making sure his squad shipped out correctly. But the rail station the day before at Ford Ord bustled with thousands of men, and orders were being barked all over. It was controlled chaos. Laird became so preoccupied putting his men in the right order, and with the right gear, that he had time for only a brief kiss for his wife. He tried but failed to keep from choking up. As soon as

Rose was out of sight, Laird thought of all the things, the more important things, he should have said. He wanted to say how much he loved her, how much he would miss her, and how much their family meant to him and their future. His wife, their daughter, and his stepdaughter were all counting on him, but the truth was that he was relying on them, too. He hoped Rose knew how much they meant to him, but as he stood in cramped quarters on a troop transport far at sea steaming toward war, he wished he had spelled it out for her exactly. They had helped him turn around his life.

He was grateful to have Rose and the girls to think about. Without them, he would think only about the enemy. The few things he did know about the Japanese were memorable and bad. While training in California, a fellow soldier had given him a photograph of a Japanese soldier decapitating a kneeling man in China. Laird kept the gruesome photo in his pack. No one would ever need to remind him about the ruthlessness of the Japanese soldier.

For the prior six months, Laird and other Americans had been stunned to watch an outmanned and outgunned Japanese force sustain a ferocious defense and counterattack on Guadalcanal in the South Pacific.

United States Navy losses were so severe that admirals had refused to release casualty figures. Americans were alarmed by the fighting spirit of the Japanese, who fought to the death and considered surrender to be the ultimate shame. When one Guadalcanal firefight resulted in the death of nearly 800 of 900 Japanese, the Imperial Army commander was so shamed that he committed suicide on the battlefield with a ritual disembowelment. The ancient samurai code of bushido, which led Japanese soldiers to value their honor over their own lives, was an alien concept to the West. Though the United States eventually won the battle, Guadalcanal led many Americans to conclude that Japanese soldiers were fanatical killing machines.

In Alaska, however, the United States commanders expected an easy fight. From his warm and comfortable headquarters at the Presidio in San Francisco, General John DeWitt predicted troops would retake Attu in just three days. Yes, the weather and the terrain might present a few extra challenges, but Attu was guarded by a garrison of just 3,000 Japanese. How difficult could it be? The Army was so confident of a quick victory that it didn't bother issuing troops the proper clothes or supplies for fighting in the

Aleutians.

This arrogance was just the latest in a series of colossal military blunders in the Aleutians.

One of the biggest problems was the leaders themselves. They did not like each other.

Son of a Confederate Army general, Major General Simon Buckner, the commander of Alaska, was a swaggering swath of testosterone who killed bears, conducted small meetings in a parade voice, and ordered a subordinate to blowtorch the ice from his outdoor bath each morning. "I don't believe in passive warfare," Buckner said. "There are two ways of dealing with a rattlesnake. One is to sit still and wait for the snake to strike. The other way is to bash in the snake's head and put it out of commission. That's what I favor."

His Navy counterpart was Rear Admiral Robert "Fuzzy" Theobald, a pudgy man who insisted on neat uniforms even as his counterparts opted in the Alaskan cold for heavily insulated clothes. Theobald had graduated near the top of his Naval Academy class, but his smarts often turned caustic. He was renowned for mocking and insulting his inferiors. He also had a weakness for conspiracy theories, later writing a book alleging that Franklin Roosevelt secretly forced the United States into World War II by suppressing intelligence about the forthcoming Pearl Harbor attack.

The rivalry between the Army and Navy was not new, but Buckner and Theobald pushed it to new depths. Buckner complained that the rear admiral was "as tender as the bottom of a teenage girl." Theobald made no secret of his desire to work elsewhere. Just four months before the Attu invasion, Theobald was replaced by Rear Admiral Thomas Kinkaid, who had gained a reputation as a fighting admiral during the triumphs at Midway and Guadalcanal. In turn, yet another rear admiral, Francis Rockwell, was assigned to command the landing of the Army's amphibious assault force in the Aleutians.

While the Navy kept replacing and adding leaders, the Army settled on Major General Albert Brown to direct the 7th Infantry Division invasion force. He was wanted by neither DeWitt, the Western Defense commander in San Francisco, nor Buckner, the Alaska commander. Brown's division was trained for trucks and tanks against Nazis in the African desert, not amphibious landings against Japanese on subarctic islands. But troops were in short supply — Roosevelt wanted manpower for a fall European offensive now that the Soviets were pushing Hitler out of Stalingrad — and the Alaska team had to take whatever it could get. Another major sticking point was DeWitt's vow of a quick and easy triumph in the Aleutians. Brown protested that a three-day victory would be impossible at Attu. Brown thought troops would need at least a week just to navigate across the black muck of the mountainous island, which was seventeen miles wide.

In other words, the United States was going to war in one of the world's most unforgiving places with a revolving door of leadership that disagreed on basic battle strategy.

Yet by the spring of 1943, the unruly United States leadership team had won some notable successes. Nearly fifty Japanese ships had been sunk in the Aleutians. Regular Air Force bombing runs cratered Japanese attempts to build a 3,500-foot runway at Attu. The main Japanese garrison at Kiska felt so under siege by air assaults that it dispatched a warning message to commanders: "Bombing is getting more violent month after month. The bomb technique used is mediocre, but when enough bombs are dropped there is bound to be damage. We are losing personnel, installations, air defense arms, fuel and firearms. Even the antiaircraft gun gradually loses its aiming efficiency."

On Attu, the last Japanese ships slipped through the fog and American blockade to deliver supplies on March 9 and 10. After that, every other transport was either turned back or sunk.

By the time Laird and the 7th Division had arrived in the Aleutians on April 30, Tatsuguchi and the Japanese on Attu had gone a month and a half without a resupply of food or ammunition. They were hungry and desperate, but still alert. Japanese code breakers had intercepted United States messages about a forthcoming invasion. They redoubled their efforts to dig foxholes and trenches.

Dug into a cave on an Attu mountainside hundreds of miles from his family, Nobuo Tatsuguchi confronted his worst fear: The country he loved was preparing to attack him. The consequences were already becoming clear. Around the clock he was in surgery performing amputations and stitching gouges to save the lives of Japanese maimed by American bombs. Crucial medical equipment was in short supply. He had vowed to his God and his wife to stay true to his Seventh-day Adventist faith and

189

remain a noncombatant. All around him, though, his suffering and dying patients moaned a different reality: This is war, they said. Kill or be killed.

Could Tatsuguchi stay true to both his faith and his country? Was it even possible to try? He had two daughters now, including one he had not even met. How could he be a father during war? What kind of example would he set? Would his daughters be proud?

The violence, the patients, the choices — it all felt overwhelming. Tatsuguchi could become frozen by fear, by the vast questions, or he could find solace in a small task that was familiar and comfortable. Over the years he had written about his travels and his wildflowers, his studies and his family. On Attu, he might not be able to fully understand his situation, but he could describe it. He felt compelled to take notes. Numerous psychological studies over the years have confirmed that writing about personal experience seems to help the brain regulate emotion. Describing a fear makes it more familiar, and, often, less frightening. No soldier in war wants to talk about emotional distress, but logging it on paper can be done privately, without judgment, as a therapeutic release.

Nobuo Tatsuguchi decided to write a war diary.

By this time, Laird felt ready for war, but he was more practiced at waiting. After six nauseous days at sea, Laird finally had arrived on the southwestern Alaska peninsula at Cold Bay. The base was accurately named. An unrelenting 20 mph wind cut through his clothes. Snow encrusted the mountains just 200 feet above the anchorage. The deep-water harbor was so small and sparsely developed that there wasn't room on shore to accommodate all the men, so they again slept in shifts on their ships. Commanders were offered the chance to bring ashore troops to introduce them to tundra, but only sixty Army officers accepted. Confined to their ships, soldiers were issued new leather boots without any way to break them in. Laird, who knew something about boots from his time in the coal mines, feared that painful blisters were in his future.

Laird was told to prepare for a May 7 invasion of Attu, but seas were so high that the battleships raised their guns to prevent swamping by monster waves. The invasion was delayed. Then dangerously high surf led the commanders to push back the assault to May 9. Another storm forced a reschedule to May 10. On May 11, four days after the original plan, a convoy of three battleships, seven cruisers, fourteen destroyers, five submarines, and an aircraft carrier finally assembled with General Brown's 7th Infantry Division on six transports in the seas off Attu. At last the order went out: Attu's beachhead would commence at 7:40 a.m.

In the fog offshore, however, two destroyers collided, punching a hole in one. The invasion was moved to 10:40 a.m. After a U.S. submarine came close to firing torpedoes at an American ship that had been misidentified as Japanese, the invasion was pushed back to 3:30 p.m. Fog was so thick on one destroyer that the captain could not see his bow from the bridge.

The element of surprise was long gone. The Japanese knew what was coming.

The Americans did not. Most of Attu remained unmapped more than a thousand yards from the shore — Air Force pilots had relied on Rand McNally road maps to fly the Aleutians, and ground troops relied on maps based on a Russian survey completed in 1864 — and uncharted reefs made for dangerous beach landings. In fact, the main Geodetic Survey map had warned that ships should not approach closer than two miles. On the rare times the fog lifted on Attu, the soldiers on the transport ships could see that about 95 percent of the island's shore ended in cliffs, some of which rose 200 feet.

On board their ships, soldiers were shown a 1/5000 scale model of Attu that had been based on aerial photographs. The Japanese were entrenched on the east end of the island, which was divided into five rocky fingers and bays. Because the beaches at the ends of the bays were treacherous, General Brown knew a complication in one spot could bottleneck the whole operation. He decided to hedge his bets by splitting the overall invasion into northern and southern waves.

First to land would be a small force of 400 scouts and reconnaissance troops on the northern shore along Scarlet Beach. Their goal was to draw out the Japanese and divert attention from the main north shore landing of US troops a few miles east, at Red Beach near the head of Holtz Bay. Meanwhile, on the island's south shore, the main US fighting force would pour onto the rocky beach at Massacre Bay, the same place the Japanese had landed during their invasion of Attu. (The ominous name of Massacre Bay came 200 years earlier from a slaughter of fifteen Aleuts by Russian fur hunters.)

The idea was to pinch the Japanese from opposite sides, north and south, and then pin them against the eastern shore at Attu Village in Chichagof Harbor. There, they would be shelled by Navy battleships and Air Force bombers. Including supply lines and reserve forces, 16,000 Americans would be assigned to retake Attu by land, air, and sea.

At least that was the plan. Much had gone wrong in unexpected ways. Fog limited visibility to a quarter-mile. Already that morning, after the destroyers collided and a friendly fire submarine sinking was narrowly averted, a northern attack force had become so lost that commanders mistakenly prepared to land on the same beach as the southern force. At Massacre Bay, a hundred landing craft converged just a hundred yards offshore. Slamming into rocks and each other, eleven boats capsized, dumping soldiers and crucial equipment into the frigid seas.

"Assault wave, man your boats!" commanders shouted through bullhorns. Laird was in the southern strike at Massacre Bay. For the past five hours offshore, the final pre-combat meal of steak and eggs had been churning in his stomach. Now the mix of rolling waves, diesel engine fumes, and raw nerves combined to finish the job. Rope ladders were pitched from tall transport ships to lower landing craft. One soldier lost balance on the ladder and plunged neck-first onto the side of his landing craft. Another slipped into the Bering Sea. Before a shot was fired, Laird saw two men die.

The first United States soldiers from the southern force touched land on Attu at 4:50 p.m., nearly ten hours behind the day's original plan. In the chaos and the fog, the second attack wave of Americans landed first, followed by the simultaneous landings of the first and third waves of men. They all were met by silence. No shots, no bombs, nothing. They stormed the shore and braced for gunfire. What confronted them instead was muck — black, sticky, volcanic muck. One step and they sank to their ankles. The next step put them to their boot tops. A third step required a mighty pull, and the fourth could strip off the boot. Before they could fight the enemy, they would be forced to fight Attu itself.

Thick clouds hovered at 1,500 feet. On Laird's right, the top of Henderson Ridge reached the base of the clouds. On his left, the heights of Gilbert Ridge were obscured.

The map said that highland rose 2,000 feet.

In the valley below, Laird knew the muck turned his men into easy targets. Why weren't the Japanese shooting? Surely they must be in the fog on the ridges above, but the Americans could see no sign of the enemy. As Laird pressed up the shore, the muck turned to muskeg. That made his boots stick less, but the elastic soil made every step uncertain. Already his feet were wet and cold. The Army's 12-inch Blucher boots were leather but not waterproof, more suited to dryland logging than crossing swampland just a few degrees from frozen. His heels were already raw with blisters. Because the boots reached halfway up his calves, chafing climbed higher up his leg with every step. He had other equipment problems. His rain pants were flimsy. Seams ripped apart with each stride. As he struggled uphill, his pants turned into chaps. The main thing keeping him warm was adrenaline. Where were the Japanese?

Behind him hundreds of men continued to land on the beach. Ahead were even more. From the model of the island on the ship he knew the terrain climbed in front of him, but fog shrouded most views of the mountains. Sometimes the fog shrouded the soldier just a few feet beside him.

At the waterline, troops struggled to lug a 105mm howitzer off the barges and up steep banks. About seventy-five yards off the water, Attu gave way, swallowing the wheels of the heavy gun, as well as the treaded truck pulling it, deep into the sticky black ooze. This was as far as the gun was going for now. Crews spun around the howitzer by hand, pointed it up the valley, and fired. "This is it, boy," Sergeant Allen Robbins proclaimed. "We're gunnin'."

They weren't hittin'. The Japanese were still nowhere to be found.

Colonel Yasuyo Yamasaki was desperate for an emergency evacuation by the Imperial Navy, but the United States naval and air blockade had proven too strong. Just three weeks earlier, the Japanese mastermind of Pearl Harbor, Admiral Isoroku Yamamoto, had been shot out of the sky and killed by an American pilot. The Imperial Navy struggled to fill his void. There would be no daring naval raid to rescue Japanese troops stranded on Attu.

In the Aleutians, Yamasaki calculated correctly that his troops would be vastly outnumbered by any attack, which he had been expecting since May 4. Rather than confronting the enemy on the beach, where the

Japanese would be in firing range of American troops and warships, Yamasaki had decided to retreat and dig in. He was trapped and he knew it. He had only 2,650 men and twelve antiaircraft guns. He had lived on Attu a month. He had enough experience in the Aleutians to realize that the weather could become his ally. When the fog and clouds cleared from the beaches, it often continued to mask the mountains. By fortifying the heights of Attu, his men could hide in the mist and shoot down at the invaders. If his men could hold out long enough, they might be rescued or at least resupplied by the Navy. Yamasaki concluded the highlands were his last best chance.

Coves on the north side of Attu were too rocky and steep to support many invading troops — Red Beach ended in a 250-foot wall so steep and crumbly that it could be climbed only by a man who had dropped to his hands and knees — so Yamasaki left it unguarded. He opted instead to fall back onto the buttresses and ridges far above the south beach at Massacre Bay.

As the Americans crawled up the Massacre Valley, sometimes literally, the Japanese watched from above in silence and waited.

Finally the northern force spotted four Japanese soldiers on patrol about 300 yards away. They held back until the soldiers cut the distance in half, then opened fire. Two Japanese soldiers dropped. Two escaped. It was 7 p.m., and the United States had killed its first enemies during the invasion of Attu.

From overhead, American bomber squadrons led by Colonel William Eareckson pounded likely Japanese positions. He was an Air Force swashbuckler — lanky, with a thin mustache and a wild streak that led one general to complain that Eareckson couldn't even spell the word discipline. Fed up with the permanent cloud cover of the Aleutians, Eareckson's pilots terrified the Japanese by dive-bombing through the mist to gain low-altitude sightings of targets.

On the southern push, Laird and other troops finally had gained their first mile up Massacre Valley without incident. The quiet stopped at the second mile. From the ridges Japanese snipers and machine gunners cut down several American troops. The job of Laird's platoon was to provide mortar support for riflemen leading the drive up the valley. He fired shells. Japanese returned fire. He fired more. They returned more. The Japanese hid themselves in the fog. When the fog line dropped, the Japanese followed the clouds to lower elevations. When the fog line went up, Japanese did, too. They turned the weather into their ally.

Laird was frustrated. The Japanese could see him but he could not see them. They fired smokeless gunpowder that could not be traced. They spread out in groups that were small and nimble and difficult to find. And worst of all, they were patient. They didn't seem to fire from anger or panic. They were deliberate and strategic. In the valley with no trees, little brush, and few boulders, Laird was an unprotected target.

And then came nightfall. He couldn't say he had seen the sun set because he had never seen the sun. Maybe the sun really had dipped below the horizon. Or maybe the fog just grew dense enough to block out all the light. Either way, it had turned dark. The temperature dipped into the 20s. Wind howled. He was exhausted and wet. His heels were raw from blisters and his legs and arms were spent from lugging his body and his gear up the steep, mushy soils. He fought to stay awake. Occasional bullets and shells reminded him to stay alert. He hunkered down, and he shivered. He had seen darkness in the depths of a coal mine, but he had never felt anything like the blackness of war on Attu at night.

1 First Sergeant Dick Laird after being awarded the Silver Star for gallantry in combat. This photo likely was taken in 1943.

2

Rose Laird at age nineteen in 1936, the year she met Dick Laird.

3

Dick, Rose, and their daughter, Peggy Laird, before Dick shipped off to combat in Alaska from California.

DICK Laird + Co.Clerk

Dick Laird and his clerk conferring with commanders on Kwajalein Atoll in the western Marshall Islands. Fierce fighting killed more than 8,000 Japanese and American soldiers and stripped the island of most vegetation.

Paul and Taeko Tatsuguchi shortly after their marriage in 1938. This photo hung on the walls of the Tatsuguchi house for decades, and was the main formal picture Taeko had together as a married couple.

6

Paul Nobuo Tatsuguchi in Imperial Army uniform.

7

Laura and Joy Tatsuguchi in Japan after the war in 1946.

8

Taeko, Laura, and Joy Tatsuguchi in Japan in 1953, shortly before moving to Hawaii.

9

Six months after bombing Pearl Harbor, Japan raised its flag over the villagers of Attu Island. It was the first U.S. soil lost since the War of 1812.

JAPANESE WINTER CLOTHING WITH
10 BOOTS, OVERCOATS & WINTER CAPS

After training in frigid Hokkaido, Japanese troops
were outfitted with clothing that could stand up to the
unforgiving climate of the Aleutian Islands of Alaska.

11

A prewar aerial view of Attu village, with the Russian Orthodox church at left and the schoolhouse and shortwave radio antenna at bottom right. This 1934 photo was released to the U.S. press on May 14, 1943, as American troops fought to reclaim the island.

12

A rare day without low fog at Attu village, photographed during a 1937 archaeological expedition by the Smithsonian Institution to the Aleutian Islands.

13

A rocky mix of islands, shoals, and reefs guards the entrance to Chichagof Harbor, making any water approach to Attu Village treacherous for invaders.

For the invasion of Attu, U.S. troops scrambled down rope ladders from their ships to landing craft that bobbed in rough seas. Dense fog sometimes blocked views of soldiers' next steps.

15

Grim U.S. troops huddle against the North Pacific cold as their landing crafts advance toward the Attu beachhead.

Chaos reigned on the beaches of Attu Island as U.S. ships struggled to navigate rocky shoals and treacherous currents.

The spongy and boggy soils of Attu made it impossible for U.S. troops to quickly move ashore men and supplies.

18

With Japanese troops firing from the highlands, U.S. troops scrambled on treeless Attu to find any protective cover.

19

Knee-deep mud prevented any swift movement across much of Attu.

Attu's slopes were so steep and spongy that troops added chains to tires and tried to winch vehicles up hillsides. Few Jeeps succeeded in making the climb.

21

Many bulldozers were swallowed by the mud of Attu. With few roads, U.S. supply lines suffered.

22

With no roads and few airdrops, the United States was forced to form man-to-man supply lines to push food and ammunition to rugged battlefronts such as Fishhook Ridge. Some lines extended two miles.

23

On the day of this photo, May 14, 1943, U.S. commanders had expected the Battle of Attu to be over. Every day after that resulted in more casualties from the enemy and the weather.

24

At aid stations, soldiers stripped their waterlogged boots and gave each other foot massages. Trench foot forced hundreds of men to stop fighting. Many were forced to have toes and feet amputated.

25

Wearing boots intended for desert warfare, U.S. troops risked their lives walking along some trails on Attu. One slip on the icy slopes of Fishhook Ridge could prove fatal.

26

When fog lifted, Japanese gunners found easy targets in the mud below. U.S. troops had to look over their shoulders while trying to extract supply vehicles from the unforgiving soils of Attu.

27

Japanese soldiers had superior clothes and fighting positions, but could not match the sheer size of the U.S. fighting force.

Major General William O. Butler (left) and Colonel William O. Eareckson (right), who directed the U.S. air war in the Aleutians. Eareckson's pilots terrified the Japanese with repeated dive-bombing through the fog and mist.

Two leaders of the U.S. Army's invasion of Attu. Best known for his vocal support of the internment of Japanese Americans in the United States, General John DeWitt (left) erroneously predicted that U.S. forces would vanquish the Japanese on Attu in three days. General Simon Buckner (right) oversaw the ultimate U.S. victory in Attu, but at Okinawa he became the highest-ranking U.S. military officer killed by enemy fire in World War II.

Rear Admiral Robert "Fuzzy" Theobald made no secret of his desire to work outside the Aleutians. Brainy and sometimes caustic, Theobald clashed with General Buckner.

Most dead American soldiers were buried at Little Falls Cemetery, near the base of a waterfall from Gilbert Ridge. Their bodies were removed and transferred to other cemeteries in 1947.

32

For decades one of the least-desired duties in the U.S. Coast Guard was working the Loran station on Attu Island. The station was decommissioned and abandoned in 2010.

33

Seventy-five years after the Battle of Attu, the island is still littered with the leftovers of war, though rust, erosion, and native grasses claim more remnants every year.

In September 2018, on a rare cloudless afternoon, the grass grows waist deep on the highlands of Attu Island. This is a view northwest from the heights of Engineer Hill toward Attu Village. The sloping shoulder to the left of Lake Cories is Buffalo Ridge, where Dick Laird and Paul Tatsuguchi met in battle. The photo is taken from the top of Engineer Hill, where scores of Japanese soldiers killed themselves with grenades after a desperate Banzai attack against U.S. troops.

In this September 2018 photo, an eighteen-foot titanium peace memorial rises atop Engineer Hill on Attu. In 1987, the Japanese government donated the sculpture, which carries an inscription in Japanese and English that reads, "In memory of all those who sacrificed their lives in the islands and seas of the North Pacific during World War II and in dedication to world peace."

12
QUAGMIRE

On the day the general said the war on Attu would end, it didn't. Instead, it turned worse.

For the Americans, none of the original military goals had been met. All three invading forces were either pinned down or far from merging. The commander of the southern push, Colonel Edward Earle, was killed by a sniper, and the commander of the northern push, Colonel Frank Culin, battled frostbite and temporarily retreated to a warm ship. Trucks and bulldozers could not move through Attu's taffy soils; several squads had been forced to withdraw when supply lines failed to keep up. There were repeated cases of soldiers on supply lines walking into the hills, dumping their loads, falling asleep, and then lollygagging their way back to the beach. Many men on the front lines went at least a full day without food and collapsed from exhaustion. Others suffered from "Aleutian malaria" — a head cold and hacking cough that would not go away. One company wasted hours of climbing when inaccurate maps led them up a canyon that dead-ended at a cliff. A battalion of reinforcements was lost in the mountains. Forty-four men had been killed and hundreds were wounded. No breakthrough was anywhere in sight. General DeWitt had predicted a victory in three days, but his men had descended into a quagmire.

The Japanese had even less hope. For eight weeks only a handful of Japanese submarines had evaded the American blockade, and Tatsuguchi and others on Attu were forced to cut back on food rations. The rigors of battle only accelerated the depletion of their reserves. Ammunition had to be conserved, too. Fighting from the ridgelines had won them a tactical advantage, but the elevation also exposed troops to stiffer winds and more dangerous cold. Air bombing against them was relentless. The number of dead and wounded soared, and the inventory of medical supplies crashed.

From a cave in a moment of downtime, Nobuo Tatsuguchi began writing his terse diary in his native Japanese. He used dates according to the Japanese calendar, which, as at Pearl Harbor, was one day ahead of the American timetable.

MAY 12 — 0155

Carrier-based plane flew over — fired at it. There is a low fog, and the summit is clear. Evacuated to the summit. Air raids carried out frequently until 1000. Heard loud noise. It is naval gun firing. Prepared battle equipment. Information — American transports begin landing at Hokkai Misaki (Red Beach). Twenty boats landed at Massacre Bay. It seems that they are going to unload heavy equipment. Day's activities — Air raid, naval gun firing, and landing of American troops.

MAY 13 — BATTLE

The United States forces landed at Shiba Dai (Hill X) and Massacre Bay. The enemy has advanced to the bottom of Missumi Yama (Buchanan Ridge) from Shiba Dai. Have engaged them. On the other hand, Massacre Bay is defended by only one platoon, but upon the unexpected attack, the antiaircraft cannon was destroyed and we have withdrawn. In night attack we have captured twenty enemy rifles. There is tremendous mountain artillery gun firing. Approximately fifteen patients came into the field hospital, which is attached to the Arai Engineers Unit.

MAY 14 — BATTLE

Our two submarines from Kiska assisting us have greatly damaged two enemy ships. The enemy has advanced to the bottom of Missumi Yama. First Lieutenant Suzuki died by shots from rifle. There is a continuous flow of wounded into the field hospital. In the evening the United States forces used gas, but no damage was done on account of strong wind. Took refuge in the trenches dug during the daytime and took care of the patients during bombardment. The enemy strength must be a division. Our desperate defense is holding up well.

On the third day, Tatsuguchi's diary was wrong on at least two accounts. No Japanese submarines had done any damage to American ships; the only damage to American ships had been done either by American ships colliding into one another, or by the shoals and rocks of Attu's harbors, which had punched holes into a number of landing craft. The stranded Japanese regiment on Attu had been praying for an Imperial Navy rescue, and Army commanders likely passed around the false story of a successful submarine attack to boost morale.

Tatsuguchi was also mistaken about the use of poison gas on Attu. Though artillery had lobbed phosphorous shells as a way to mark Japanese positions, the smoke was not toxic. Sherman Montrose, an independent cameraman for Acme Newspictures, reported that Americans in a supply line had seen the gas and panicked, believing that it had been fired by the Japanese. When troops began fleeing to save themselves, the journalist reassured them that the gas was safe, and only a way to highlight enemy targets for Americans. The men returned to battle, and the civilian journalist was later awarded a citation from the secretary of war.

Behind Japanese lines, however, rumors of American use of poison gas only heightened the siege mentality. For Tatsuguchi and his fellow stranded troops, the stakes could not be higher. This was a fight without mercy.

Laird felt no sympathy. Fighting in Massacre Valley had ground to a standoff. He blasted mortars for the riflemen ahead, but the Japanese in the heights fired mortars right back. He often wasn't sure where to aim. The fog was the enemy's best friend. Laird may as well have been trying to blast birds from a cloud. With the Japanese hunkered down in trenches, foxholes, and caves, American commanders began to concede the difficulty of the task ahead. "The infantry will have to go in there with corkscrews to dig out the Japs," warned the Alaska commander, General Buckner.

Like many infantrymen, Laird had come ashore with just two cold meals in his pack. They were long gone. He ached with hunger. There were repeated rumors of resupply, but the Army struggled to move inland the required tons of ammunition and food without machinery. Laird and the 7th Division had trained on level ground in the desert. Their legs weren't used to climbing, and they'd weakened further during the weeks-long sea journey from San Francisco. Most men simply weren't in the physical shape necessary to hump heavy loads of supplies up valleys of mush and mountains of snow. Both the fighters, and the men who reinforced them, were spent.

They also were dangerously cold. The same leather boots that caused so many blisters on the first two days were now creating hundreds of debilitating injuries. The leader of the scouts, Captain William Willoughby, was a macho man who had prided himself on his men's preparation. "You come to this outfit, you train your asses off, or you go back to the Women's Corps," he warned. But on their first night on Attu, many of his troops had catnapped in wet boots and woken up with frostbite. Now many soldiers struggled to stand, much less walk. The mountains of Alaska didn't care how many push-ups a soldier could do while training in the desert.

Even more widespread than frostbite was a painful malady called trench foot. First described by Napoleon's troops during their 1812 retreat from Russia, trench foot had claimed more than 70,000 Allied troops during World War I. Trench foot was a fungal infection that resulted from long immersion in cold water or mud, two of the fundamental ingredients of Attu. The first sign was a numb and swollen foot that turned white as blood vessels constricted. As numbness gave way to constant pins-and-needles prickling, the foot exuded a rotten smell and turned red, blue, and black. Skin died. Gangrene festered. In severe cases, amputation was required, but even the milder cases could take weeks to heal. On Attu, trench foot spread with the speed of an epidemic. By the second day of battle, a few men with black feet were being ushered back from the front lines. By the third day, a few cases had turned to dozens. By the fifth day, only forty of the 320 survivors of one provisional scout battalion were able to walk. Several soldiers lost both feet to amputation.

War correspondent Russell Annabel described the miserable conditions for *The Saturday Evening Post:* "Your outfit would move into a position under cover of fog and darkness, and you would dig a foxhole and put up a breastwork of cut sod and rocks. You were already wet from fording streams and falling into sinkholes in the dark, and now seepage begins trickling into the foxhole, so that presently you were standing in a foot or more of bitterly cold water. You couldn't search for a drier place, because by this time the Jap snipers and mortar crews had spotted you. So you crouched there, returning their fire, and after a while, strangely, your feet and legs no longer ached."

The three-day promise of victory was broken. Little ground had been won. Every hour brought more casualties by either the Japanese or the weather. In many places the slopes were so steep and slippery that Americans required eight soldiers to evacuate a single injured comrade; officers were forced to assign a detail of four hundred men to stretcher duty. Nothing on Attu moved easily. Twenty men needed half a day to haul a single piece of artillery six hundred yards through the muck. Such wretched terrain was easier to defend than attack. From the ridges above Massacre Valley, two Japanese companies with less than a hundred men each had stymied the progress of 3,000 American infantrymen backed by artillery and battleship fire.

General Brown swallowed his pride and asked his superiors for help.

"Evidence of greater enemy strength than anticipated," Brown wrote. "Indication of lack of sufficient force to accomplish mission."

Admiral Rockwell was reluctant to give the general what he wanted. Landing beaches remained a serious bottleneck. With tractors and trailers mired in Attu's muck, supply crates from ships piled up on shore. Some transports, such as the *Chirikof* and *Perida,* had managed to unload less than a third of their cargo. A flotilla of forty still bobbed offshore, and Rockwell feared the Imperial Navy could launch a surprise counterattack through the fog. Japanese torpedoes that narrowly missed the 600-foot battleship *Pennsylvania* and the 377-foot destroyer *Bell* only escalated the admiral's worries.

The Army commander believed the Navy

was holding back the manpower he needed to win the battle. The Navy commander believed the Army was turning the North Pacific fleet into sitting ducks. When the Army commander pushed the dispute up to the next level, General DeWitt, who had finally arrived in the Aleutians from San Francisco, wondered why his three-day victory promise wasn't being kept. Admiral Kincaid questioned Brown's "aggressiveness." When the Army commander discussed further plans for Attu that might require six months, generals and admirals recoiled.

The result: The Army commander of the invasion of Attu was sacked.

Major General Brown was out, and Major General Eugene Landrum, a Florida native who had previously led troops in the Aleutians, was in. The revolving door of leadership at Attu spun again.

There was irony in the transition. In the hours while the sacked general was still in command — but before the new general arrived — United States troops won their first notable ground victory on Attu. Colonel Culin had recovered enough from his frostbite to push his men on a bold nighttime charge up a sniper-filled ridge that had tormented troops for days. The Japanese were caught unaware, and fled in a retreat to Chichagof Harbor so swift that they left behind stockpiles of food and ammunition.

Yet even triumph came with tragedy. The successful sneak attack had done more than startle the Japanese — it also surprised the Americans. As the sun rose on the first Americans to have won a heavily defended Japanese ridgeline, Culin's troops were bombed and strafed by America's own Wildcat fighter planes. Several soldiers were wounded before the friendly fire could be halted.

With their own supply lines struggling — ninety of the available ninety-three landing craft had been lost to shoals, reefs, and williwaws — Americans turned to their bounty of seized Japanese grenades. Several times in different firefights, American soldiers pulled the pin of a captured grenade, hurled it, and watched in dread as it landed unexploded. Japanese soldiers picked up the same grenade and threw it back, killing and wounding many American soldiers. The 7th Infantry had not been trained to properly operate an enemy grenade, which, unlike their own, required a separate fuse to be struck to activate detonation.

The new American general was under no illusions about the difficulty of the task ahead. "I know this country and my heart bled for the boys I had to send up there," General Landrum said. "I knew how cold and bitter it was on the mountains. But I knew death was more bitter. I gave them a terrible task. I believed it kinder to send them into the mountains to whip the Japs than to hold them in the valley where Jap snipers could cut them down."

MAY 15 — BATTLE

Continuous flow of casualties to our field hospital caused by the fierce bombardment of enemy land and naval forces. The enemy has a great number of Negroes and Indians. The west arm units have withdrawn to near Shitigata Dai (Moore Ridge.) During a raid I was ordered to the west arm, but it was called off. Just lay down from fatigue in the barracks. Facial expressions of soldiers back from the west arm is tense. They all went back to the firing line soon.

MAY 16 — BATTLE

If Shitigata Dai is occupied by the enemy, the fate of the east arm is decided. So burned documents and prepared to destroy the patients at the last moment. There was an order from Headquarters of

Sector Unit. Proceeded to Chichagof Harbor by way of Umanose (Fishhook Ridge), 0100 in the morning. Patients from Second Infantry were lost, so accompanied the patients. There was an air raid, so took refuge in the former field hospital cave. The guns of a Lockheed [fighter plane] spitted fire as it flew past our cave.

MAY 17 — BATTLE

At night about 1800, under cover of darkness, left the cave. The stretcher went over muddy roads and steep hills of no-man's-land. No matter how far or how fast we went, we did not get to the pass. Was rather irritated in the fog by the thought of getting lost. Sat down every twenty or thirty steps. Would sleep, dream, and wake up again. Same thing over and over again. The frostbitten patient on the stretcher does not move. After all the effort, met Sector Commander Yamasaki. The pass is a straight line without any width and a steep incline toward Chichagof Harbor. Sitting on the butt and lifting the feet, I slid down very smoothly and changed direction with the sword. Slid down in about twenty minutes. After that, arrived in Chichagof Harbor after struggling. The time expended was nine hours for all this, without leaving any patients. Opened a new field hospital. Walking is now extremely difficult from left knee rheumatism which reoccurred on the pass. The results of our navy — the submarine and special underwater craft [midget submarines] in the vicinity of Chichagof Harbor since the fourteenth: sunk battleship, cruisers three, destroyers, transports of airborne troops, and six other transports. By the favorable turn since the battle of the east arm, reserves come back. Off shore of Shiba Dai, six destroyers are guarding one transport.

For Tatsuguchi, the toll of battle was setting in. Americans may have been hungry and cold, but they had reinforcements. The Japanese had only themselves.

Despite Tatsuguchi's claim, the United States had lost no ships to the Japanese. Any talk of a sunken battleship was either a misunderstanding or a false claim by Imperial Army commanders to improve morale, which the Japanese needed. On the morning of May 15 (May 16 Japanese time), two United States battalions had captured the Imperial Army base at Holtz Bay. The Japanese fled so quickly that they left behind large stockpiles of food and ammunition, plus six light artillery guns, as well as several machine guns and mortars. The fleeing survivors would soon feel the loss of these supplies.

The May 16 diary entry saying Tatsuguchi "prepared to destroy the patients at the last moment" is chilling. Japanese military men had been indoctrinated for centuries in the samurai code of bushido — valuing honor more than one's own life. Among the worse humiliations for a Japanese soldier was to be captured alive as a prisoner. Under the bushido code, a noble warrior always chose suicide over surrender. If capture by an enemy was inevitable, a Japanese patient in a military field hospital was expected to ask for a way to kill himself as a way to save his personal and family honor. His commander might even order it.

It's hard to imagine Tatsuguchi obeying it. In the front of the personal Bible he had brought to Attu, Tatsuguchi had inscribed his favorite verse, Deuteronomy 30:19: "Choose life." For Tatsuguchi, the tension between his Japanese and Christian identities could face few challenges greater than the idea of honorable suicide.

At the moment, Dick Laird's main challenge was staying alive. His company had gained some ground up Massacre Valley, which helped the overall objective but hurt his chances for cover. At lower elevations, Laird's standard olive trousers and field jacket had camouflaged him in the willows and mud. Now he was climbing higher. The snowline on Attu was as low as 300 feet. Against the white landscape, his military drabs may as well have been a flashing red light. It turned Laird and all other Americans into easy targets for the Japanese firing from above.

Snow also caused more boot-related problems. The soles were smooth, with little traction. Time and again Laird would try to scale a steep slope, only to slip and slide back down the same grade. The same snow that had allowed Tatsuguchi to glissade down a mountain slope with speed was now blocking Americans from chasing him.

Lieutenant Donald Dwinell of the 32nd Infantry led a charge up Point Able, which towered 2,000 feet above Massacre Valley. The Japanese had fortified the point to rain shells on the invaders below. The point could be gained only by crossing a ridgeline four feet wide with sheer plunges of hundreds of feet on either side. On the exhausting climb upward, Dwinell passed the bodies of four Japanese killed by artillery fire four days prior. Fog swirled. The American soldiers inched along the ridgeline unseen and unheard until the wind shifted and the air cleared without warning. Exposed directly in front of them was a group of Japanese soldiers. Dwinell and his men fired but the Japanese fired back. He leaped with his sergeant and his radioman, William Rehfeld, down into the crater of an artillery shell for protection. Weighed down by his heavy communications equipment, Rehfeld was just a second slower. The Japanese cut him down with a spray of machine gun fire as he jumped into the hole. Bullets had bisected his body from left to right. While his lieutenant and sergeant frantically dug deeper for cover with their hands and a trench knife, Rehfeld lay on top of them, bleeding and asking where he was hit. A few minutes later Rehfeld died on top of his commanders. Enemy fire remained too heavy to permit escape, so the lieutenant and sergeant were forced to lie in the crater on their bellies with their dead comrade pressed across their backs, blood pouring onto their uniforms. They survived hours that way. With nightfall drawing near, the two men were able to roll the body aside and crawl and run from the trailing hail of bullets. The Japanese held Point Able that day.

MAY 18 — BATTLE

The Yonekawa Detachment abandoned east and west arms and withdrew to Umanose [Fish Hook Ridge]. About sixty wounded came to the field hospital. I had to care for all of them by myself all through the night. Heard that the enemy carried out a landing in Chichagof Harbor. Everyone made combat preparations and waited. Had two grenades ready. Second Lieutenant Omura left for the line on Hokuchin Yama. Said farewell. At night a patient came in who had engaged a friendly unit by mistake and who had received a wound on the wrist. The countersign is "Isshi Hoke."

MAY 19 — BATTLE

At night there was a phone call from Sector Unit Headquarters. In some spots on the beach there are some friendly float-type planes waiting. Went into Attu Village church — felt like someone's home — some blankets were scattered around. Was told to translate a field order presumed to have been dropped by an enemy officer in Massacre Bay. Was ordered to

218

evaluate a detailed sketch map of Massacre and Holtz Bay which was in possession of Captain Robert Edward, adjutant of Colonel Smith. Got tired and went to sleep. First Lieutenant Ujile is now in charge of translation.

MAY 20 — BATTLE

The hard fighting of our 303rd Battalion in Massacre Bay is fierce, and it is to our advantage. Have captured enemy weapons and have used for fighting. Mowed down ten enemy closing in under the fog. Five of our men and one medical noncommissioned officer died. Heard that enemy pilots' faces can be seen around Umanose. The enemy naval gun fire near our hospital drops about twenty meters away.

The Japanese northern force was prowling up the coast of Holtz Bay when Sergeant Arthur Benevich and Private First Class Walter Imbirowicz spotted it: a machine gun outpost, surrounded by snow. Imbirowicz sneaked to within thirty-five yards of the enemy when an unseen Japanese rifleman fired. The company dove for cover, but Imbirowicz was exposed on a snowbank. The air exploded with the blasts of machine guns, rifles, and grenades, and Imbirowicz collapsed into the snow. For the next fifteen hours, the Americans remained pinned down by relentless Japanese fire and were unable to retrieve the body.

Finally the Japanese withdrew for the night. When American medics bent over to check on their comrade's dog tags, they witnessed a miracle: Imbirowicz jumped up and ran down the hill to safety. The fallen soldier had only minor wounds on the hand and arm from a hand grenade. He had played dead throughout the fifteen-hour firefight, and lived to tell the tale.

In the opening days of fighting, American surgeons reported treating an unusual number of belly wounds, mainly because troops were inexperienced and reluctant to dive hard for protection against the muck. As the battle progressed, however, surgeons found the common wound had shifted to the buttocks. Better wet and miserable than dead.

That was for the Americans. The Japanese, however, seemed to know no injury. Time and again, Laird and other troops would approach a wounded Japanese soldier, only to hear the crack of a rifle or a blast of a grenade. The first two times he witnessed this, Laird thought the wounded enemy was setting off one final counterattack. A few steps closer and he learned otherwise. The Japanese would not surrender. If they could not flee, they would kill themselves. Despite many attempts, the Americans captured only a handful of prisoners. In the United States, editorialists expressed shock and respect at the devotion of the Japanese fighter on Attu. "Unlike their Nazi imitators, whose synthetic savagery merely produced a bully who cracks when the odds are against him, the Japanese are aboriginal savages who will fight to the death and to the last man, and in that respect are even tougher enemies than the Germans," wrote *The New York Times.*

MAY 21 — BATTLE

Was strafed while amputating a patient's arm. It is the first time since moving over to Chichagof Harbor that I went into an air raid shelter. Enemy plane was a Martin. Nervousness of our commanding officer is severe, and he has said his last word to his officers and noncommissioned officers — that he will die tomorrow. Gave all his articles away. Hasty chap, this fellow. The officers on the front are doing a fine job. Everyone who heard about the actions of the commanding officer became desperate and things became disorderly.

At 0600 — Air raid again. Strafing killed one medical man. Medical man Okasaki wounded in right thigh and fractured arm. During the night a mortar shell came awfully close.

Laird had shot and been shot at more times than he could remember. Fighting was intense. He spent hours blasting mortars up the valley, and he spent hours with his belly pinned into the mud, making himself as small as possible. One of the four men in his foxhole had his penis blown off by shrapnel. Another had survived, barely, after being shot through his helmet by a machine gun. Laird himself felt lucky. His toenails had turned black, and the side of his feet had, too. It hurt to walk, but so far his trench foot had not been debilitating. For American troops, the biggest prize anyone could find in an abandoned enemy foxhole was dry socks. The cold had become so persistent, and so miserable, that some US soldiers risked mistaken identity on the battlefield by seizing the superior Japanese clothes and wearing them.

At one point Laird had unfurled his sleeping bag for the night near a creek. Basic supplies were still scarce. He and his troops lived off occasional K rations eaten cold. He was usually on his own for drinking water, but the combination of rain and snowmelt on Attu kept the creeks brimming. After an exhausting day of fighting and climbing, Laird dipped his canteen into the cold mountain stream. He washed his face, and he drank. He didn't know when he'd have access to mountain water again, so he drank some more.

The next day, Laird woke and refilled his canteen. As he advanced a hundred yards up the creek, ready to fight, he found the body of a Japanese solider, dead, facedown, and bleeding into the current. This was the source of Laird's drinking water. He emptied his canteen and retched.

The battle toll on both Americans and Japanese was brutal. Time magazine correspondent Robert Sherrod found one Army company being led by its fourth commander. The company had started with 192 men. Twelve were killed and 28 wounded. Another 43 were lost to exposure, frostbite, and trench foot. Forty-eight more were sick, shell-shocked, missing, or otherwise unable to fight. That meant only 61 of the original 192 could still fight. The survivors were taken aback by the dedication of the Japanese. "I thought I was going to capture one of the sons of bitches the other day," a private told Sherrod. "I was standing over his foxhole and he was badly wounded. But he reached for his gun and I had to shoot him. I don't care whether you call it fanaticism or just plain guts, they fight to the last man. They are tough bastards." The next day the company mounted its second assault on a high Japanese machine gun and mortar nest known as Buffalo Nose. Of the 61 Americans who attacked Buffalo Nose, only 25 returned. They did not win Buffalo Nose. They could not fight again without reinforcements. The weather on Attu was a powerful foe. The Japanese were even tougher.

MAY 23 — BATTLE

Seventeen friendly medium bombers destroyed a cruiser offshore. By naval gun firing, a hit was scored on the pillar pole of our tent for patients, and the tent gave in and two died instantly. From 0200 in the morning until 1600 stayed in foxholes. The day's rations about 1 go, 5 hakies (a pound and a half), nothing more. Officers and men alike in frost. Everybody looked around for food and stole everything they could find.

MAY 24 — BATTLE

It sleeted and was extremely cold.
Stayed at Misumi barracks alone. A great
number of shells were dropped by naval
gunfire. Rocks and mud fell all over the
roof. It fell down. In a foxhole about five
yards away Hayasaka, a medical man,
died instantly by a piece of shrapnel
through his heart.

13
SUNDAY

A day of Laird's fighting was chronicled at the time in an official War Department book, *The Capture of Attu: Tales of World War II in Alaska, As Told by the Men Who Fought There.* The book was reported and written as a group project by Alaska soldiers, led by Lieutenant Robert Mitchell and including Dashiell Hammett, the dean of the hard-boiled detective novel and author of best-sellers such as *The Maltese Falcon, The Thin Man,* and *Red Harvest.* During the war, Hammett was stationed for eighteen months in the Aleutians and edited the Army news-paper on Adak Island. Though the specific author of the section on Laird is unclear, the writing is much jauntier than typical Army fare. Laird was proud to be featured.

Here is the account:

AN ATTU SUNDAY
1st Sgt. Charles W. Laird
Company H, 32nd Infantry

A little thing like a war wasn't going to stop 1st Sgt. Charles W. Laird from spending a good old American Sunday, although he admits it took a few field expeditions to get it done. The battle had pushed through Clevesy Pass and down into Jim Fish Valley by Sunday, May 23. It was a very cold miserable morning: an icy drizzle of half rain, half snow was falling while Lt. Dean Galles and Sergeant Laird slopped around in the mud, digging in Company H's CP. (Command Post.) They could keep their bodies warm but their hands and feet were freezing off. Sergeant Laird worked as long as he could, with mud sticking to his shovel, then he told Lieutenant Galles he was about to give up. He said he was going to take a walk and keep walking until he got warm. Lieutenant Galles told him to go ahead so Laird started off. He planned to visit all of his machine-gun squads, and during his tour he got farther off to the right than he planned. It was very foggy and unless you were careful you would suddenly look around and discover yourself lost. Laird did just that. He looked up into

227

a draw and saw four well-hidden Jap tents. From the distance he couldn't be sure, but he thought he saw two men near one of the tents. The company had been firing into that area the evening before and Laird wasn't sure how far the riflemen had advanced. Those men might be Japanese, was the cautioning thought he gave himself; but Jap tents always meant stores of dry socks, canned heat, and maybe matches and dry insoles. He decided to take a chance and go on to the tents.

When he got close enough to see some detail through the fog he saw smoke coming from the top of the nearest tent. He hurried up to it and then he heard American voices. He pulled back the flap and looked in. In the center of the tent in a large tin box, some soldiers had built a small, very smoky fire. Sgt. R. L. ("Pinky") Holman and Lt. William B. Frost from Company F were there and several others too, huddled around the little fire. Their faces were grimy and whiskered and haggard, but they were smiling and muttering over the meager warmth of the fire. Pinky even had his shoes off and was painfully wiggling his doughy looking toes over the can. Laird went in and stood by the fire a few minutes.

228

Before long another character came in. He was just an ordinary looking soldier, beat-up, muddy, the weight of fatigue pulling hard at the edges of his face. He spoke to the men inside and added comments to the trickle of conversation about the fight, like any GI. Men were snooping through the litter in the tent, picking up a dry sock or a glove and then returning to the fire. For a small moment all the sound in the tent stopped and the newcomer was the only man standing.

He said, "Well, it isn't exactly an appropriate place to hold a service, I guess, but this is Sunday . . ." The circle of ragged roughnecks looked at him. No one spoke, and Sergeant Laird quickly thought, What is this? Some GI pulling a wise one. Pinky courteously lowered his bare feet and shoved them down into his boots. Chaplain Clarence J. Merriman, the muddy, tired soldier, pulled out his small book of scriptures and read. The circle of lined, gaunt faces watched the chaplain, and they listened. They didn't hear the words, the words weren't important then. But they heard what each of them needed to hear for himself. And then as the helmeted heads bowed over their rifles, the chaplain said The Lord's Prayer.

Lieutenant Frost coughed, and Pinky hung his feet over the fire again. The chaplain said, "If you find any written documents or things around here, give them to me and I'll take them to G-2." The men turned over several manuals and postcards and things to the chaplain as he left to look for some matches. Church was over. Sergeant Laird went in search of matches himself, and he and the chaplain and a fat soldier were in the tent across from the "chapel" when a Jap machine gun opened up. The tent popped as the bullets ripped into it and the paper on the floor hopped around like leaves in a whirlwind. The three men dived for the floor as another burst sang over their heads, tearing gashes in the fat boy's parka. The doorway was blocked by the fire so the chaplain ripped a hole in the back of the tent and rushed through it, with the fat boy on his heels. Laird stayed low while the third burst struck, then he made a dash for the hole. Everyone else had miraculously disappeared. Laird jumped over a bank at the back of the tent and dashed to a creek bed in the flat below. He considered the possibility that his own guns were firing at him and thought he might even show himself and perhaps the firing would stop. He got up out of the creek and waved, then dived back into the creek bed as a burst of bullets ripped the tundra close to where he had been standing. For several long minutes he lay still, then slowly and carefully he began working his way down the creek and toward Engineer Hill.

It was about 20 minutes after the first burst had hit the tent and Laird was on his belly moving across an exposed part of the creek bed, when he saw a flash in the creek. His eyes lit up and he whistled through his teeth. The biggest trout he had ever seen had ducked under the bank right below where he was lying. Laird pulled up the sleeves of his shirt and jacket as high as he could get them and carefully slipped his outspread fingers into the water. Slowly he worked his hands over the bank and back under the overhanging grass and tundra. Then he felt the big fish. He made a grab with his right hand and caught the trout around the gills. After a round of violent splashes and grabs and grunts he rolled back from the creek holding a fine, big, solid three-and-a-half pounder tight in both hands. He wanted to holler "Yippee!" and jump up but he remembered his little slant-eyed buddy with the machine gun.

So, holding his fish tightly, he worked his way cautiously back along the creek until he was sure he was out of sight in the fog. Then he got up and quickly cut across to where Lieutenant Galles and the CP were located.

Lieutenant Galles was tickled to see the fish and suggested they roll it in mud and bake it. They had a helluva time. The mud wasn't the right kind and it kept crumbling off, and the fire wouldn't burn, but finally they got the fish baked and even without salt it was the best fish dinner either one of them had ever had. "Just like Sunday back home," Sergeant Laird was saying. "Go to church in the morning and then go fishing, come home and have a good supper, and then . . ." A Jap 70mm from somewhere up on the mountain had spotted them. A piece of shrapnel from the first shell ripped through a box of ammunition that Sergeant Laird had been sitting on. Lieutenant Galles looked up from his hole a few minutes later. "Laird, this may be like a Sunday back at *your* home," he said, and Sergeant Laird replied from his hole, "Well I was going to add 'with some slight variations,' sir, but I was interrupted."

Laird was thrilled to be featured, but the

story wasn't entirely accurate. For starters, Laird was the one who cooked the fish, not Lieutenant Galles. The bigger issue, of course, was the depiction of Laird's typical Sunday back home as something out of a Norman Rockwell painting. That certainly wasn't the case while Laird grew up in Appalachia, where there was rarely enough food for a comfortable family dinner, the mother was hardly ever home, and the family did not regularly attend church. It also wasn't true in California, where Laird lived on the Army base and only occasionally was able to see his wife and her daughter. Still, Laird enjoyed the story enough to send it to family and friends. He liked it better than ducking gunfire.

14
"Come On! Let's Go!"

Naval gun firing, aerial bombardment, trench warfare — the worst is yet to come. The enemy is constructing his posts and positions. Battalion commander died at Umanose. They cannot fully accommodate their patients. It has been said that at Massacre Bay district, the road coming to Sector Unit Headquarters is isolated. Am suffering from diarrhea and feeling dizzy.

MAY 26 — BATTLE

By naval gun firing, it felt like the Misumi barracks blew up, and things shook tremendously. Consciousness becomes vague. One tent burned down by a hit from incendiary bombs. Strafing planes hit the next room. Two hits by a .50 caliber gun; one stopped in the ceiling and the other penetrated. My room looks like an awful mess from the sand and pebbles that have come from the roof. Hirose, first lieutenant from the medical corps, is wounded. There was a ceremony of granting the Imperial Edict. The last line of Umanose was broken through. No hope for reinforcements. Will die for cause of Imperial Edict.

Even in retreat, the Japanese Army was ferocious. For two days, soldiers had killed and wounded dozens of Americans trying to scale Fishhook Ridge, the stark geographic barrier protecting the Japanese base at Chichagof Harbor. Fishhook was 1,500 feet high, caked with snow, and steep enough to set off avalanches. At this point in the battle, Fishhook was the main strategic advantage left for the Japanese. In white coveralls, machine gunners camouflaged themselves in the snow and sprayed ruin on the invaders below. Others rolled hand grenades down snowy slopes to explode on climbing attackers. For Americans, the flat area below Fishhook Ridge became known as Suicide Basin.

On May 26, however, Private Joe Martinez decided that he'd had enough. Disgusted by the stalemate, he stood with his Browning Automatic Rifle and charged the hill.

"Come on! Let's go!" he yelled to his Company K of the 32nd Infantry.

A man possessed, Martinez blasted automatic fire into every hole he found. When he ran out of ammunition he grabbed a service rifle from someone else and rained more hell. Men followed. "Come on! Let's go!" he cried again.

At the top of the pass, the Japanese were holed up beneath a rock overhang. Their rifles and machine guns once again pinned down the Americans. Martinez decided he hadn't come so far, and risked so much, to be ground down to another stalemate. He stood on an exposed rock and emptied a magazine of bullets into the Japanese trench. He stopped to reload and fired again. With his next round came a crack in response. Martinez fell backward. He was mortally wounded. His courage and sacrifice inspired the 3rd Battalion to press onward. The battle for Fishhook Ridge tilted in favor of the Americans.

The whole charge was so unexpected and so chaotic that no one managed to record an accurate count of the casualties inflicted by Martinez. Some GIs say he killed six Japanese; others believe his toll was as high as thirty. No one disputed his valor. "It was a one-man charge," said Lieutenant Morton Solot, his commanding officer. "He didn't have any cover."

Martinez was awarded the Congressional Medal of Honor posthumously. The native of Taos, New Mexico, was the first Hispanic to win the nation's highest military decoration, and the first private to win it in World War II. His final rallying cry — "Come on! Let's go!" — was used for years as a slogan to sell United States savings bonds.

As the battle turned in favor of the Americans, some troops regained their swagger. When Private Joe Mendoza found an unarmed Japanese soldier huddled behind a rock, he aimed his M1 rifle but doubted the morality of what he was about to do. Mendoza then decided to make it a fair fight. He dropped his rifle. According to *Time* magazine, he pulled out one knife, pitched another knife to the enemy, and challenged him to a fight. When the Japanese soldier instead ran for his life, Mendoza shot him with no regrets.

At a horrible cost to both sides, the Japanese had been blasted out of Massacre Valley, Point Able, Jarmin Pass, Hill X, and the east arm and west arms of Holtz Bay. Surviving fighters were concentrated on a low plateau between the fortified heights of Buffalo Ridge and the base and old Attu village at Chichagof Harbor. There was no easy way for the Americans to push forward, or for the Japanese to escape. Tatsuguchi was grim and desperate.

MAY 27 — BATTLE

Diarrhea continues. Pain is severe. Took everything — pills, opium, morphine — then slept pretty well. Strafing by planes. Roof broke through. There is less than a thousand left of more than two thousand troops. Wounded from Coast Defense, Unit Field Hospital Headquarters are here. The rest are on the front lines.

MAY 28 — BATTLE

The remaining ration is for only two days. Our artillery has been completely destroyed. There is a sound of trench mortar — also of antiaircraft gun. The company on the bottom of Attu Fuji (Cold Mountain) has been completely annihilated except one man. Rations for about two days. I wonder if Commander Yonegawa and some of his men are still living. Other companies have been completely annihilated except one or two. The 303rd Battalion has been defeated. Yonegawa is still holding Umanose. Continuous cases of suicide. Half of Sector Unit Headquarters has been blown away. Hear that they gave four hundred shots of morphine to seriously wounded and killed them. Ate half-fried thistle. It is the first time I have eaten something fresh in six months. It is a delicacy. Order from the sector commander to move the field hospital to the inland, but it was called off.

15
BUSHIDO

No help was coming. He hadn't wanted to believe it, but now he had to admit it. All those promises of rescuing submarines, counter-attacking battleships, supporting fighter planes, even backup food and ammunition — they were all a lie. Any hope was false. Tatsuguchi and his fellow troops were on their own. For seventeen days they had fought fiercely, even nobly, but fewer than half of their original brigade survived. They were down to a thousand men. Perhaps two days of food and ammunition remained. They had been assaulted by 42,000 artillery shells, dozens of warplanes, and tens of thousands of bullets. They were surrounded.

The day before an American plane had dropped leaflets with this message:

Your attention is called to the fact that your forces are now in a hopeless position, and that because the United States forces control the air and sea lanes, there is no chance of reinforcements for your troops. Therefore, in accordance with the rules of land warfare, I ask for the unconditional surrender of the Japanese Garrison of Attu Island. Your defense and soldierly conduct of your troops have been worthy of the highest military traditions. It is requested that the Commanding Officer, accompanied by not to exceed four staff officers, proceed openly in broad daylight under white flags in a southerly direction in Chichagof Valley to the vicinity of the South End of Lake Cories. This party will not be fired upon and will be met by guides who will conduct you to the place where the surrender will be received. After the surrender, your forces will be entitled to and will receive all privileges due prisoners of war according to the rules of land warfare.

Colonel Yamasaki, the Japanese commander, was dubious. Just who did the Americans think they were fighting? Japan did not surrender. Even when an Imperial Army soldier was caught behind lines, he refused to lay down his rifle. He turned it on himself, or pressed a grenade to his chest. Surrendering was an insult to his emperor, the sacred spirits, and his family honor. The few Japanese captured as prisoners of war, almost to the man, asked to be killed or sent permanently to a place where no family member could ever see them.

When Yamasaki gathered his men that evening outside their besieged command post, hope had been replaced by duty. They could not win. They could not surrender.

They could, however, mount the biggest banzai attack the United States Army had ever seen.

"By the combined attack of the enemy land, sea, and air units, the battalions on the front line have been defeated," said Yamasaki's order to his troops. "However, our morale is excellent and we are holding some important points. We will attack and annihilate the United States Forces."

The goal was to break through the front line, seize U.S. food and weapons, especially artillery, and then use it all to crush United States troops with a retooled offensive. Because Yamasaki knew the plan was unlikely to succeed, he directed his cryptographers to destroy all remaining documents at the Japanese base. He then ordered his soldiers to reconvene before dawn the next day.

MAY 29 — BATTLE

Today at 2000 o'clock we assembled in front of Headquarters. The field hospital took part too. The last assault is to be carried out. All the patients in the hospital were made to commit suicide. Only thirty-three years of living and I am to die here. I have no regrets, Banzai to the Emperor. I am grateful that I have kept the peace of my soul which Christ bestowed upon me. At 1800 took care of all the patients with grenades. Goodbye Taeko, my beloved wife, who loved me to the last. Until we meet again, grant you Godspeed. Misako, who just became three years old, will grow up unhindered. I feel sorry for you, Mut-suko, born February of this year and never will see your father. Well, goodbye, Machan [brother]. Goodbye Sat-chan, Teshi-chan, Mitchan [nicknames for sisters]. The number participating in this attack is a little over a thousand, to take enemy artillery positions. It seems that the enemy will make an all-out attack tomorrow.

Dick Laird heard something. He wasn't sure what, but it was out there, beyond his pup tent, a noise in the dark that jostled him awake. Maybe it was just footsteps from his company runner returning from head-quarters with the day's fighting orders. Or maybe it was something worse. He couldn't ignore it. He grabbed his M1 service rifle, his .45 caliber pistol, two grenades, and he rolled on the ground outside.

His Company H was camped just below the crest of Buffalo Ridge, a strategic point that allowed his soldiers to blast mortars onto the Japanese encampment below at Chichagof Harbor. Now it was 5 a.m., before sunrise, and fog shrouded everything. Laird couldn't see much, but he could hear a noise, a scuffling, not far away.

Then the gloom erupted.

"Banzai! You die! We die!"

A squad of Japanese soldiers descended upon his tent and slashed it with bayonets. It was chaotic and confusing and Laird wasn't even sure what was happening. In the fog, he could hardly see the enemy, and they could hardly see him. He raised his rifle for a shot, but they disappeared back into the fog.

Laird frantically tore at the remnants of his tent. Under the shreds he found his tent mate groaning and soaked in blood. He convulsed, then grew still. He was dead.

From behind Laird came another noise. He grabbed his rifle again, bracing for another attack, when he turned and saw a fellow American soldier stumbling toward him. It was a platoon sergeant with a deep slash from his ear into his mouth. The sergeant's jaw dangled with every step. He could not calm himself. Laird pressed the jaw back into place, but the soldier was unwilling or unable to hold it. Laird sat the man on the ground. This time the man seemed to comprehend. He held his own jaw in place. Laird promised to get help.

His tent mate was dead and his platoon sergeant was slashed through the bone. Laird needed medics, and fast.

From the ridge rose the screams of the attackers and the moans of the wounded. With dawn the sky lightened, but the fog continued to drift through, offering only unpredictable glimpses of his surroundings.

From the corner of his eye he detected movement, then heard an unearthly groaning sound racing toward him. Had the Banzai attackers returned to finish him off? This time he would not be caught off-guard. He raised his rifle and fired.

After the crack of the shot he heard a weight drop to the muskeg. He tensed. Would a shot be fired in return? Nothing. He paused a second more. Still quiet. He waited for a squad of banzai warriors to burst from the fog, but nothing moved. He pressed ahead and found a body slumped on the ground, wearing not the tan woolens of the Japanese, but the combat helmet of an American.

Laird had killed his own Army runner, who, it turned out, had been bayoneted earlier in the banzai attack.

He collapsed in grief. My God, what had he done? He was trying to defend himself. He couldn't see clearly and he didn't think clearly. It all happened so fast. He made an awful mistake. It was so final. His own man sprawled lifeless at his feet.

Friendly fire has always been a horrible partner of war — the Army estimated 12 to 14 percent of all deaths in World War II came from friendly fire — but this fact didn't make Laird feel any better. He felt like a monster. He looked around and panicked. He didn't know what to do.

He had little time for guilt, and even less for hand-wringing. Above him in the fog he heard more noises, more men. He could not see if they were friend or foe. His self-confidence was weak, but his instinct for self-preservation took over. He moved slowly, cautiously, through the fog and toward the disturbance. This time, Laird promised himself, he would be certain of his target.

Toward the top of the ridge the clouds lifted, just for a second, but it was enough for Laird to confirm what he was up against. A squad of Japanese had claimed the American mortar position, which was dug into a knoll along Buffalo Ridge. Instead of being aimed at Chichagof Harbor, the mortar was being spun around by the Japanese and pointed in the opposite direction — at the Americans.

Laird was joined by his company clerk, and together they heard the clunk of a shell being dropped by the Japanese into the 81mm mortar. "Oh, boy, it's going to come down right on our troops," Laird whispered. "It's got to be stopped." Laird and the clerk raced around the side of the knoll and watched the Japanese maneuver the mortar into position. Their squad had too many men for Laird to defeat with his rifle. He had already thrown his two grenades during the earlier assault, so he asked the clerk for more.

His clerk handed him two. Laird pulled the pin on one and held it two seconds to let the fuse burn down. The clerk was so terrified by the delay that he crawled as fast as he could away from Laird, who lobbed the grenade over his shoulder and toward the Japanese and dug his face into the dirt for cover.

The tundra shook with the force of the blast. Ears ringing, Laird stood to survey the damage.

His grenade scored a direct hit, but some troops survived. One Japanese soldier stood and trained his pistol at Laird, who was ready with his rifle. He squeezed the trigger and shot the pistol from the soldier's hand. Laird had been aiming for the body, but was still grateful that he hit something. He charged the enemy and let his M1 finish the job.

He had killed eight Japanese. In the frenzy his clerk had run in the opposite direction, but another soldier had come across the mayhem and sprayed more bullets from his Browning Automatic Rifle into the corpses. The soldier had lost control of himself, and kept firing and firing and firing. Chunks of flesh exploded into the air. Laird screamed. "If you fire one more shot, I'm going to kill you!" he barked. "We're not barbarians!"

The soldier stopped. Laird tried not to gag.

At his boots was a twisted pile of human futility — soldiers who had given all for a place that no leader of their country would ever see. They were here only because men

248

from the opposite side of the Pacific were here, too. In time Laird would leave this place. The corpses around his feet would not.

More men from Company H had heard the firefight and joined the battle. They stood in awe at what Laird had accomplished. He had single-handedly wiped out a squad of eight enemy soldiers. In the mortar commandeered by the Japanese there was a shell, pointed at U.S. troops below, that remained unfired. It was the worst day of Laird's life, but it had turned him into a hero. He had killed, and he had spared.

Laird and the other soldiers inspected the bodies. They were supposed to look for papers and maps and anything else that might reveal enemy war plans. At this point in their cold and brutal fight, however, many soldiers also were desperate for booty — dry socks, food, warm hats and gloves. Laird tried to stay true to his training. He studied the bodies as a policeman would view a crime scene. He struggled to keep his eyes clinical and dispassionate. The scene around the mortar was gruesome.

Like many of his fellow soldiers, Laird claimed a Japanese gunto sword as a war prize. On one dead soldier, however, Laird noticed something unusual. The soldier carried a satchel. Laird looked inside and found books and a document that was handwritten in Japanese. It might be important, it might not. Laird stuffed it in his pocket to give to his superiors.

He had no time to look for anything else. Down the slope the Japanese assault continued. Bullets and shells flew around Laird and his men. Over the explosions he heard men yipping like coyotes and screaming curses.

"Banzai! You die! We die!"

"Die Yankee dogs, die!"

And then, a furious cry in response: "The Japs are here! They've broken through!"

Led by Colonel Yamasaki, who wielded his sword in the center of the attack just behind the front line, a thousand Japanese soldiers poured up the Chichagof Valley, across Buffalo Ridge, and overran the first of two United States command posts.

The next hours were a fury of screams and blood and adrenaline. Japanese blasted into an American medical tent and sprayed the wounded with bullets and grenades. Attackers bayoneted the bedridden to death. Whole camps of fighting men were detonated. A soldier fleeing a grenade in his tent ran for his life outside and was impaled by a sword. The Japanese captured a Browning Automatic Rifle and turned it on its owners. Another wounded American tried to defend himself by grabbing an abandoned Japanese rifle, but he tripped and fell with his chest onto the bayonet. The Japanese shot and pressed on, shot and pressed on, stopping only when they came across a supply dump or kitchen, where they paused to load up on food, cigarettes, and grenades. The Japanese were so short of ammunition that some mounted the banzai charge with only the bayonets on their unloaded rifles, or knives lashed to sticks, their determination stronger than their firepower.

Caught by surprise, the Americans regrouped and mounted a furious counterattack. After Captain Albert Pence killed and stunned a handful of attackers with a grenade, he raced in to finish the job with his combat knife. In his anger Pence lost control of himself and plunged his knife again and again and again into the back of a Japanese soldier, only to realize that the blade had snapped several thrusts ago inside the man's spine. Pence moved on.

Yamasaki's men overwhelmed Company L of the 17th Infantry and seized every available weapon. For the first time the full might of American firepower was trained back on Americans. The fog lit up with .30 caliber tracer bullets, then the bigger and louder .37 calibers. Every tracer shot illuminated a landscape of men running for the lives, diving for cover, collapsing in their tracks.

Through the Japanese onslaught Alvin Mahaffey played dead in a hole as squads of Banzai attackers charged by. At least three separate squads of Japanese had kicked him or run over him, but Mahaffey's act was so convincing that no one had thought to bayonet him. Finally Mahaffey could bear it no longer. He up and ran for the closest English speakers he could find, Company B of the 32nd Infantry and Colonel Lawrence Kelley. When Mahaffey saw his fellow Americans, he stopped running, stood up straight, and broke into a giant grin. "Get down!" the men shouted, but Mahaffey continued walking in relief until a bullet dropped him twenty feet from his rescuers. He was shot in the arm, but he rolled into a creek for cover and survived.

At an aid station for the frostbitten and wounded near the base of what came to be known as Engineer Hill, Japanese pockmarked the tent with a fusillade of bullets, then stormed on to other targets without checking inside. Captain George Buehler gasped. Had he really survived? He surveyed the tent and found that four of the thirteen soldiers inside were still able to move. Only one had been killed — a frostbitten soldier whose skull had been exploded by a bullet. Fearing a return of the Japanese, Buehler dragged the mangled body of the slain American serviceman to the front of the tent, hoping the enemy would see it and conclude that the others inside had been killed as well. The ruse worked. Five successive Japanese patrols pulled back the tent flap, saw the slain soldier sprawled in the doorway, and turned around without further investigation. When his wounded brethren moaned with pain, Buehler had medics inject them with morphine to restore silence. When the doped-up soldiers snored, Buehler jostled them to stop the noise. Hours later they were all rescued. "What a nightmare — a madness of noise and confusion and deadliness," Buehler said.

As the banzai charge continued, the Japanese tired. Though still potent, they were too outnumbered to capture the American artillery and ammunition needed to survive. The attack stalled.

At the top of Engineer Hill, the Army had stationed several platoons of noncombatant support troops — construction engineers, medics, and supply workers. When the Japanese broke through the front lines, General Archibald Arnold quickly organized the rear echelon into a defense force that grabbed any possible weapon. They blocked the Japanese with the few available grenades, then pushed back the attackers with a hand-to-hand fight to the death in a fury of bayonets and rifle butts. On the snowy flanks of Engineer Hill, Colonel Yamasaki was killed with sword in hand by an American bullet.

Decimated and in disarray, the banzai attack collapsed. The Japanese realized they had lost their chance to seize American artillery and supplies. They knew their training. They knew their obligation. They knew the code of bushido — death before defeat. At the foot of Engineer Hill, as many as 500 Japanese soldiers massed together, pressed grenades to their chests, and, with a relentless series of explosions, committed mass suicide. Afterward one U.S. soldier described the scene as an uprooted graveyard.

Night fell. Shooting paused. The few Japanese who survived the day crumpled with exhaustion. Laird did, too. He had never seen anything like May 29, 1943, on Attu. He hoped he never would again.

■ ■ ■ ■

The next morning the Americans found that the Japanese fighting spirit was all but gone. Troops who had mounted a fearless attack the day before now hid and hunkered down in caves and tunnels. Not all were ready to quit, however.

Captain Albert Pence led five men in what was supposed to be a mop-up operation on an approach to Chichagof Harbor. As they approached a draw, a Japanese machine gun sprayed, and two of the five in Pence's patrol fell to the tundra. Andrew Mezei was hit in the hip and lived; Staff Sergeant Harold J. Hunter took a bullet in the forehead and died. Pence was distraught and furious. This was no mop-up. This was still war.

From the top of the hill the machine gunner fired on Pence, then lobbed a grenade, which bounced off Pence's side and rolled down the slope. He pushed himself hard enough into the dirt to survive the blast, then he saw two more grenades, including a purloined American device, flying back at him. This time Pence was injured slightly in the face. In retaliation, he hurled two of his own grenades back up at the Japanese. He was not prepared for the result.

A massive eruption of arms, heads, and boots cascaded down the hill. Astounded, Pence raced to the machine gun nest only to find that his grenades weren't the cause of the carnage. In a twenty-yard circle around the gun, thirty-six Japanese men had held grenades to their chests and blown themselves up.

The closer the Americans progressed to the Japanese base at Chichagof Harbor, the more suicides they witnessed. When Pence killed one sniper, two others in the same foxhole detonated themselves. When Sergeant Roger Carpentier wounded another sniper, the Japanese soldier yelled in English, "I'm going to die." He blew himself up, too. Sergeant Carmen Calabrese rolled one grenade into a cave and heard two blasts in response. He waited a minute, rolled in another grenade, and received two more blasts. The Americans had never seen or heard anything like it.

What awaited the Americans at the Japanese base on Attu was even worse.

Inside the field hospital were corpses — hundreds of corpses. Americans had not fired a single shot here.

Sakae Horiguchi was a Japanese patient

who witnessed what had happened. Just before the banzai attack, after Yamasaki's final orders, the wounded were directed to end their own lives. "I pulled the pin on my grenade," Horiguchi explained later to a reporter for NBC News. "I tried to commit suicide but the grenade never went off. Had it exploded I wouldn't be here today."

Dozens of others, however, were successful.

"Everyone had tears in their eyes, especially those who had to burn photos of their wives and children," Horiguchi said. "Those who weren't able to walk committed suicide. For those who couldn't on their own, soldiers helped them go through with it."

Of the 2,900 Japanese men stationed on Attu, only 28 survived battle as prisoners of war. The shame of capture was so great that many asked to be taken to America or someplace where they would never see their families or countrymen. The prisoners were unusually cooperative. Japanese soldiers were not trained to resist enemy interrogators because it was presumed they would kill themselves before questioning started. And so many did commit suicide that Laird and the Americans required days to find the Japanese corpses. The United States Army recorded burying 2,351 Japanese, usually eight to a trench, though an exact count was challenging because suicides by hand grenade had left behind so few intact bodies. The piles of casualties were so vast that many burials were carried out by bulldozer.

The toll on the Americans was horrific as well. There were 549 killed; 1,148 wounded; 1,200 with frostbite, trench foot, and other severe weather-related injuries; 614 with severe illnesses; and 318 with psychological breakdowns, self-inflicted wounds, and accidents. Hundreds of soldiers on Attu required amputations. All this was for a battle that the generals had predicted would require only three days of fighting.

About one of every four American soldiers became a casualty on Attu. For the United States, it was the worst casualty rate up to that point in the war in the Pacific. (It was exceeded later only at Iwo Jima.) For every 100 Japanese found on the island, 71 Americans were killed or wounded. Few fights in modern warfare had more suffering than the Battle of Attu.

The Army brass vowed to learn from the lessons of Attu by issuing better equipment for cold weather. The reality, however, was that no place on earth had comparable weather. Other battlefields in World War II offered a strategic location, or natural resources to seize, or a population to protect. Attu had none of these. The island was unknown before the war, and it would be forgotten soon after.

In Washington, D.C., the military was embarrassed by the initial loss of territory at Attu and the costly, ill-prepared drive to reclaim it. As a result, the War Department saw little reason to publicize the victory. Eventually many Aleutian veterans would return home and be greeted with blank stares when describing how they fought in Alaska. Americans didn't know about Attu because the brass didn't want them to know about Attu.

In Tokyo, the government issued a terse statement on the day after Attu was lost: "It is assumed the entire Japanese force has preferred death to dishonor." Though Radio Tokyo stressed the heroism and selfless sacrifice that turned Attu into a kind of Japanese Alamo, the reality was that few citizens wanted to hear much about a crushing defeat. Public attention in Japan moved on.

On the Fourth of July, after a vast new cemetery was dug and the bodies were buried, the United States Army conducted a memorial service. A major read all 549 names of the American dead. A sergeant sang "My Buddy." Prayers were recited and a salute of gunfire echoed up the valley and onto the mountains. Two buglers played taps. When it came time to dismiss the assembled troops, Captain Robert Foulston called, "Forward," but a reservoir of despair cracked in his throat and prevented him from finishing with the next word, "march."

A soldier sniffled. The shoulders of another rocked. Dick Laird could stand it no longer. He let his tears flow.

For his valor killing eight Japanese who had wrested control of an American mortar, Laird was awarded the Silver Star, the Army's third-highest commendation for soldiers in battle. He felt no joy and little pride. His conscience was heavy with the friendly fire death of his runner. He had buried too many friends. He also didn't feel right about the incident that had won him the Silver Star.

In the hours after the doomed Japanese counterattack, the war diary of Nobuo Tatsuguchi was translated behind battle lines at division headquarters by Army Sergeant Yasuo Sam Umetani, a Nisei, or the America-born son of Japanese American immigrants. The Nisei translator reportedly wept bitterly when he read Tatsuguchi's final diary entry that bade farewell to his family. At the request of Laird, the translator had returned an English version of the diary to him.

Laird cradled his mimeographed copy of the diary days after the battle was over. His first reading disappointed him. He had hoped the journal would give away some Japanese code, some secret plan, that would help bring this war to an end. No such luck there.

But the more he read the diary, the more he considered the man behind it. Laird could not help but imagine himself in the same situation. He had been delivering the bombardment, not taking it. What if Laird were the one facing certain death? Would he maintain the same quiet dignity? Laird did not want to contemplate his own last words. He was a man who talked little, wrote less, and was self-conscious when he did either. The mere idea of writing something permanent, under pressure, that likely would be read by strangers, turned Laird's stomach.

He thought of Rose, and he thought of their daughter. They needed him. Surrounded by mud and agony and so many bodies, Laird realized he needed them, too. They gave him reason to push on.

Then the gravity of the document began to sink in. According to the diary, this writer, this Nobuo Tatsuguchi, had family who depended on him, too. He was a trained surgeon with many years of education. Laird had been forced to quit school for the coal mines at age fourteen. The surgeon was a healer. Laird was a warrior. Pushed forward by their countries, the two men had ended up on the same battlefield. And Laird had killed him.

Tatsuguchi had concluded his diary with a terse listing of his personal résumé, or, as he called them, "Life Facts." Two entries, in particular, gnawed at Laird: *September 15, 1929, to May 22, 1932, Pacific Union College, Medical Department, Angwin, California.* And: *September 1, 1933, to June 1937, College of Medical Evangelists, [Loma Linda University]. Received California Medical License September 8, 1938 (USA).*

Laird already carried the dark burden of having killed his own runner in a battlefield friendly fire accident. Now here was a diary describing another man killed by Laird who had attended college in California and earned a California medical license. Had Laird killed a second American as well? The question was almost unbearable.

Through an almost unbelievable series of coincidences, Laird soon faced his dread.

After Tatsuguchi was killed and Laird had

moved on to the next firefight, other American soldiers recognized the medical bags of a doctor strewn on the tundra. The soldiers brought the bags to their own battalion surgeon, Dr. Lawrence Whitaker, who was startled to find they contained an English-language version of the classic physician's textbook *Gray's Anatomy.*

Even more shocking — the inside cover of the book held the handwritten name of Ed Lee, a former classmate of Whitaker's at the College of Medical Evangelists at Loma Linda University in California. Beneath Lee's name was handwriting with another name: Paul Tatsuguchi.

Whitaker had a hard time believing his own eyes. He ventured from his sick bay to the battlefield and identified the body of the man he knew as Tatsy, a fellow graduate of Loma Linda.

In medical school, Tatsuguchi had bought the used *Gray's Anatomy* from his classmate Lee. The guide had served Tatsuguchi at peace in California and at war in Attu. (Amazingly, another Loma Linda classmate, Dr. Joseph Mudry, who had once called Tatsuguchi "quite an American," was also stationed on Attu. Whitaker showed him the textbook, too.) Whitaker thought the book deserved a better fate than its owner. Years later, after the war, he made it a point to return Tatsuguchi's book to Lee at his home in Downey, California.

The surviving classmates could not help but wonder if the world had turned upside down. In a prewar letter months earlier from his Imperial Army base in Hokkaido, Tatsuguchi had joked to his wife that he might soon be reunited with former medical school classmates. In the worst possible way, his prediction had come true.

The whole notion of a California-trained surgeon slain in battle in a Japanese uniform was fascinating to United States servicemen. The Tatsuguchi diary quickly became a coveted war souvenir. First dozens and then hundreds of copies were circulated among soldiers in the Pacific, then back in the continental United States when transports returned home. Some copies were mimeographed onto thin onion-skin paper and stuffed into rucksacks. Other soldiers created their own versions on typewriters. And still others may have resulted from a subsequent translation.

All told, at least ten separate versions of Nobuo Tatsuguchi's diary were eventually distributed. Some versions varied by just a word or two. Others added or deleted whole phrases and sentences. There were typos and mangled words that bore little resemblance to anything in Japanese. Names were misspelled in ways that weren't even close to phonetic pronunciations. Years later, the differences in the translations of a few words would fuel a vast controversy for the Tatsuguchi family and the Seventh-day Adventist community.

One controversy was immediate. The Alaska commander, Simon Buckner, was concerned about the diary's false claim that the United States had deployed gas against the Japanese. Buckner called for the original diary to be pulled out of circulation and sent to his headquarters. He also demanded that souvenir copies of all other translations be confiscated.

Both orders were botched. Somewhere in transit from Attu to the Alaska headquarters, Tatsuguchi's handwritten diary was apparently lost, never to be found again. And the confiscation order for translated copies went widely ignored or unenforced.

The result was that Tatsuguchi's true handwritten words — and the Army's first field translation — could never be checked for accuracy. What remained in circulation, however, were hundreds of copies of different versions of conflicting translations.

For now, Laird and other U.S. servicemen

were less concerned with translation errors, but fascinated by the private account of the enemy. They had been told for months that the Japanese were ruthless killers, fanatics with an inhuman thirst for blood and destruction. Seventeen days of furious battle only helped to confirm that stereotype for Laird.

Tatsuguchi's diary, however, proved to Laird that the Japanese were human, too. Like U.S. soldiers on Attu, Tatsuguchi was cold and scared and hungry and sick and brave. Most of all, Tatsuguchi had offered a heartfelt confession of love for his wife and their daughters. Regardless of his native country, a long-deployed soldier could not help but be moved by a man bidding farewell to a three-month-old daughter he had never met. They also were struck by the one undisputed truth: Neither the American GI nor the Japanese Army surgeon wanted to be on Attu.

In the aftermath of the battle, soldiers learned even more about Tatsuguchi and his background. As the Americans sorted through the detritus of war, they found other possessions of the Japanese surgeon that gave them pause.

The first was Tatsuguchi's personal Bible. Inscribed with the doctor's favorite verse,

"Choose life," the recovered scripture made Laird doubt his belief that the enemy in the Pacific was a pagan murderer. Just as in Japan, military brass in the United States did little to discourage racist hatred of the enemy. The realization that a Japanese and American soldier could share the same religion made Laird think twice about exactly who he was trying to kill.

Second was Tatsuguchi's address book, which also was found on the battlefield. It was written partially in English, and contained the names and addresses for dozens of his former college and medical school classmates in California and across the United States. Tatsuguchi had more contact information for Americans than Laird. The Tatsuguchi address book made Laird wonder even more about what he had done on Attu. His body had survived war, but his conscience battled on.

16
Fog

The Japanese stationed 6,000 troops on Kiska, and the extra manpower allowed them to convert the island into a fortress, with miles of tunnels, an underground mess hall and hospital, an airfield, submarine base, seaplane base, observation tower, and antiaircraft guns around the perimeter. In other words, on Kiska, the Japanese had twice the troop strength of Attu, but with many multiples more weaponry.

Both the United States and Japan were determined to learn some lessons from the Battle of Attu.

For the United States, this meant steady leadership, a marked improvement in cold-weather gear for troops; longer and better training for the harsh Aleutians climate; much greater support via Air Force and Navy bombing; and a vast increase in troop numbers.

For the Japanese, it meant an audacious trick.

Dick Laird and the other survivors of Company H spent the weeks after the Battle of Attu trying to make the island livable. They built a camp. They hauled in supplies. They ate hot food and drank hot coffee. They nursed back their feet and hands and ears and everything else that had turned black and frostbitten. And they slept.

For the first few days it was hard to describe what Laird did at night as sleep. It was a surrendering to exhaustion, an unconsciousness, even a hibernation. He would awake with a jolt and not know where he was. He felt like he had crawled into an extremely deep and dark cave.

And then the nightmares started.

Always there was fog and foreboding. Sometimes he saw his runner approaching. Other times a pile of Japanese bodies was rocking and bursting with the slam of each incoming bullet. Too often it all ended with the faces of the men he had killed.

He began to wake nightly in a cold sweat. Laird knew he must try to fall back asleep, but he dreaded it. He had done his job. He had been courageous. He had won a top medal. Yet the nightmares would not go away.

In his waking hours Laird threw himself into his work. Attu was a vastly different place when people weren't trying to kill you. In June and July, winter finally faded, and the Aleutians were reborn. It still rained daily, but now willows sprouted. Wildflowers bloomed. Cliffs and rocks bustled with the comings and goings of thousands of nesting seabirds. Salmon massed in bays and creeks in numbers so thick that Laird could catch a fish with his hands, a daily rerun of his story in *The Capture of Attu.* During hard times in Appalachia, Laird had learned to live off nature, but he had never imagined a bounty as vast as Alaska in the summer.

On a whim, the Army had brought in some garden seeds, and Laird volunteered to plant them. The results startled him. Seeds didn't sprout — they exploded. In June and July the sun never set completely on Attu. The sky just dimmed gray about four hours a day. Even with clouds and fog, the near-constant sunlight, combined with daily rains, made plants grow rapidly. Laird was gorging on fresh radishes and turnips and carrots. Could this really be the same place where, just weeks before, men had launched a desperate suicide attack in part because they could find no food?

While Laird tended his garden, his superiors braced for an even more intensive war. They were assembling a force of 35,000 men — nearly triple the size of the Attu invaders — to overthrow the Japanese on Kiska. This time, the men would have clothes designed for the frigid and wet. They also would be trained to fight in Alaska, not the desert sands of Africa. They would be backed by formidable naval and air power. They would be aided by a lengthy naval blockade of Kiska that would isolate the Japanese. The commanders prepared for an August invasion.

Before they could bring the fire, however, they worried about a Japanese resupply — or a counterattack. Imperial Navy ships had been gathering in the Kurile Islands port of Paramushiro north of Japan. Though the United States Air Force and Navy had been pounding Kiska for months — the Japanese had withstood more than seven million pounds of bombs — the generals could not afford to have the enemy sneak up on them.

On July 21, an armada of fifteen Japanese ships cast off from Paramushiro toward the Aleutians. The next day, seventeen United States battleships, cruisers, and destroyers arrived at Kiska to bolster the existing blockade. The Americans spent the next hours pounding the island with hundreds of thousands of pounds of shells from 5-, 6-, and 14-inch guns. Just as their assault was concluding, however, the admirals received a disturbing report: An American plane had detected seven enemy ships in the seas between Paramushiro and the Aleutians.

Fearing an attack from behind, Admiral Kinkaid abruptly pulled his warships from Kiska and ordered them to find and destroy the approaching Japanese fleet. His decision left the harbor at Kiska unguarded.

In the predawn hours of July 26, U.S. warships detected seven radar blips just fifteen miles away from Kiska. Sailors girded for battle. The war at sea was on.

The U.S. fleet navigated west of the island to better intercept the moving targets. Guns roared at a range of eight to twelve miles. Each 14-inch gun weighed 180,000 pounds. It required a quarter ton of propellant to blast a 1,400-pound projectile up to thirteen miles. Even after firing 518 rounds from the big guns, and 487 shells from the 8-inch guns, the radars still showed seven pips. There were no explosions or any other evidence that the enemy had been hit. On radar, the targets still moved. More shots yielded no change. After a half hour of fury, the guns were silenced. The seven pips blinked on the radar, then disappeared.

At sunrise the American fleet and warplanes scoured the area for crippled and destroyed ships. They found nothing — no flotsam, no oil slicks, no lifeboats.

All seven pips had been detected repeatedly by radars on five separate U.S. ships. It was hard to believe all were faulty. Had the Imperial Navy outwitted them? Were the Americans firing on Japanese submarines? How could so much firepower be trained on seven different targets without any apparent damage?

The whole mystery became known as the Battle of the Pips. It wasn't until years later that the admirals believed they had finally figured out what had happened.

Postwar investigations found that no Japanese ship was within a hundred miles of any of the American blasts. Instead, the world's greatest navy was targeting rafts of seabirds, sooty shearwaters that migrated through the Aleutians every July in numbers so vast they could be detected by radar. (Years later, film director Alfred Hitchcock would see another mass of sooty shearwaters so large and so crazed in Monterey Bay, California, that he was inspired to make a horror film called *The Birds*.) During the war in the Aleutians, sea radar was still a relatively new invention, and the Navy did not have enough experience viewing pips on a screen to be able to distinguish feathered creatures from warships.

The Battle of the Pips had no known human casualties. It did, however, set up an even bigger embarrassment for the U.S. military.

Dick Laird was scared again. For the second time in three months, he was jammed into a troop transport and headed for a frigid landing beach. It was August 15. His destination was Kiska. The word was that the Japanese would be twice as strong here as on Attu.

He and his Company H had been assured that the job would be done right this time. Their invasion force was vast — 29,000 Americans and 5,300 Canadians. In the four days before the assault, U.S. warplanes had dropped 400 tons of bombs on Kiska. The enemy should be softened, but that's the same thing the commanders said last time.

Through the fog the transport motored, then abruptly halted. The Navy had miscalculated local tides, which were low, not high, and several boats ran aground on volcanic rock. Others, including Laird's, bobbed in wait behind them. They were stuck in a traffic jam and were sitting ducks. A shot from the enemy in the highlands would kill or cripple them all. For the first time Laird was grateful for the Aleutian fog, which shrouded him and his men.

Slowly, painfully, and behind schedule, Laird and his men landed on the beach. They found an eerie calm. No snipers fired at them. He advanced forward. Still nothing. Was this Attu all over again? Were the Japanese conceding the beaches, only to remain hidden in the fog and strategic heights of the mountains? Laird shuddered. He heard gunshots in the distance, just as he had two months earlier. If they were going to repeat the Battle of Attu, he at least knew what to expect. He would dig in. He would do his best to stay dry. He carried enough food to last for days. At the same time, he hoped the much larger invasion force would make for a much shorter firefight.

With every step deeper into Kiska he expected to hear a blast from mortars or grenades or artillery. Instead, there was only sporadic gunfire. All they found moving by the end of the first day was a half dozen dogs, including the one named Explosion, which had belonged to American troops captured during the original Japanese take-over of Kiska.

Laird's second day on Kiska dawned with the rattle of machine gun fire and shelling from offshore American naval ships. Some soldiers swore they saw Japanese dug into bunkers, but Laird hadn't seen any. In the fog it was easy to mistake rocks for men, or, worse, Americans for Japanese.

Soon Laird heard the whispers among his men: Where was the enemy? Had the Japanese evacuated?

It turned out they had. While the United States refueled after waging war against seabirds during the Battle of the Pips, a convoy of Japanese ships had sneaked into the unguarded harbor at Kiska and started whisking away troops. The Japanese had learned their lesson on Attu. Their position in the Aleutians was indefensible. They did not want to fight to the last man, again, in a place with no strategic value. In their rush to leave the island before being discovered, the Japanese troops did their best to quietly destroy anything of value. They also scrawled insults on the walls of their barracks, such as, "We shall come again and kill out separately, Yanki-joker," and, "You are dancing by foolische order of Rousebelt." Then the Japanese filed onto the beach with their rucksacks and rifles. Because their convoy was short of space — in the Aleutian fog, five of the rescuing Japanese ships had collided and rendered two unusable — troops were ordered to pitch their rifles into the sea before coming aboard. In just an hour, 5,183 soldiers crammed onto eight ships and set off from Kiska.

Four days later, the Japanese transport arrived peacefully with all troops in the Kurile Islands at Paramushiro. Kiska had been vacant for nearly three weeks before the Allies invaded.

In the fog, Americans saw none of this. The commanders could not believe so many soldiers could escape without detection. For nearly a week, Laird and the other troops were ordered to scour Kiska for hiding Japanese. In the dense fog, many shots were fired at unclear targets, though never by Laird.

At the end of the week, twenty-four American and four Canadian soldiers had been killed by friendly fire. Four more lost their lives to Japanese booby traps. Seventy-one died when their ship, the *Abner Read,* struck a floating mine. Another 168 were wounded, injured, or sick.

All told, the Allies suffered more than 300

casualties to claim a deserted island a thousand miles from the Alaska mainland. According to war correspondent Robert Sherrod, the ridiculous operation gave birth to a new word — JANFU, an acronym that *Time* magazine cleaned up for readers as a Joint Army Navy Foul Up.

Nevertheless, the United States had reclaimed Alaska. Six thousand men were dead — about 1,000 Americans and Canadians, and 5,000 Japanese — but the maps of North America did not have to be changed. In the coming months, the United States would try to build airstrips and harbors in the Aleutians to aid a projected northern attack against Japan, but ultimately the militarization of Alaska had little consequence on the overall war. Winds blew. Waves rolled. Snow drifted. In time the village and barracks on Attu were abandoned by the Army. No flag could survive the williwaws of the Bering Sea. On the landscape of Attu, the biggest lasting change caused by World War II was the cemetery.

Dick Laird knew there was a fine line separating him from that cemetery. He had done his best on two beachheads, and he had escaped without injury, but he had killed foe and friend. The harsh climate would reclaim most war scars on the landscape of Attu. Laird's scars were not healing. His nightmares continued. His feet hurt. His hacking cough continued. Not long ago, while dropping deep into the blackness of the Powhatan Coal Mine in Ohio, Laird had dreamed of an escape to a new life. This was not the life he had envisioned. This life was filled with dread. He was committed to destroying the enemy, but he hoped he would not destroy himself in the process.

Shortly after Kiska had been secured, Laird and his men received their new orders. They were being shipped to Hawaii. Laird knew little about it. He hoped it was better than war in Alaska. He doubted it could be worse.

17
NEWS

Taeko Tatsuguchi heard the news in the same way as the rest of Japan. There was a government announcement: Attu had been lost, and there were no survivors. She didn't know what to make of it. It had been months since she had heard from her husband. She didn't know where he was. For security reasons, military censors had banned Nobuo in his letters home from disclosing his field location. Based on his interest in books on Alaska, and his postcard joke that he might soon see classmates from medical school, Taeko guessed her husband might be headed to the Aleutians. However, the Japanese force was split between two islands, Attu and Kiska, with the main force deployed at Kiska. If her husband really was in Alaska, she could only hope that he was deployed 200 miles from Attu at Kiska.

"I still believed he would come back as I saw some people who had been reported as dead returned after several years," Taeko told a reporter years later.

When the telegram finally arrived, Taeko didn't have to read it to know what it said. Her weeks of praying and worrying and crying had come to this.

Nobuo Tatsuguchi had been dead nearly three months before anyone told Taeko. The Imperial Army waited until all soldiers had been evacuated from Kiska before revealing the fate of those on Attu. His body would remain on Attu, an island she had never heard of. She had no idea her husband had written a diary, which was in the hands of the Americans. Her last physical evidence of Nobuo was the lock of hair he had sent months earlier.

She wavered between despair and emptiness. He did not want to fight this war. He was pulled into it by duty and obligation. Both Nobuo and Taeko thought he could remain true to his faith by serving as a healer, not a warrior. She could not say whether his life had ended as a pacifist. She could say only that it had ended.

Every time she looked at her young daughters, she saw his face. She missed his quiet strength, his gentleness, his quirky insistence on discerning the correct name of every living creature in the wilderness. His side of the bed would never be warm again.

Taeko had no obvious path to survival. She had given up her college education to follow him. Now she had two girls to support, the youngest only six months old. In the depths of war, Japan's economy was in a shambles. Food, clothes, electricity — everything had strict limits. She had no easy access to anything. But there was no time to feel sorry for herself. "I dried my eyes and finally started to move forward. I had to raise my two daughters."

Worst of all, she would have to do it alone. Before Pearl Harbor, Taeko's parents had moved from Japan to Hawaii as missionaries for the Seventh-day Adventists. Because of the war, she could not contact them in the American islands. She needed their love and advice. Her parents did not know Taeko had a second child. They also didn't know she was a war widow.

As the weeks passed, Taeko's longing increased. She needed emotional help and financial help. Without parents, she had few options. What she did have, however, was a dream. If she could get through this — raising two young children as a single mother during a war she didn't believe in — then she would set out to rejoin her parents in Hawaii.

■ ■ ■ ■

Dick Laird couldn't believe it. He'd heard they existed, but all he'd ever seen were photographs. Now he was holding one in his hands, proof that even an Appalachian boy could bask in an exotic tropical locale.

He was in Hawaii with his first coconut.

More specifically, he was stationed at Schofield Barracks in Honolulu. After the agony of Attu and Kiska, the 7th Infantry Division had been redeployed to Laird's version of paradise. He could think of no better symbol of his contentment than the coconut. Honolulu was so lush that he could find a coconut on the sidewalk, slash it with his knife, and drink the coconut water as refreshment. It sure beat shooting squirrels back home.

Enthralled with the whole idea of the coconut, Laird shared it with the people he loved. He taped an address tag on the hairy shell and mailed it, unboxed, to his daughter Peggy. The postman who delivered it to her at home in Ohio was thrilled. He, too, had never held a coconut.

Keeping in touch with his wife was trickier. Laird was intensely self-conscious about his eighth-grade education. He hated to write letters home that he knew would be filled with spelling and grammar mistakes. Rose had graduated from high school and, Laird believed, she was smart enough for college. Writing made him feel stupid. Plus, he wasn't even sure what to say. He told his wife about his Silver Star, but would not describe how and why he had won it. He was afraid his wife might see him as an animal. Though he would write an occasional note to Rose, he felt better sending a package with a grass skirt or sea shells.

In Hawaii, Laird and his troops walked the streets with pride. They had seen the enemy and defeated him. Their generals and admirals may have issued some poor orders, but the fighting men on the ground overcame them. Laird felt a kinship with anyone else who fought in the Aleutians. If they could win in Alaska, they could win anywhere. No wise soldier ever felt invincible, but Laird did feel mighty.

Sometimes, though, pride boiled over into trouble. On a weekend pass, Laird started drinking and did not stop until he ran into a Marine. Neither needed a reason to insult the other; the Army vs. Marines service rivalry was that intense. Marines thought they were tougher. Army Joes thought the Marines were glory hounds. In fact, after

Attu, some Army commanders grumbled that their heroics went largely unnoticed in the press back home partly because they weren't as skilled at self-promotion as the Marines.

When the Marine called Laird a dogface, the alcohol and testosterone took over. Outside the bar, under a giant banyan tree, and surrounded by dozens of cheering soldiers, Laird and the Marine went at it. "Get him, Sarge!" the Army men cried. "Get him good, Sarge!"

Laird expected a fight but got a jumping. The Marine leveled him with a kick to the groin, then pounded his ears and face and demanded that Laird say quit. Laird wouldn't. With the Marine still pummeling him, Laird managed to stand and rear back until he forced the man onto the hood of a parked car. Fortunes reversed, Laird was about to slam the man into the bumper when the crowd called out, "MPs! MPs coming!"

The Military Police found an ugly sight: two soldiers with faces of bloody hamburger. The MPs didn't want to deal with formal charges, so they threw Laird into a taxi and sent him back to his barracks.

That night, word spread of Laird's savage brawl. By reveille the next morning, troops were trying to catch a glimpse of the man who had fought so hard to uphold the honor of the Army.

They were not disappointed. Laird showed up with one black eye, two blackened ears, and a cheekbone that looked as if it had been used as a battering ram against a hard-pack of rocks and broken sea shells. Which it had been.

The chaplain of his outfit gave Laird a nickname — Marine Killer. Laird shrugged it off, but the other men noticed, and the story circulated throughout his company and battalion. Sergeant Dick Laird was the guy you wanted fighting at your side. Company H had a celebrity.

For the next months, through December 1943, Laird and the 7th Division trained intensively in Hawaii. They practiced shore landings and fast dig-ins and jungle warfare and moving heavy equipment across beaches. Captured Japanese weapons were fired for troops to be able to recognize them by sound. They knew there must be a reason for all this repetition. Soon after the New Year, they would find out.

Remarkably, just twenty miles from Laird's base at Schofield Barracks lived the in-laws of the man Laird had killed in Attu. Shohei and Toshi Miyake, parents of Taeko Tatsu-guchi, had been in Honolulu for ten years. In 1940, they founded the first Japanese Seventh-day Adventist Church in Hawaii, across from Cartwright Park.

Because of an inconsistency in United States policy, few Japanese in Hawaii were imprisoned in internment camps. At the time of the Pearl Harbor attack, about a third of the people living in Hawaii were of Japanese ancestry. That was 157,000 people. Yet fewer than 2,000 were sent to intern-ment camps. By contrast, of the 126,000 people of Japanese ancestry who lived on the United States mainland, about 110,000 were confined in internment camps.

The only real justification for the detain-ment of Japanese Americans on the main-land was flat-out racism. Japanese Ameri-cans on the mainland were vastly outnumbered, and could be bullied politi-cally in ways that German Americans and Italian Americans could not. However, Japanese Americans in Hawaii were by far the largest ethnic group, controlling many of the key business and government jobs that made the islands work. Hawaii's econ-omy could not afford to single out Japanese for persecution. Though some congressmen on the mainland grumbled about the favorable treatment of Japanese Americans in Hawaii, the policy continued. To appease those racist congressmen, Hawaiians noted that their islands remained under martial law, with strict curfews for everyone to head off sabotage.

Taeko's parents made the most of their freedom. They cared about faith, not politics, and worked hard with the thirty founding members of their church to establish a strong foothold for Japanese Adventism in Honolulu. Taeko's father served first as a pastor and then an elder for the church. He shuddered at the sneak attack on Pearl Harbor. The resulting clampdown on communications between Hawaii and Japan sickened him. He had no idea what was happening to his daughter, son-in-law, and granddaughter back in Tokyo. He and his wife could hope and pray only for a swift conclusion to the war.

18
FURY

For Dick Laird, the next thirteen months were a chaotic rush of blood, guts, and heartbreak. On February 1, 1944, Laird and more than 40,000 soldiers and Marines descended upon Kwajalein Atoll, a spit of coral and sand in the Marshall Islands about 2,400 miles southwest of Honolulu. It was one of the most intensive bombardments in the history of warfare. Onto an island only 2.5 miles long and 800 yards wide, Navy ships unleashed a torrent of 7,000 rounds of 14-, 8-, and 5-inch shells; the 7th Infantry blasted 29,000 rounds of artillery fire; and six B-24 bombers unloaded fifteen 1,000- and 2,000-pound bombs. Another sixty warplanes from United States carriers flew ninety-six sorties against the Japanese.

Kwajalein looked like a gravel parking lot after a cyclone hit. The dense jungle Laird and his men had trained to fight in had been converted instead into a moonscape of palms without fronds and shrubs without leaves. As veterans of Attu, however, Laird's men knew the Japanese were tougher than any landscape.

The Imperial Army had stationed 5,000 men on Kwajalein as a sacrifice squad. They held out for four days. In the daylight the Japanese retreated through a well-constructed defense of pillboxes, block-houses, and logjams, and in the nighttime they sneaked behind U.S. lines with deadly sniper and grenade counterattacks.

Laird was stuffed in a foxhole alongside his company clerk with a sheet of corrugated metal above for protection. A Japanese bullet somehow ricocheted off the edge of the metal and ripped a deep gash into the clerk's buttocks. The clerk screamed in pain and panic as his blood splattered across Laird's face and the rest of the foxhole. Hoping to muffle the noise, Laird gave the man a strap to bite on until the medics arrived. He survived.

Another soldier in Laird's company was lost to sniper fire. The Americans braced for another last-ditch suicide attack, but there may not have been enough Japanese survivors to mount one. After the initial American bombing onslaught, the little vegetation that survived on the island was dispatched by dozens of flamethrowers. So were the Japanese blockhouses.

Of the 5,000 Japanese who defended the island, only 49 Japanese and 125 Korean slave laborers survived as prisoners of war. Once again, the bushido code of death before dishonor had prevailed. The first time Laird had seen bushido, on Attu, he was horrified. The second time, on Kwajalein, he felt dread. It meant the battle in the Aleutians was no fluke. Laird and his fellow Americans faced an enemy who would not surrender.

On Kwajalein, 177 American lives were lost, with an additional 1,000 men injured.

Even when the fighting was over, Kwajalein exacted a toll. As they exited the island, Laird and several men with full packs were climbing a rope ladder from a landing craft to a transport when the ladder gave way. Men high on the ladder fell backward onto men below. More than a dozen troops were hurt, including two with broken backs and several with serious fractures. Victory could be dangerous, too.

All told, the Battle of Kwajalein extinguished about one human life per minute over the course of nearly four days, all for a remote tropical atoll with just 1.2 miles of surface area.

For the United States, Kwajalein marked a significant strategic and psychological victory. It was the first time Japan had lost an outer ring defense island.

For Laird, Kwajalein added a darker cloud to his nightmares. On top of his nightly dreams about the killings of his runner and Nobuo Tatsuguchi in Attu, Laird now heard the screams of his company clerk in the foxhole on Kwajalein. He could never be sure when the nightmares would strike. Sometimes the same dream would repeat twice in the same night. Sometimes he could go days without dreaming at all, but then be rocked by the worst yet night terrors. The winner of the Silver Star feared his bedroll.

His superiors, however, knew nothing of Laird's inner turmoil. They watched him fight on Attu and Kwajalein — and Hawaii — and came away impressed. His commander recommended him for promotion as an officer.

"During the entire operation on Attu, Sergeant Laird proved himself to be an exceptional combat leader," wrote Captain Robert Foulston in his recommendation letter. "During the recent operation on Kwajalein, he performed the duties of company executive officer in a superior manner. . . . Sgt. Laird displayed the highest type of individual courage and leadership at all times."

His lieutenant colonel concurred, and recommended Laird for Officers Candidate School.

Laird had his doubts. He was flattered by the recommendations, but he worried about the "school" part of officer training. He was self-consciously Appalachian. What if he started officer's school but flunked out? He couldn't bear the shame.

When Laird was interviewed about his nomination to officer's school, he was too embarrassed to talk about his lack of schooling. Instead, he voiced doubts about leaving battle for school in the middle of the war, and whether the Army life was really for him. "Although this non-commissioned officer undoubtedly possesses all requisites for commissioned grade, at interview he expressed doubts to desire to serve in that category," wrote Lieutenant Colonel Francis Pachler. He rescinded the recommendation. Laird remained a first sergeant.

With the rest of his division, Laird returned to Schofield Barracks in Hawaii to heal and train. This time the work felt more urgent. Laird thought the troops were spending unusual amounts of time on non-battlefield routines, such as marching in formation. On July 27, 1944, Laird and the other soldiers were ordered to assemble for two important visitors.

"Officers and men of the 7th Division," President Franklin D. Roosevelt told the troops while seated in a convertible with General Douglas MacArthur, "I want you to feel that, at least in theory, I am bringing to each and every man, greetings from his own family and his own home, at this spot, which thank God is still a part of the United States. I have heard much of what the 7th Division has done. We're all proud of the 7th, in what it has done and what it is doing. And that's another reason why I give you all the good luck in the world."

Between the 7th Division at Schofield and the Navy at Pearl Harbor, Roosevelt witnessed a massive show of force on Oahu. The road along his drive to the Army base was lined with 40,000 troops. None of them missed the significance of the president meeting directly with General MacArthur. Twenty-eight months earlier, MacArthur had fled the Japanese invasion of the Philippines with his famous farewell promise: "I shall return."

Reporters in Honolulu pressed the president about the meaning of his meetings with the general. "When General MacArthur was about to leave the Philippines," a reporter asked, "he said something to the general effect that 'I will return.' In view of the setting of this meeting with him, is there anything that you could tell us? Is that true now?"

Roosevelt's answer: "We are going to get the Philippines back, and without question General MacArthur will take a part in it."

Laird considered the president's words. He saw his own future.

Ducking bullets and leaping from mortar shells, Dick Laird was running for his life, when he heard a fearsome explosion behind him. He turned and saw that his landing ship was hit by a Japanese fighter plane. A vast hole opened, and the ship took on water. He could not retreat now.

On October 20, Laird was one of 132,000 men invading the beaches of Leyte, one of the largest of 7,500 islands in the Philippines. He knew from the start this would be a beachhead like no other. For as far as Laird could see, there was United States naval power — carriers, battleships, destroyers, cruisers, PT boats — more than 300 ships in all, and one of the greatest displays of military and industrial might in world history. If the Japanese were intimidated, they did not show it. Gone were the days of granting the invading troops a foothold at the shore and then beating down on them from fortified positions in the heights. Now the Japanese were dive-bombing ships in the water and men on the shore. Laird and his men raced through the open sand and dove for cover.

The first protection he found made him shudder. It was a cemetery outside the town of Dulag. Laird crouched behind monuments and pressed himself flat between graves. He did not want to dig a foxhole here.

He and his unit managed to push beyond the graveyard to the edge of a clearing. He dug a slit trench with a Latino soldier from Los Angeles. Laird wasn't sure of the man's name, but with bullets crossing overhead, there was no time for introductions. A mortar crashed beside them. The other soldier, blown open, collapsed dead onto Laird, before another blast of shrapnel ricocheted and ripped into him. The body shielded Laird. The dead man saved his life. Laird froze in shock and horror. When the firefight ebbed, another soldier helped pull off the corpse. Laird had no choice: He had to move on. Leyte was much bigger and more complicated than anyplace Laird had fought before. One hundred ten miles long and forty wide, the island was bisected by a densely forested volcanic mountain range with peaks that jutted 3,600 feet. Leyte offered a million hiding places for snipers and bunkers, and the Japanese had garrisoned Leyte with 16,000 troops, though as the battle ground on they would be reinforced with another 45,000.

A few hours behind Laird and seventeen miles up the beachhead, General MacArthur had waded through knee-deep surf to the beach on Leyte. "People of the Philippines, I have returned," MacArthur announced. "The hour of your redemption is here." His proclamation was followed by the largest battle in the history of sea warfare.

On October 23, the Imperial Navy launched a massive counterattack in the Leyte Gulf. Already facing severe oil shortages at home and in their war effort, the Japanese correctly feared that an American takeover of the Philippines would cut off shipping lanes to their conquered East Indies petroleum supplies. Since its overwhelming victory at Pearl Harbor, the Imperial Navy had been rocked by devastating losses at the Battle of Midway and the Battle of the Philippine Sea. The United States' vast industrial capacity allowed it to rebuild its Navy. Japan, however, could not come close to matching the output of America's steel mills and shipyards. Every passing week allowed the United States shipyards to add to the country's advantage. The Battle of Leyte Gulf was the last chance for Japan to regain the upper hand in the Pacific War.

The gambit did not work. After four days of furious fighting, the Japanese lost four aircraft carriers, three battleships, ten cruisers, twelve destroyers, 300 warplanes — and more than 10,000 men. The Allies suffered about one-third the destruction, losing one light carrier, two escort carriers, two destroyers, one destroyer escort, and 200 warplanes. About 3,000 sailors were killed or injured. Leyte Gulf marked the first time the Japanese made extensive use of kamikaze warplane pilots, sinking one ship and damaging at least seven others.

It was the most costly battle in the history of naval warfare, and Japan's military had been irrevocably crippled. Japan had entered the Pacific War with one of the world's most advanced navies, but after the Battle of Leyte Gulf concluded on October 26, it would never again dictate the terms of a battle at sea. Japan also lost easy access to the oil fields of Indonesia, a deprivation that would throttle the remainder of Japan's war efforts.

The defeat at sea did not stop the battles on land. If anything, the Imperial Army redoubled their defense with tens of thousands of reinforcements.

Then it started — rain. In the same way that Attu had fog and cold, Leyte had rain. On November 8, the island was engulfed in a typhoon, forty days of warfare drenched in thirty-five inches of rain. Trees crashed, mudslides ruined roads, and paths became wallowing trenches of knee-deep mud. It was as if the ocean had come ashore.

When Laird dug a foxhole, it filled with water. He dug deeper and stacked ammo boxes on the bottom to keep his feet above water. That worked until he had to dig again. Trench foot was mostly a malady of the cold, which the Philippines did not have, but after Attu he never wanted to repeat that experience. He worked to keep his feet dry.

The elements played with his mind. The pelting rain made it easy to mistake targets. Leyte was thick with wild pigs, monkeys, and flying fox (a bat with a five-foot wingspan), and more than one animal lost its life for moving too much like a Japanese soldier at the wrong time. Someone in Laird's company accidentally shot and killed a domestic water buffalo.

Laird was on patrol in a storm along a sugarcane field near Baybay on the western coast when he saw stalks quivering in an unusual way. He raised his rifle and braced.

From the tall cane emerged two figures, dark in the rain, and staying pressed against the dense cover. They looked both ways. Laird saw them first. He was ready for them.

His finger moved over the trigger when he noticed that one of the figures was unusually short.

The two men raised their hands. Laird moved closer.

They were two Filipinos, a teenager and his younger brother. One was maybe fourteen years old and the other was perhaps nine. He was overcome with shame and anger. He had almost killed two innocent boys. Laird gave the boys rations and cigarettes, which were worth more than money, and sent them on their way.

The boys didn't want to go. For the next several days, they found Laird before sunset and built him a sleeping shelter with straw mats above the wet ground. Laird repaid them with food. They also gave him a set of teardrop pearls. Laird kept those for Rose. Before he slept at night, as he listened to the rain pelt the palm frond roof constructed by the boys, Laird could not get beyond the fact that he had nearly shot them to death.

In the Philippines, Laird would acquire another medal, a Bronze Star, for bravery. He also acquired more grist for his mill of nightmares.

By New Year's Day 1945, Leyte had been secured by United States troops. The death toll for Japan was 49,000, or about four times greater than the combination of 3,504 dead for the United States, with an additional 12,000 casualties.

Japan still had more than 250,000 troops stationed on the largest Philippine island of Luzon, the home of Manila. However, the crushing loss on sea and land at Leyte had limited Japan's military options. With little naval or air support, the vast army on Luzon had few tools left to defend itself. By April 1945, the Imperial Army on Luzon was vanquished in the second-deadliest battle in the Pacific for the United States.

Laird, however, was spared that fight in the Philippines. Instead, he was shipped out to a fight even worse — Okinawa.

A large island just 350 miles southwest of

mainland Japan, Okinawa was the linchpin to any U.S. invasion of Tokyo, the key stepping-stone to the final confrontation. It offered airfields for warplanes and anchorage for ships. Until this point in the war, Japan could fight a defensive war on perimeter islands without jeopardizing the homeland. Losing Okinawa would put the emperor in the crosshairs.

Okinawa was Laird's fifth beachhead. Repetition did not make it easier.

Determined to fight on their own terms, the Japanese allowed the massive Allied force — 180,000 men, plus 40 aircraft carriers and 18 battleships — to land largely unmolested on Okinawa beaches. (An overwhelming Allied flotilla of 1,500 naval vessels and 350,000 men bobbed offshore.) The Japanese waited patiently. They were holed up in a confounding network of tunnels, pillboxes, and limestone caves, scattered through the dense jungle and the island's 1,600-foot highlands. The Allied force was led by Lieutenant General Simon Buckner, who had directed the Alaskan Defense Command.

Laird and the Americans landed on April 1, which was both Easter Sunday and April Fool's Day. For the first three days, he faced only light fighting. On April 4, however, he had advanced about halfway up the island from the western shore when he and his buddy from Fort Ord in California, Sergeant Harold Gellein, approached a fortified line of Japanese defense. Laird stood on one side of a knoll and Gellein stood twelve feet away on the other side. With no warning the air exploded with a wild mix of bullets and mortars. Laird and Gellein both hit the ground, but Gellein did not get up. When the shooting subsided, Laird checked on his friend. He had been ripped apart by a chunk of shrapnel. He didn't survive long enough for last words.

Laird was overcome with grief. His friend was one of the few in his unit roughly the same age. Laird admired him for his smarts. Just before his Army induction, Gellein graduated from the University of Idaho. The two men had fought side by side on Attu, Kiska, Kwajalein, Leyte, and now Okinawa. Gellein had never met his two-year-old son, who lived with his wife, Hildreth, in Weiser, Idaho. Laird could not stop thinking about Gellein's widow and child. He also could not help but wonder what would have happened if Laird had been two steps closer to his Army buddy.

His friend's death was terrible, but it could have been even worse. Gellein's body was recovered. As days and weeks of battle rocked Okinawa, bullets and bombardments became so intense that it became impossible to retrieve fallen colleagues. Hundreds of bodies piled up in the thick tropical air cut daily by drenching rains. Allies and Japanese remained confined to the same foxholes for days, and relied on ammo boxes for latrines. Okinawa reeked of fecund death and sewage. Laird learned to breathe through his mouth. Years later, survivors would still gag when asked about the battlefield smell of Okinawa.

With relentless shelling and so many bodies decomposing in the tropical heat for so long, the Allies suffered unprecedented battle fatigue and mental damage. More than 26,000 American troops had to be pulled from the front lines in Okinawa as psychiatric casualties.

Horrific tactics by the Japanese caused many of the mental breakdowns. Before the Allies landed, the Japanese Army ordered 1,700 Okinawan teenagers, age fourteen to seventeen, into battle as the Blood and Iron Student Corps. Hundreds were forced into suicide attacks. U.S. servicemen had to shoot children or be blown up by them.

Offshore the Japanese embraced even more suicide attacks. Dozens of sixteen-foot speedboats were crammed with 600 pounds of explosives and rammed by individual Japanese sailors into American ships; several shinyo, or suicide boats, succeeded because the boats were deliberately constructed of wood to evade detection by radar. At least three American ships were sunk by shinyo.

The hellfire from the sky was even worse. From April through June, nearly 2,000 kamikaze pilots ended their own lives trying to crash into Allied ships. On April 6 alone, more than 300 Japanese planes set off on a one-way trip for the United States Fifth Fleet off Okinawa. John Chapman was a gunner on the stern of the USS *Newcomb* when four dozen kamikaze planes approached. "Well, it was a scary situation, because you knew that they were going to dive on you," Chapman said. "You could be firing on the aircraft, and they'd come right on, just keep coming right on through that. And you'd see pieces flying over the planes and everything else, and they'd just keep right on a-coming." His ship shot down four planes but five other kamikazes plowed into the 376-foot destroyer. Ninety-one sailors were killed or wounded on the *Newcomb.* The surviving crew managed to keep the ship afloat, and she was towed twenty miles to another harbor for repairs under more gunfire.

At Okinawa, kamikazes killed 5,000 Allied sailors and wounded another 5,000. The suicide attacks sank thirty ships and damaged 400.

On shore the battle was even bloodier. Increasingly desperate, the Japanese began to suspect many Okinawans of spying. When natives were heard conversing in a local dialect that the Japanese could not understand, they shot them. A thousand Okinawans were executed for speaking their own language.

Many more natives were either forced or coerced to kill themselves. Okinawans described hundreds of cases of family members and natives being handed grenades and forced to hold them against their chests for detonation.

Sumie Oshiro gathered with her friends in a tight circle, pulled the pin on a grenade, and waited for it to explode. It didn't. Like the Americans on Attu, she could not figure out how to detonate a Japanese grenade. She was rescued by American soldiers before it could go off.

Japanese soldiers also spread rumors of Americans binding the hands and feet of civilians to run over them with tanks. As a result, when American soldiers approached, many Okinawan citizens panicked and killed themselves to avoid capture. On the nearby island of Geruma, where 58 of 130 residents committed suicide, Takejiro Nakamura was hiding in a cave with his mother and sister when the Americans approached. "Kill me now, hurry," his twenty-year-old sister told his mother, who tightened a rope around the neck until her daughter was dead. Takejiro tried self-suffocation but failed. "It's really tough to kill yourself," he later told *The New York Times.* When American soldiers found Takejiro and his mother alive in the cave, they gave them candy and cigarettes.

His mother lived into her eighties. She and her son would talk later about the war, but she never uttered a word about killing her daughter.

As days turned to weeks and then to months on Okinawa, frustration and despair mounted. The Japanese used hundreds of civilians as human shields. The Americans claimed they had a difficult time telling civilians from enemy soldiers, and many were shot. Okinawans reported many cases of American troops firing indiscriminately on their houses.

Laird had taken cover near dusk in a cave

when he became convinced that an enemy soldier was sneaking up. He opened fire, but saw nothing fall. He waited. No movement. He organized a squad and they filed out slowly in diminishing light. They found that Laird had obliterated a tree stump.

The next night Laird was standing watch when someone with a knapsack walked swiftly along a dirt road. "Stop!" Laird called, but the person said nothing and picked up the pace. Laird released the safety on his .45 caliber autoloader and aimed.

Then he hesitated. What if that knapsack wasn't filled with grenades? What if that person wasn't a Japanese soldier? "Stop!" he called again, to no effect. He could see that it wasn't a soldier. It was a woman.

He still panicked. Was she a suicide bomber? He had put other soldiers at risk. He had let an Okinawan woman laden with explosives pass through his watch. He quickly phoned his battalion headquarters and warned of the bomber moving up the road.

A few minutes later, before she could detonate her bomb, other American soldiers jumped from both sides of the road and pounced on the woman. They pinned back her arms and wrestled her to the ground. They grabbed the backpack.

Inside was a baby. The bomber Laird had called in turned out to be a mother with a baby in a backpack.

In the night air the mother screamed. The baby bawled.

Laird broke out in cold sweat. He had come within a millimeter's squeeze on a trigger of killing mother and child. He could not bear it. That night he was so afraid of nightmares that he did not let himself fall asleep. He did not think of falling back from the front for a rest. Strong men, he believed, fought on. He had seen men collapsed in a shivering mess from horrors they had seen, and men who had shot themselves in the foot or hand to escape duty. He could not allow himself to be seen as someone who admitted weakness, especially when so many others had fallen.

When headquarters sent reinforcements, Laird was grateful. His men were spent. Two soldiers, however, were green. Laird was wary of newcomers with little experience, but figured they were better than shell-shocked veterans. The new soldiers were friends. One was blond and 200 pounds; the other had dark hair and weighed about 165. Both looked strong, and Laird hoped they could hump more than their share of gear. Laird told them which soldiers to replace and where they were positioned, and then he sent them off with a word of caution: Stay in single file on the trail.

There was a lull in the shelling and the new men became distracted. The smaller soldier wandered a couple feet of the trail and set off a landmine. He and his buddy were blown to pieces. They had lasted just hours in the field. Laird either could not or would not remember their names — it hurt too much.

After their experience on Attu, Laird and other soldiers from the 7th Division kept waiting for the enemy banzai attack. The Japanese, however, changed tactics. The Okinawa commander, General Mitsuru Ushijima, decided that his best shot was to withdraw troops facing imminent defeat instead of sacrificing them with banzai charges. By pulling back soldiers, Ushijima wanted to prolong the battle on Okinawa as long as possible to give his superiors more time to prepare for the imminent Allied invasion of the Japanese homeland. Surrounded by a massive enemy force, Ushijima did everything he could to make a war of attrition as costly as possible.

By the beginning of May, there were hundreds of bodies at the base of every hill. In the confusing maze of fortified underground tunnels and bunkers, the Japanese furiously defended every inch, then set booby traps before they fled. The Americans found that guns weren't enough to win battles in underground tunnels, forcing them to resort to explosives and flamethrowers. Some tunnels were cleared only after Americans poured hot oil into them to scald the enemy to death. Maggots became a part of everyday life.

While reporting on the Battle of Okinawa, beloved war correspondent Ernie Pyle was riding in a jeep with a commander on the nearby isle of Iejima when sniper fire broke out. Pyle was struck in the temple and died instantly.

Laird thought Okinawa couldn't get worse, but it did. Two men from his outfit were killed when their jeep ran over a landmine. He encountered dozens of Okinawans, women and children, who were walking skeletons dying of starvation. Another civilian blew herself up with a grenade as he approached.

Finally his unit was pulled back off the lines for a rest near Ginoza in the northern end of the island. His mind was as exhausted as his body. Even miles from the battle, he still smelled death.

His company was watching a movie when

there was an interruption: Laird's name was called over the public address system. He was ordered to report immediately to battalion headquarters.

What had he done wrong? Did he forget some assignment? Was there bad news from home?

It was May 17, 1945, and Laird was being sent home.

Troops had talked for months about an Army point system that allowed soldiers to accumulate enough credit to leave the war. Under the Advanced Service Rating system, soldiers earned one point for every month of service; one point for every month in service overseas; five points for every combat award and theater stars worn on campaign ribbons; and twelve points for every child at home under the age of eighteen. Laird had earned more than the magic number, which was 85 points. As far as he knew, he was in the first group of thirty servicemen in the 7th Infantry Division to be released from the war under the point system.

He turned in his guns and gear and boarded a C-54 airplane.

He was done with war.

He was going home.

The Battle of Okinawa raged on for weeks

after Laird left the island. On June 18, General Buckner was inspecting American troops at a forward observation post when a Japanese artillery shell blasted into a rock outcropping and splintered shards of coral. Buckner was struck in the chest. He was rushed away on a stretcher to a field aid station, where he died on the operating table. The former Alaska commander who oversaw the Battle of Attu, Buckner was the highest-ranking United States military officer killed by enemy fire in World War II.

The next day, June 19, Japanese General Mitsuru Ushijima realized all hope was lost. He ordered his remaining troops to convert to guerrilla warfare. "With a burning desire to destroy the arrogant enemy, the men in my command have fought the invaders for almost three months," Ushijima wrote in a farewell letter. "We have failed to crush the enemy, despite our death-defying resistance, and now we are doomed."

Ushijima's colonel asked to commit suicide to prevent capture by the Americans, but Ushijima refused: "If you die, there will be no one left who knows the truth about the battle of Okinawa," Ushijima told him. "Bear the temporary shame but endure it. This is an order from your Army commander."

The colonel said he followed Ushijima and his chief of staff, Lieutenant General Isamu Cho, into a cave, where the two top commanders exchanged poems. Ushijima wrote, "We spend arrows and bullets to stain heaven and earth, defending our homeland forever." Cho's poem concluded, "We have used up our withered lives. But our souls race to heaven." Each man plunged a ceremonial dagger into his belly, and a captain with a razor-sharp sword sliced off the head of Ushijima first, then Cho, under the seppuku suicide ritual.

In three months, more than eight million rounds of artillery and mortar had been fired, the equivalent of nearly one shell per second. Okinawa was the bloodiest battle of the Pacific War. More than 14,000 Allied troops were killed, including 12,500 Americans, and another 50,000 were wounded, with an additional 26,000 psychological casualties. Estimates of the Japanese dead ranged from 77,000 to 110,000. Another 10,000 were captured as prisoners of war, the first time large numbers of Japanese soldiers had surrendered instead of fighting to the death.

The biggest single loss, however, were the civilians of Okinawa. An estimated 100,000 noncombatants died either by war or suicide, forced and coerced. That was one of every three residents of Okinawa. After the shooting ceased on June 23, Okinawan women reported frequent rapes by American soldiers.

Many historians believe it was the sheer savagery and brutality of Okinawa that dissuaded the United States from launching an American ground invasion of mainland Japan. If 100,000 Japanese troops could render such atrocity and heartbreak on an outlying island, what kind of death and destruction could result from as many as two million troops defending their homeland? The atrocities of Okinawa would fester as a frightening caution to civilized society.

■ ■ ■ ■

PART FOUR: PEACE

■ ■ ■ ■

19
JOY AND LAURA

By now, Taeko Tatsuguchi was used to hardship. The government rationed all the basics — food, shoes, medicine, bandages, sewing needles, nails, cooking oil. Clothes were extremely difficult to come by; textile production for anyone except the military was all but halted in 1941. Like many mothers, though, she was able to make do. Through friends from her church she could swap booties as daughters outgrew theirs. Her clothes could be cut down and refashioned into children's clothes, which could then be either swapped or converted into diapers, depending on which need was more pressing at the time. As food shortages increased, so, too, did the popularity of a street black market. Everyone wanted rice, but it was in short supply. Taeko was lucky to have developed a taste for different food when she lived with her husband in the United States. She was surviving.

And then came the telegram. Before that notification from the Imperial Army she did not have many material goods, but she did have hope. One piece of paper changed that.

She dreamed of reuniting with her parents in Hawaii, but war meant she could not send them a letter, much less visit.

Tokyo did not seem safe. Like her husband, Taeko had seen the might of the United States, and she feared it soon would be trained on the capital city of Japan. She could not afford her current apartment, and she could not find enough food for herself and two daughters.

She left Tokyo with the girls and moved seventy miles north to Ibaraki Prefecture, where an uncle offered them a wooden shed to live in. It was one room, with no indoor plumbing, but they had a garden with vegetables and wood to burn for cooking. Misako remembered two main things about living in Ibaraki. The first was her mother, thin and sullen, claiming she wasn't hungry as she watched her daughters eat. The second thing Misako remembered was that the shed's earthen floor was covered with tatami, the traditional rice straw mat. Misako would fall asleep listening to a massive infestation of lice jumping up and down on the straw mat.

Taeko was disgusted by all the lice, which she worked mightily to eradicate, but she was grateful to be out of Tokyo. On March 10, 1945, just after the Battle of Kwajalein but before the invasion of Okinawa, the United States sent a squadron of 334 B-29 bombers on a night raid of Tokyo. It turned out to be the most destructive bombing raid in history.

In a city where most homes were constructed of wood and paper, the United States dropped 1,165 tons of explosives that were mostly filled with napalm and gelled gasoline. The main targets were the densely populated Chuo and Koto neighborhoods near the Tokyo docks. Flames were whipped into a frenzy by prevailing 20 mph winds, and the resulting firestorm was so powerful and intense that it sucked in at least one American bomber.

The Tokyo firebombing killed 100,000 people, almost all civilians, injured 40,000, and left one million people homeless. About fifteen square miles of Tokyo were destroyed. Historians say more people were killed in a single day by the Tokyo firebombing than by the Dresden firebombing — or the atomic bombs dropped later on Hiroshima and Nagasaki.

Taeko knew the odds were that some of

her friends, neighbors, or church congregation members in Tokyo were killed in the firebombing, but wartime communications were difficult, and she never knew for sure. In some ways, she was grateful for her ignorance. She had never been a country girl, but living in Ibaraki at least meant she was not a likely military target.

On June 22, Okinawa fell. Six days later, General MacArthur declared the end of Japanese resistance in the Philippines. For the rest of June and July, the United States led hundreds of bombing and firebombing raids across Japan. In more than sixty cities, at least one of every five buildings was destroyed. In thirty cities, at least half of all structures were destroyed. As many as 500,000 people were killed and five million were left homeless. Much of the country's oil, armaments, and shipping industry was destroyed, crippling the country's defense.

In Washington, Harry Truman, who had become president upon FDR's death in April, conferred with his military advisors about the next step. At this point in the war, they believed Japan had about five million troops remaining, including two million in the home islands; two million in Korea, Manchuria, China, and Formosa; 200,000 in French Indochina, Thailand, and Burma;

and 500,000 in the East Indies.

After Japan's fight-to-the-death battles on Okinawa and Iwo Jima, Secretary of War Henry Stimson believed an American invasion of the Japanese home islands would exact an almost unbearable toll on both countries.

"If we once land on one of the main islands and begin a forceful occupation of Japan, we shall probably have cast the die of last ditch resistance," Stimson wrote in a July 2, 1945, memo to President Truman.

The Japanese are highly patriotic and certainly susceptible to calls for fanatical resistance to repel an invasion. Once started in actual invasion, we shall in my opinion have to go through an even more bitter finish fight than in Germany. We shall incur the losses incident to such a war and we shall have to leave the Japanese islands even more thoroughly destroyed than was the case with Germany. This would be due both to the difference in the Japanese and German personal character and the difference in the size and character of the terrain through which the operations will take place.

Stimson estimated one million Americans

would be killed or wounded in an invasion of Japan.

That price, Truman decided, was too high. In the July 26 Potsdam Declaration with Winston Churchill and Chiang Kai-shek, Truman opted instead to give Japan a last-ditch warning:

> We call upon the government of Japan to proclaim now the unconditional surrender of all Japanese armed forces, and to provide proper and adequate assurances of their good faith in such action. The alternative for Japan is prompt and utter destruction.

Japan did not officially respond to the Potsdam Declaration, but at a press conference in Tokyo, Prime Minister Kantaro Suzuki dismissed the demand with the word *mokusatsu,* which U.S. officials translated as meaning, "unworthy of public notice."

United States responded by sending warplanes that dropped millions of leaflets over Japan urging citizens to evacuate:

> Read this carefully as it may save your life or the life of a relative or a friend. In the next few days, four or more of the cities named on the reverse side of this leaflet

will be destroyed by American bombs. These cities contain military installations and workshops or factories, which produce military goods. We are determined to destroy all of the tools of the military clique that they are using to prolong this useless war. Unfortunately, bombs have no eyes. So, in accordance with America's well-known humanitarian policies, the American Air Force, which does not wish to injure innocent people, now gives you warning to evacuate the cities named and save your lives.

America is not fighting the Japanese people but is fighting the military clique, which has enslaved the Japanese people. The peace, which America will bring, will free the people from the oppression of the Japanese military clique and mean the emergence of a new and better Japan.

You can restore peace by demanding new and better leaders who will end the War.

We cannot promise that only these cities will be among those attacked, but at least four will be, so heed this warning and evacuate these cities immediately.

On August 6, the first atomic bomb was dropped on Hiroshima, a city chosen by

United States leaders because it was head-quarters of the Army defending southern Japan and a major military storage and assembly point.

On August 8, the Soviet Union declared war on Japan and invaded Manchuria.

On August 9, a second atomic bomb was dropped, on Nagasaki, a major seaport with several large industrial facilities.

For weeks, as the war turned against Japan, local extremists had been trying to build support for a death-before-dishonor mass suicide. Soldiers had always been trained that surrender would be too shameful to bear. Families at home braced. Would they, too, be expected to give their lives to protect the emperor?

Though the masses did not know it at the time, Emperor Hirohito had been conferring behind the scenes with top government officials to consider an end to the war. After the U.S. nuclear bombs and Soviet declaration of war, the emperor and cabinet officials concluded their chances for victory were over.

On August 13, at 11:25 p.m., the emperor entered a bunker at the Imperial Palace and recorded on disc a four-and-a-half-minute speech of surrender. The plan was for the record to be broadcast on Japanese radio stations, but a cadre of ultranationalist military officers, adamantly opposed to surrender, stormed the palace in the pre-dawn hours of August 14 in an attempted coup. After successfully disarming most palace guards and severing outside communications lines, the rebels searched frantically for hours for the emperor's recording. They did not find it. Loyalists to the emperor had hidden the recording first among a stack of papers, and then, legend held, in a basket of dirty laundry. By dawn, the coup had been defeated. Many rebel leaders took their own lives.

On August 15, radios across Japan broadcast the recorded voice of Hirohito, the man descended from the gods, announcing the end of war. For almost every resident of Japan, including Taeko, it was the first time they had heard the emperor's voice. "To our good and loyal subjects," Hirohito began in the speech that became known as the Jewel Voice Broadcast. "After pondering deeply the general trends in the world, and the actual conditions obtaining in our empire today, we have decided to effect a settlement of the present situation by resorting to an extraordinary measure."

Hirohito went on to explain that Japan had accepted the terms of the Potsdam

Declaration. He did not describe it as unconditional surrender, but he did offer an explanation.

Despite the best that has been done by everyone — the gallant fighting of the military and naval forces, the diligence and assiduity of our servants of the state, and the devoted service of our one hundred million people — the war situation has developed not necessarily to Japan's advantage, while the general trends of the world have all turned against her interest.

Moreover, the enemy has begun to employ a new and most cruel bomb, the power of which to do damage is, indeed, incalculable, taking the toll of many innocent lives. Should we continue to fight, not only would it result in an ultimate collapse and obliteration of the Japanese nation, but also it would lead to the total extinction of human civilization.

Such being the case, how are we to save the millions of our subjects, or to atone ourselves before the hallowed spirits of our Imperial ancestors? This is the reason why we have ordered the acceptance of the provisions of the Joint Declaration of the Powers.

The bombing stopped. Guns fell silent. The war was over.

Most estimates placed the number of dead Japanese, military and civilian, at 2.6 million to 3.1 million. The war had killed at least three of every 100 Japanese.

Japan had exacted a far more costly toll on its enemies. As many as 20 million were dead in China; three million in the Dutch East Indies; one million in French Indochina; 380,000 in Korea; and up to one million in the Philippines. The overwhelming majority of those killed were civilians, not soldiers.

Taeko Tatsuguchi had lost her husband and her home. She was living in a shed where the lice on the floor were as loud as the rain dripping through the roof. She still had her daughters, though. She could pick up Misako and Mutsuko, and she could hug them.

The end of the war did not end the bad times. Food shortages were severe. Starvation was rampant, and some cities advised citizens to eat worms, acorns, and peanut shells. Medicine was in short supply. Many died of treatable diseases.

At her uncle's house, Taeko felt like she was wearing out her welcome. The uncle's vegetable garden would go only so far. Besides, Taeko did not see much of a future for her in a place with few jobs or even opportunities.

She earned enough money through odd jobs for a train ticket out. She moved nearly 500 miles southwest to Okayama, where they moved in with an aunt. Misako remembers being required to carry her own bowl on the train for sanitation; the train was so crowded that she could not move far enough to use a bathroom.

In Okayama they were given another one-room shack with a dirt floor. There was no electricity or indoor plumbing, but also no lice. The vegetables they grew in their small but manicured garden were cooked in a clay pot shichirin, which was fired with bamboo or anything else that would burn. On windy days, the shed shook.

Taeko's aunt ran out of food at about the same time that Misako was old enough to enroll in school. So Taeko moved her family to Kobe, where Allied bombing campaigns had destroyed 55 percent of the city and left a half million people homeless. Postwar reconstruction, combined with the luck of finding a friend of a friend of a relative with connections, allowed Taeko to move herself and her girls into another shack on the outskirts of town.

The best part about Kobe was the school, where Misako learned to read. Each day she was given one hot meal, which was almost always whale-in-miso soup. The smell made Misako retch, but it was her only guarantee of daily food. She saw others eating out of trash cans.

With Misako in school, Taeko would entrust the younger Mutsuko to an elderly woman. Taeko then would work with businessmen learning to speak English. The extra money meant she could skip fewer meals.

At this point after the war, it was possible to write letters to Taeko's parents in Hawaii. One day a surprise package arrived in the mail. Taeko's mother sent her a hand-me-down maroon sweater, her first piece of new clothing in more than a year. Misako and Mutsuko watched their mother joyfully dismantle the sweater to make two new sweaters for the girls. After washing the yarn, Taeko hung it to dry outside, where it was stolen.

Taeko wanted out, badly. Her parents could afford to send her somebody else's used sweater, but not tickets for Taeko and the girls to move to Hawaii. Besides, her parents may not have understood the true desperation of postwar Japan. In her letters home, Taeko downplayed problems. The Japanese way was to grit through the hard times of war, and also to grit through the hard times of peace.

After several months, Misako's school began struggling to keep students and find teachers. Taeko moved the family to Osaka, where the school was more stable and Misako and Mutsuko could walk to classes together. Taeko found more businessmen to tutor in English, but all she could afford was a shanty next to an extremely loud business that, in hindsight, was likely a brothel. With a parade of men and music and drunkenness just outside their door, Taeko and the girls learned to focus on the task at hand.

In Osaka, Taeko's fortunes began to change. Two American soldiers, Pete Roehl and Melvin Baker, had visited her father's Seventh-day Adventist church in Honolulu and pledged to find Taeko in Japan and help her, which they did. They secured her a job at the local Army Post Exchange, or PX, where consumer goods were sold to American servicemen. The two soldiers opened their hearts to Taeko and the girls, bringing them food and clothes and supplying the girls with a steady supply of chewing gum and chocolate. For the first time, other kids in school had reason to be jealous of the Tatsuguchi girls.

Even better was the access to the U.S. base. On weekends, when few people were around, the two soldiers would stand watch outside the locker rooms and let the mother and daughters inside to take showers. Accustomed to either bathing with a pot at home or standing in line once a week at bathhouses, a private shower was an unimaginable luxury. "It was so hot and I felt so good," Misako said. "It was an incredible treat."

For the first time in years, Taeko was able to save some money. She began to feel some hope. Things stayed steady, but the Seventh-day Adventist soldiers eventually moved on. They left Misako and Mutsuko with great respect and curiosity about the United States.

And then, in November 1954, they didn't have to feel curious any longer. Taeko and her parents had saved enough money — and secured the necessary U.S. visas — to move everyone to Honolulu. "We landed in Hawaii and they welcomed us with a lei," Misako said. "The sun was so bright and shiny and the people were happy and jolly and not gloomy. It was so different than Japan."

With the move to Hawaii, Taeko repeated a tradition that her husband had adopted. Now that they were in America, the girls would use the American middle names they had been given at birth.

Misako became Joy. Mutsuko became Laura.

Both girls enrolled in the local Adventist school. Though Joy had just completed eighth grade in Japan, she started in third grade in Hawaii to learn English. She towered over her much younger classmates, but learned the new language easily enough to move quickly through fourth and fifth grades. She had difficulty speaking English, but could understand it.

Laura adjusted more easily. She remained in classes mainly with children closer to her own age, and had more of an aptitude for English.

To earn tuition, Taeko, Joy, and Laura cleaned and did maintenance work at the school. Taeko taught Japanese to Hawaiians, and earned money going door-to-door selling church books and Bibles. Her father, who had retired from the ministry, helped support them.

For many months, neither Joy nor Laura could say she fit right in. They still felt more Japanese than American. But they were with their grandparents, who loved them, and a supportive church community, and they lived in a beautiful place where tropical fruit grew in backyards and the ocean water was warm enough for swimming. If Americans were prejudiced against Japanese, Joy and Laura couldn't feel it. Hawaii was filled with enough different kinds of people to make them feel tolerated, if not accepted. The girls could not imagine a better start. "It was paradise," Joy said.

As the girls grew older, they wanted to know more about their father. Taeko had told them he was a surgeon opposed to war who was killed in Alaska. At the time, that was all Taeko knew. No one else really knew more, either. The only Japanese survivors of Attu were a handful of prisoners of war too ashamed to show their faces, much less say anything about what they saw. In fact, nobody in Japan was saying much about the war. They were trying to move on.

In the United States, however, classmates of Paul Tatsuguchi did not want to forget the past. They wanted to change the description of it. After the Battle of Attu, dozens of newspapers across the United States had printed stories about Tatsuguchi, almost all highlighting the final entry of his diary.

Most stories accused the Japanese doctor of an unthinkable act. "Japs Slew Own Patients on Attu, Diary Discloses," said the headline on a September 9, 1943, story in the *Chicago Tribune.* "How Japanese medical officers on Attu blew up their own field hospitals with grenades, killing the patients, and then killed themselves as American invaders tightened their hold on that Aleutian island late in May was revealed today in a bloodstained diary." None of the stories said anything about Tatsuguchi's background, his religious devotion to pacifism, or his time living in the United States as a college and medical student. In all likelihood, journalists at the time knew nothing about Tatsuguchi beyond his diary. It was the thick of war, and American newspapers were all too willing to promote stories portraying Japanese as fanatical killing machines.

However, Tatsuguchi's old medical school classmates read the same stories and were infuriated. The published descriptions of Tatsy as a heartless murderer did not fit with their remembrances of a gentle, careful, and devout physician. His classmates took the accusations as an affront to their Seventh-day Adventist faith. They did not believe a man who inscribed his Bible with

Deuteronomy 30:19, "Choose Life," could kill the wounded so heartlessly.

They set out to clear the name of Paul Tatsuguchi.

In September 1944, with the war in the Pacific still raging, the death of Tatsuguchi was noted in *The Medical Evangelist,* the Seventh-day Adventist journal from his alma mater at the College of Medical Evangelists at Loma Linda University. The original mention of his death in the school newspaper was straightforward and not controversial. However, the newspaper followed up the first story with a second article that disputed the way Tatsuguchi's death was reported in the popular press.

"We have received the following in a letter from a responsible source," *The Medical Evangelist* said without further identifying the writer. "This letter is being written in an effort to straighten out some of the facts regarding the conduct and manner of death of Dr. Paul Nobuo Tatsuguchi, Class of '38, on Attu in the Aleutian Islands."

The editorialist said he had

obtained copies of the New York, Chicago, and Seattle newspapers, which have had lengthy articles on this news story. In practically all of those articles the context of statements in his diary have been so changed as to imply conduct by him for which there is no factual foundation.

I had occasion to talk with officers in the Alaskan Intelligence, who were actually on Attu during this action, and who assisted in the translation of the original diary. I believe that there is nothing in this information that I am giving you which has any military significance, so it should pass the censor.

First, the doctor was not a suicide. He was killed in action in the last major counterattack conducted by the Japanese troops. Also there is no foundation to believe that he had any personal part in the destruction of any Japanese patients. It seems to be customary among Japanese troops for grenades to be issued to helpless patients, making it possible for them to commit suicide if they so wish. If an administrative order were given from higher headquarters to the effect that grenades should be furnished all patients, the Japanese medical officer, regardless of his personal views, would be helpless to do anything but see that it was carried out. However, there is absolutely no foundation for the statement, as carried in the newspapers, that Dr. Tatsuguchi personally contributed to the murder of any patients.

There were both personal and professional reasons to challenge the press narrative of Tatsuguchi's diary. For starters, Tatsuguchi had many friends at Loma Linda who knew him and liked him, but had lost touch with him during the war years. In their memory, Tatsy was a faith-centered surgeon who devoted himself to healing the infirm, not lobbing grenades at them. They wanted to clear Tatsy's name.

The professional reasons were serious, too. Though some practices set Seventh-day Adventists apart from traditional Christian faiths in the United States — the Saturday Sabbath, the promotion of vegetarianism, the door-to-door evangelizing — Adventists wanted to be viewed in the mainstream of religions. The church had always put strong emphasis on wholeness and health. The version of the Tatsuguchi story in the popular press was completely at odds with the Adventist view of its Loma Linda–trained physicians. Classmates did not want the reputation of the church or the medical school to be sullied, especially if the Attu headlines about Tatsuguchi were not true.

The year before Taeko Tatsuguchi had

moved to Hawaii, she had been visited in Japan by Adventist elder B. P. Hoffman. He had been an instructor of Paul Tatsuguchi at Pacific Union College. The instructor told Taeko that his name and contact information had been in Tatsuguchi's address book on Attu, and that an FBI agent had conducted an interview on the relationship between the men.

The church elder told Taeko a different story about her husband's death. Hoffman said the FBI agent told him the doctor had been killed as he emerged from a field hospital. The church official told Taeko that her husband had been waving a Bible and calling out, "Don't shoot! I am a Christian!" but that an American soldier could not understand the words through the Aleutian wind. The soldier mistook the Bible for a gun and shot Tatsuguchi, the church official told Taeko.

Which version of the death of her husband was true? At the time, Taeko hadn't yet heard Dick Laird's telling of the Attu story. She would only see her husband's diary for the first time eight years after his death, when the Japanese government passed along a version it had translated from English — a translation of a translation. Taeko had no reason to doubt the church elder's version.

She told her daughters about it. It's what they all believed.

She told her daughters about it. It's what they all shared.

20
HOME

Dick Laird returned home to Ohio a war hero. He had a Silver Star, Bronze Star, Presidential Unit Citation Medal, Asiatic Pacific Theatre Ribbon with Four Bronze Stars and Arrowhead, Philippine Liberation Ribbon with Two Bronze Stars, and Army Achievement Medal, among others. He had so much hardware that he needed four standard picture frames to hold it all for display on the walls of his home.

He soon learned, however, that there was one tough truth about all his recognition: Medals didn't pay.

Yes, he was thrilled to be living in Columbus, Ohio, with Rose and the kids. He couldn't believe how much how much Peggy and Nancy Lou had grown. He also couldn't believe how difficult it was to find a good job.

He arrived home on June 16, 1945, the day the first atomic bomb was tested in

Alamagordo, New Mexico, and he found the country was still geared up for war. His one job offer was as an ROTC instructor, which he rejected, because he'd had his fill of the Army. He eventually hired on driving a gasoline tanker for Shell Oil, but long days in a truck seat hurt his back and, frankly, the work was boring. It was hard to be interested in driving the same route on city streets, day after day after day, when he had gone to war and risked all.

Civilian life was not easy for Laird. In the Army, he was used to giving orders and having them followed. Now his voice was just one of four in the family, though his was the loudest and sternest. The daughters were in grade school, and had minds of their own. Life in a foxhole could be more predictable than life at home with a wife and children — in war he knew when to fight and when to duck.

Laird worried that he was letting down Rose. For all of his time away overseas, he felt that he owed her a better life. Driving a truck wasn't going to do it. He had earned the opportunity of an education through the GI Bill, but college had no appeal to him. Rose had the brains and the drive for school. Laird insisted that she start taking classes at Ohio State University. The Army buddy who was killed next to Laird in Okinawa, Sergeant Harold Gellein, had convinced him of the power of a college diploma. Laird vowed to make sure his wife would get one. He opened an appliance-repair shop for a day job, worked at a roller-bearing factory at night, and installed home insulation on the weekends. Meanwhile, after attending her daytime classes, Rose worked another three hours a day for professors and typed term papers for graduate students. In 1953, Rose and Dick's combined work paid off: She earned a bachelor's degree in education from Ohio State. As a fourteen-year-old dropout from Appalachia, Laird felt proud and a little in awe to see his wife earn a college diploma. He also felt like he had lived up to his end of the deal. Not long after Rose had earned her degree, Laird walked up to his night-shift boss at the Timken Roller Bearing Company and quit his job. When his boss asked why, Laird told him, "I'm a number and in ten or more years I'll still be a number."

Quitting his night job gave him more free time, which did not turn out to be a good thing. Without something to keep him constantly busy, Laird's mind raced. At night he lay awake and rehashed the events of the day. He also relived the war. When he fell asleep, the nightmares returned.

Pointing his gun at the mother and baby. Finger on the trigger with the two boys at the sugarcane fields. An Army buddy mangled beside him. The soldier hit in the backside in his foxhole. Pieces of the two fresh young soldiers at the landmine. Drinking from the creek with the dead soldier's body. And the American-trained surgeon with the wife and the kids and the diary, Nobuo Tatsuguchi.

Rose knew about her husband's night terrors because he was thrashing and moaning in bed. Still, Laird wouldn't say much. He didn't want to burden her with his problems. He was also embarrassed. Soldiers, he thought, should not show weakness or even feel it. He was supposed to be brave, and he had the medals to prove it. He definitely did not want his daughters to know what made him scream at night.

Still, the whole family was ready for a change. Ohio was just too familiar. He couldn't see a big future here. He wanted a fresh start.

During his time training in the Army, Laird had learned to love the desert. Rose had a cousin who lived in Tucson. So the Lairds loaded up a trailer and moved cross-country from Ohio to Arizona. Laird was accepted to the Asbestos Workers Local No. 73, and began working at power plants, nuclear missile silos, and other industrial construction jobs across the Southwest. Rose hired on as a schoolteacher and began working on her master's degree in education from the University of Arizona. They had another daughter, Ellie, in 1955. They were well on their way to a comfortable, middle-class life.

And yet Laird did not take well to domestication. He loved the four females in his house, but he could never quite shed the give-orders-or-take-orders structure of military life. He could be a stern taskmaster. For years around the house, his own daughters did not naturally refer to him as Dad or Father or Pop. They called him Laird.

Laird missed the camaraderie of Army life. He tried a VFW hall. It wasn't the same. He didn't want to be an old guy reliving his glory days. He wanted to fix things in the here and now. He and Rose bought four acres near what was then Saguaro National Monument. Laird then designed and spent hundreds of hours building the family's new three-bedroom brick house. Laird was busy again, and he was happy.

Rose earned her master's degree and started teaching at the Arizona School for the Deaf and Blind. They bought a few acres in the White Mountains, and Laird fixed up a mobile home to withstand local snows. By the mid-1970s, the girls had grown up and moved into their own homes, which Laird renovated. Laird added a greenhouse to the family home in Tucson and spent hours collecting and growing orchids. Without the kids, the house turned quiet. Rose and Dick sat on the sofa in the living room and adjusted slowly to their empty nest. So many of the family issues that had consumed so much energy for so many years — the kids' grades, their driving, their curfews — were all gone. Through the 1980s, Rose and Dick were happy grandparents. The days had dragged, but the years had flown by.

On February 3, 1992, the Lairds were reading in their living room when the phone rang. "Are you Rose?" the caller asked. "Are you from Columbus, Ohio?"

Yes, Rose answered.

"Did you have a baby girl in Columbus, Ohio, on December 31, 1934, and give her up for adoption?"

"Yes."

"I am that girl."

Her name was Marty. She lived in Bluffton, Ohio. After her adoptive parents died, she began looking for her birth mother. She was middle-aged now, and with children of her own. She and her husband traveled to Tucson to meet Rose and Dick and their daughters. The ice was broken when Dick and Rose's daughter Peggy met her new-found sister and said, "Well, I'm not the oldest anymore." The two families joined for boisterous barbecues, a tour of blooming cacti, and long stories about unfamiliar relatives. Rose and Marty spent hours together catching up on their years apart while Dick and Marty's husband, Bruno, who had a shared love of landscape and wildflower photography, drove across the southern Arizona desert exposing hundreds of frames of 35mm film. For an event so unexpected, the reunion went amazingly well.

Laird had unsettled history, too. He still had nightmares from the war. They weren't as frequent as they used to be, but in some ways that made them worse. He could never predict when they would happen. They always were terrifying. It troubled him to realize that three years of combat decades ago still had such sway over his life. The Army medals displayed in a large custom frame on his wall reminded him daily of how the war made him rise up and become a hero. Yet war's dark chapters were lodged in his conscience.

He found his box of wartime memorabilia and pulled out his copy of the Tatsuguchi diary. The man had a family. Laird wondered if he could find them.

In Honolulu, Taeko knew it was time for a change. Joy was reaching college age, and Laura was close behind. Taeko moved the family to California so the girls could attend the same Seventh-day Adventist schools as their parents.

The transition from Hawaii to the mainland United States was difficult. The family found California to be much less racially tolerant than Hawaii. In Honolulu, the girls' schools were filled with more Japanese, Chinese, and Korean immigrants than Anglos, but Laura was the only Asian student in her California high school. Her isolation hit home during a history lesson in her senior year, when Laura's teacher lectured on World War II. After the discussion, a white classmate turned in his desk and pointed a finger at Laura. "You bombed Pearl Harbor!" he shouted at her in front of the class. Neither the teacher nor classmates did anything to contradict the accuser. Laura was horrified. The year before, at age seventeen, she had completed all the studies and tests to become an official United States citizen. She had not bombed Pearl Harbor. She had not even been alive for the bombing of Pearl Harbor. She wanted to tell off the accuser, set him straight, but she realized she was all alone on the front lines of racism with no backup. She kept her head down and stewed in silence. The confrontation defused, but Laura boiled inside.

Laura had no doubt that the United States offered far more opportunities than her native Japan. In California, the girls never went hungry. In fact, the postwar boom was turning the parents of many of her friends rich. The California parks offered regular free concerts. The libraries loaned books. And the beaches, mountains, and Sequoia forests were full of free paths and adventures. The Tatsuguchis could practice their religion without fear of persecution. Their lives brimmed with optimism.

In their new country, the two sisters earned educations far superior to those available to most girls in Japan, with Joy enrolling at Pacific Union College and Laura attending Loma Linda University. Both studied to become nurses, and both, in the footsteps of their father, worked at White Memorial in Los Angeles. Both girls believed they were living the American dream.

And yet . . .

No matter their accomplishments in school or at work, Laura and Joy often faced reminders that they, like their mother and father before them, were outsiders in a new land. In California, Laura had several Japanese American friends who had lost everything — their homes, their businesses, their cars — while being ordered to internment camps during the war. Her friends talked often of the humiliations of daily life in the camps — the searing heat of the desert, the dust that caked everything, the stench of unsanitary toilets, the children who sobbed at night, the hacking coughs that would not go away. Their shame only intensified with the knowledge that their German and Italian former neighbors were still living free of barbed wire. Years after the war, the father of one of Laura's friends was invited to a business conference in Palm Springs. He refused because, after years in an internment camp, he could not stand the sight of the desert.

Even the most accomplished members of the Japanese American community battled discrimination. In Los Angeles, Laura worked for a top American-born orthopedic surgeon who wanted to buy a house in the tony Brentwood neighborhood. The surgeon had the same personal wealth, prestigious career, and elite diplomas as many of the surrounding homeowners. What the surgeon did not have was the same skin color. After being rejected by one real estate agent after another, the surgeon finally found a white friend to stage a straw purchase of a Brentwood house for him. Laura could not forget the pain and anger of a boss who performed daily miracles in the surgical bay, but whose race prevented him from buying the home of his choice in the land of the free.

Still, Laura and her mother were often taken aback by the curiosity and friendliness of American strangers. While living first in Hawaii and then in California, Taeko started to see one consequence of having an unusual last name — she was easy to find in the phone book. Several times a month the family mailbox would fill with letters from former American soldiers that all asked the same questions: Do you know the Tatsuguchi soldier who wrote the diary on Attu? Are you related? Have you ever seen the diary? Can I send you a copy? Years after their service, soldiers from the Aleutians were still haunted by the writings of the man who had changed their beliefs about the enemy.

Over the years she had received dozens and maybe hundreds of letters from former GIs. Usually she answered with a brief thank-you, but didn't do much beyond that. She was living in America now, and what happened in the war and Alaska and Attu was long in the past. She let it drop. Eventually the inquiring soldiers let it drop, too.

One day, however, she received a letter from someone more persistent. Floyd Watkins was an Emory University literature professor from Atlanta who had been an Army cryptographer in the Aleutians during the war. Like hundreds of other soldiers, he ended up with several copies of the Tatsuguchi diary. Watkins, however, was a curious academic who noticed differences between versions. He wanted to discuss them with the Tatsuguchi family.

Taeko's first instinct was to say no. Her heart had suffered enough. She was a war widow and saw little need to rip the stitches off that wound.

But the professor persisted. He assured Taeko that he was not some voyeuristic ex-GI on a nostalgia trip. He was an English professor whose life's work was the analysis of William Faulkner, Robert Penn Warren, Eudora Welty, and other celebrated Southern writers. Yes, the professor had a personal interest in the topic of the Tatsuguchi diary, but he felt it deserved serious scholarship. He embraced academic rigor. He promised to be respectful and open-minded.

Taeko softened. She was interested in what the man from Georgia might find. She just didn't know if she could bear it. She asked for more information.

In another heartfelt letter, the professor assured Taeko that he was not out for sensationalism. Acknowledging Taeko's deep Christian beliefs, the professor noted that he was a church elder who studied the scriptures. He told how the Book of Job had helped him to make sense of the pain and suffering in the war.

Taeko was curious, but Laura was ready. If this man from Georgia knew something about her father, then she wanted to hear it. The Tatsuguchis agreed to meet with Watkins in Los Angeles.

When the professor walked into their home in Los Angeles, Taeko was overwhelmed with memories. Here was a man who, like her husband, had gone to war in Alaska and seen man at his worst. But this soldier had returned home. He had a wife and children and a rewarding career. He had gray hair. He was standing in her living room now.

It was hard not to like Floyd Watkins. He was polite and gentle and spoke with a soothing voice. He was like an earnest, favorite uncle. He also knew something about the diary of Nobuo Tatsuguchi.

The professor had canvassed other soldiers who served in the Aleutians and accumulated ten different copies of the diary. The mistakes between versions were myriad.

The name of the youngest Tatsuguchi daughter, Mutsuko, was incorrectly spelled as Fokiko, Takiko, Tekiko, Tokiko, and Tokkiko. Taeko's name was misspelled as Faeke, Tacke, Taeke, Taoko, and Toeko. Only one translation correctly lists Tatsuguchi's use of the word Christ; others either omit the passage or repeat the word as Ehkist, Enkist, and Edict. Different versions say he ate a half-friend thistle, a dried thistle, a friend thistle, and half-a-fried thistle. Two versions of the diary omit Tatsuguchi's claim that the Americans had used poison gas on Attu, raising the question of whether the diary was censored by military officials.

To the heartbreak of Taeko, two versions of her husband's translated diary read, "Two hours ago I took care of all the patients with grenades." Four other versions do not include a subject in the sentence, saying only, "Took care of all the patients with grenades." In the mind of Taeko and other church officials, this difference was crucial: It left open the possibility that Tatsuguchi himself did not kill the patients. If he "took care of all patients with grenades," then perhaps Tatsuguchi — or even someone else — had merely distributed grenades for soldiers to detonate themselves. There also was the chance that "took care of all patients with grenades" meant that he had just attended to them as a physician. Either way, Tatsuguchi would have been able to stay true to the biblical commandment of thou shalt not kill.

Taeko told the professor some details of her husband's life — the man behind the diary.

"Wherever he was, he wanted to be a good Christian," Taeko told the professor. "He wanted to do the best he could.

"He never would kill all those boys. For sure he would not. I would like to get that clear by getting the original [diary] if possible."

The professor promised to try his hardest, but ultimately he could not recover the diary. The U.S. Army said the original was lost.

In his paper about the diary, published in

the academic *Journal of Ethnic Studies,* the professor repeated the unverified story of Tatsuguchi trying to surrender on Attu with a Bible in his hand. The story was reprinted in the alumni magazine of Pacific Union College under the headline, "Don't Shoot! I am a Christian!"

For a story on the fortieth anniversary of the Battle of Attu, the Associated Press published in May 1983 a story on Tatsuguchi that ran in newspapers across America with the quote, "Don't shoot! I'm a Christian."

The AP story was read in Tucson by a man named Dick Laird.

That's not right, Laird thought. That's not what happened at all.

357

21
QUEST

He wasn't really sure what he wanted to do. Through the help of a Japanese journalist, he had found the house of a woman in Sherman Oaks, California, named Laura Tatsuguchi Davis. He was told it was also the home of a widow named Taeko Tatsuguchi. Laird had called ahead to say he had some items from the Battle of Attu, and he wondered if any belonged to the family.

Laird was too nervous to tell anyone the true reason for his visit — he was the American soldier who had killed Nobuo Tatsuguchi.

When Laird arrived at the home, Taeko was polite, but not friendly. Laird opened his box of battlefield souvenirs, but Taeko said she didn't recognize anything. Just looking inside the box seemed to bother her. She thanked Laird, then excused herself to the backyard, where she said twins were playing.

Laird could tell that Taeko was uncomfortable. He couldn't blame her. Her husband had been dead for four decades. She had a new life in a new country. Laird was the one who wanted to revisit the past.

With Taeko in the backyard, it was now just Laird and Laura in the living room. There was an awkward pause. Laird wondered: What now? He fumbled and fidgeted. He was never a man of many words, and he was even less at ease with strangers. To the Tatsuguchi family, Laird was worse than a stranger, though only he knew it.

He tried to break the ice by talking a little about himself, about his life in Tucson, about his cultivation of bromeliads in the greenhouse he built. Laird could tell, however, that his chitchat wasn't going over well.

Laura didn't have to say it. Laird knew she wanted him to leave. But he still hadn't done it. There was one thing he had come here to do, and it remained undone. Laird couldn't bear to say it to the face of the widow of Paul Nobuo Tatsuguchi, but he knew he owed it to the family. Laird owed it to himself.

"By the way," he told Laura Tatsuguchi Davis as he entered his car, "I'm the one who killed your father."

And he drove off.

■ ■ ■ ■

Laura was thunderstruck. She was forty years old and had never known much about her father. Her main source of information was her mother, who, in the words of Laura, "did not like to dwell on sad stories." Laura knew her father had been killed in World War II in Alaska. She knew he was born in Japan but studied in America, and that he loved both countries. She knew he was devout, and a pacifist, and had been drafted against his will, and had served as a surgeon. She had heard the story of how her father had tried to surrender with a Bible in his hand.

Her older sister, Joy, who had lived with Laura in the United States but had married and moved back to Japan, had one memory of their father. That was playing hide-and-seek with him as a young girl in an apartment in Tokyo. But Laura was born after her father had been sent to war. She had never seen or heard her father. She knew little about his life, and even less about his death.

Outside her house, Laura struggled to breathe. She did not want to go back inside to tell her mother. She did not want to return to the house, period. She slumped in her car and cried. She had shaken the hand of the man who killed her father. She had offered him tea. Laura turned the ignition of her car and drove.

She didn't know where to go. She didn't know what to do. Truth be told, she didn't know what to think. She had not thought about her father in a serious way for a long time. Besides her mother's sparse stories, and some pictures on the wall, he had never been a part of her life. She had wanted to know more about him, but life got in the way — school, marriage, job, house, twins, elderly mother at home. She barely had time to think about herself.

The more she drove, the more she realized she needed help. Luckily, she knew someone.

A friend who had served in the Vietnam War was now a psychiatrist. She called him.

"Oh my God," she told him. "I just talked to the man who killed my father. My stomach is churning. I feel terrible. What should I do?"

Her friend listened to the details of Laird's visit, as well as the story of her father's death. "I think he came over to relieve himself of a burden," the friend told her.

That analysis was a shocker. Laura hadn't

considered this. She had always thought that growing up without a father had been a burden for her life. But what if the man who killed her father had regrets? What if he carried a burden, too? The guilt might be unbearable. It made her think.

Laura spent more than a decade on a quest to figure it all out. When her own marriage ended in divorce, she became a single mom with little unscheduled time, but she worked hard to open up some hours to learn about her father. She asked her mother lots of detailed questions about her life, her father's life, and their life together. Her mother opened up a little, but still did not want to talk much about the past. Taeko wanted to spare her daughter the pain. Laura, however, felt compelled. A stranger who knocked on her door knew something important that Laura did not know about her father. She wanted to know the story of the man who made her.

She doubled back to talk with the Emory University professor who in 1971 had interviewed her mother and investigated the Battle of Attu.

"You are the daughter in the closing lines of Nobuo Tatsuguchi's diary?" he asked her.

"I am," Laura told him.

"My goodness," he replied.

History had come to life for the professor.

Laura was thrilled with the way the professor had put her father into historical context. He had written: "Since the time of the American Civil War probably no lover of America has been assigned to such burdensome military service. He was loyal to two peoples and two cultures, who were warring against each other." She had learned about her father as a man from Taeko. The professor helped Laura understand her father as a symbol of the tragedy of war and the clash of cultures.

The professor helped Laura hash out the similarities and differences in the conflicting versions of her father's diary. She came to understand how, in the chaos of war, a competing translation of a single Japanese phrase or symbol could raise questions that would persist for decades.

She wrote letters to her father's medical school classmates and even attended a class reunion. At first she was nervous to walk into the ballroom. She knew no one. Everyone at the reunion was considerably older — the same age as her father would have been.

As attendees clustered in groups — some were old friends, some were reintroducing themselves for the first time in years — people began to notice her nametag: Laura, daughter of Paul Tatsuguchi. First she was greeted by a few individual doctors. Then whole groups came. The gravity inside the room shifted.

The reunion turned into a de facto Tatsy tribute, with Laura as the star attraction. Old classmates buzzed around and introduced themselves. They told Laura how her father had loved his wife, America, and Japan. For many classmates, he had been a walking, talking example that disproved America's racist propaganda against the Japanese during World War II. They told Laura that he was humble and hardworking, serious in school but fun outside it, with a wry sense of humor. Everyone had a Tatsy story. Everyone shared grief over his fate in Attu. Everyone also agreed that he was a devout man of peace, though the classmates who served in the military during the war must have known that horrible things happened in battle that could not be easily explained or understood back home.

They were proud to have known him. The more she heard, Laura was, too.

For the first time in her life, Laura started to understand her father as a person and not just as a framed picture on the wall.

She wished she had met him. When Laura was a girl in Japan, she knew many other children without fathers. In the United States, however, casualties had not been as common. Many of her friends in California grew up with fathers who could offer advice or help with school or just be there when needed. Laura had never known what it was like to have a father. The more she learned about hers, the more she felt loss.

Like the Emory University professor, Laura tried to recover her father's original diary, but the Army gave her the same response — it could not be found. A U.S. senator lent the power of his office to the diary hunt. No luck. Laura concluded that her father's battlefield writings truly were lost.

When Laura felt she had uncovered as much as possible about her father's life, she was ready to learn about his death. She called Dick Laird to arrange a meeting.

22
DELIVERANCE

It had been thirteen years since Laird rang the doorbell at the home of Laura Tatsuguchi Davis in California. The kindergartener twins who had been playing in the backyard on the day of Laird's visit were now grown, and one boy, Brian, had enrolled as a student at the University of Arizona in Tucson. Laura was going to visit her son at school.

Laird lived just a few miles from campus.

As a career intensive care nurse, Laura was not easily flustered, but she felt on edge as she drove up to Laird's home. Her mind raced. The last time she had seen him, Laird was so strong and stern and blunt — he had frightened her.

Now that hardly seemed possible. Laird was eighty-four years old and he looked like it. He lived in an assisted care facility. He shuffled his feet as he walked and he needed help entering Laura's car.

Laura's son had suggested dinner at a nearby family restaurant packed with customers.

The soldier and the daughter sat across the table from each other, with Laura's son at her side, just in case she needed support. To others in the Arizona restaurant, it might have looked like a daughter and grandson taking their grandfather out to dinner — Laird was twenty-seven years older than Laura — except that few family dinners were this serious and careful.

Laird listened quietly as Laura described the way her father grew up, why he came to the United States, and how he was conscripted against his will to serve as a surgeon in the Imperial Army. She also talked about her own personal quest to learn about the father she had never met.

In return, Laird recounted his own past. He talked about his daughters, his photography, and his orchids. He'd had a full life, a good life, but war lurked behind it. He couldn't move past it. Sometimes he dwelled on it. Laird told Laura about the hellhole of Attu and why he had killed her father.

The more he talked, the more Laird seemed to unburden himself. Still, Laura could sense that something was still on his mind. She asked how he was doing — how he was really doing.

He wasn't well. The love of his life, Rose, had died little more than a year earlier, and Laird still hadn't recovered. "Now I know why husbands and wives die shortly after a spouse dies," Laird said. "Boredom. No one to talk to and argue with. No one to turn over to in bed in the middle of the night."

The late hours, especially, were a problem for Laird. His nightmares were more frequent and worse. He had seen friends killed in war. He had killed dozens of Japanese in war. He had killed his own runner in war. He had nearly killed innocent civilians in war. He had seen soldiers do savage things. And, oh, the things he had heard — screaming, moaning, weeping. Sometimes he would wake with the voices of anguish in his ears. Of all the misery he had caused and witnessed, the one that still gave rise to the worst nightmares, Laird told Laura, was his killing of Paul Tatsuguchi.

"I killed your father and seven other men and they gave me a medal for it," Laird said. "I still can't sleep because of it. I didn't have any other choice, but that doesn't mean it was right. I keep thinking about your father and your mother and you and your sister. I think about it all the time."

He believed Laura's father, like other

368

Japanese soldiers in the final banzai attack, was trying to kill him. But what if he wasn't? What if he was just a pacifist running along with a banzai charge because those were his orders? The truth was that Laird didn't know for sure. At the very least, Tatsuguchi was with the people who were trying to kill Laird and his fellow soldiers. Laird believed everyone atop that knoll on Buffalo Ridge at Attu was a mortal threat, so he lobbed his grenade and shot at them all. It was easy to kill an enemy who was a symbol, yet another uniform in an unrelenting army attacking Laird and his country and his way of life. But it was much harder to have killed a person. Laird knew now that Paul Tatsuguchi was a man torn between two countries, a husband who loved his wife and his children. He was a doctor who opposed war. His daughter said he loved America. "I was a professional soldier," Laird told Laura, "but your father was not. Your father was not."

All these years later, Laird still didn't think he had done the wrong thing. He just could not identify the right thing. He feared he had killed an American.

"When I read the diary," Laird told her, "I felt like I'd killed a husband, a father, and a Japanese man that had no business where he was at."

Laura and Laird looked at each other. Their eyes welled. Laura did not know what to say, so she told Laird the first thing that came to her mind: "It was war. It was a long time ago and you did what you thought you had to do."

In the middle of the restaurant, Laura knew it: The man who killed her father did bear a burden. He had carried it inside himself for more than five decades. He could not rid himself of it. And now Laura knew what she wanted to do about it. She could not give him peace, but she could give him atonement. After dinner, she sat down and wrote him a letter:

Dear Mr. Laird,
It was so good to have had a chance to talk to you tonight. I am writing this letter to express even more completely my gratitude to you for coming to my home so many years ago, and to ask you to let go of any feelings of guilt or pain you still have over what happened between you and my father at Attu. What happened there was neither your fault nor his. Neither you nor any of your comrades chose that particular battle or that particular time to fight. If fault lies with

anyone, it lies with those commanding generals, all long dead, who decided to spend the lives of their men in what many believe to be a stupid battle over a useless and barren piece of land. That includes the Japanese generals who invaded, for what must have been symbolic purposes, small and frozen islands that they could neither defend nor use, and who left men stranded there. It also includes the American military commanders who chose the worst of seasons to stage a battle that never needed fighting.

The only thing that dignifies and sanctifies that terrible battle was the bravery, duty, and loyalty to country that those of you who were left to fight that battle displayed under the most terrible circumstances. You were an American soldier. Your native land had been attacked, and you accepted the task of defending it. You did the duty thrust upon you bravely and ably. So did your comrades. So did the men on the other side. None of you, on either side, chose to make this horrible war happen. When others did, it fell upon you and your comrades, and my father and his, to do what was left to you to do.

My father's medical school classmates told me how my father felt in the later '30's about the then-brewing conflict between Japan and the United States. My father loved America, and would have happily remained here to practice had family necessities not required him to return to Japan. He had traveled all over this country. He thought it would be insanity for Japan to get into a war with the United States, and told his classmates so. He said, "America is such a huge and powerful country. All of Japan is not as large as California. War with America would be insane. Japan could never survive it." Had he lived to see it, he would have grieved, but hardly been surprised at the devastation Japan suffered before the war was over.

When you confronted my father he appeared to be, and was in the eyes of the conflict, one of the enemy. You and your comrades were all in a "kill or be killed" conflict. When interviewed almost 60 years later, you remarked that what hurt about the memory of my father's death was that my father had no business being there and neither did you. But that could be said for most if not all of the men who fought and suffered and died there. None of you should have been there. But you were, and that fact cast upon you terrible duties, duties you discharged the only way you could. What happened, happened. You were not at fault. The men you fired upon that day would have fired upon you. Had you not fired when you did, you and more of your own comrades may have died. How could you know that there was an American trained physician, and a father and husband facing you? And what could you have done, other than what you did, even had you known?

Whatever happened out there that day, and whatever painful flashes of memory still visit you, I ask you to let them go. I ask you to accept what happened and forgive yourself and to be at peace. And I want you to know that the daughter and the wife of Paul Tatsuguchi both hold you in honor and gratitude for coming forward and visiting our home that day, and wish you peace and happiness.

With Best Regards
Laura Tatsuguchi Davis

When Laura returned home to California, she read her letter aloud to her mother.

Together they wept, but Taeko's tears turned into a smile.

"I miss my husband terribly," she told her daughter. "Life was not easy without him, but life went on. We had to keep on. If you hold on to anger and animosity, it's going to eat you alive. You have to let it go.

"The guilt was eating at Mr. Laird. At his age he wanted to feel peace. As Christians we believe in forgiveness. I hope you have helped Mr. Laird move on."

Laura's heart swelled. Her mother brimmed with so much grace. Faith may have given Taeko her roadmap to life, but she still chose every turn at every intersection. Laura wished she could match her mother's model of empathy.

Of course, meeting with the man who killed her father required some courage by Laura, too. Her mother's serenity about the decision helped convince Laura that she had done the right thing.

Laura wondered how Laird would react when he read her letter. Home alone in his elder care complex, Laird had plenty of time to hash over history. Laura knew Laird was the kind of man who drew a strong line between right and wrong, but the gray fog of war had blurred so many judgments. She had forgiven him. Could he forgive himself?

A few days later, Laird wrote back to Laura with his answer: "I don't mind telling you that your letter brought a tear to these eyes. I think you understand just what went on during the war."

The night after the restaurant, Laird told Laura, he slept without nightmares.

23
RETURN

Taeko Tatsuguchi and Laura Tatsuguchi Davis didn't have to be told that the fiftieth anniversary of the Battle of Attu was approaching. In the months before, letters from retired American servicemen packed their mailbox. Many enclosed copies of their own version of the Tatsuguchi war diary. All their letters were roughly the same: *Hello, you don't know me, but I was a U.S. soldier in Alaska, and I found this diary. Are you related to the man who wrote it? I thought you might want it. I always wondered what happened to the man who wrote it.*

Laura responded with brief but polite letters explaining who her father was and how he died on Attu. By now, all the Aleutian veterans had reached retirement age, and they had the time and interest to reconnect with the formative events of their youth.

Then Laura received two letters that required more consideration. The first invited her to a reunion in Hokkaido of Japanese troops evacuated from Kiska. The second invited her to speak at a commemoration ceremony on Attu. She attended both.

The Japanese reunion was somber. Yes, the Imperial Army soldiers had managed to outsmart the Americans with a daring escape from Kiska, but all their colleagues had been killed on Attu, and many of the Kiska survivors had been killed later in other battles across the Pacific. At the reunion they all swapped war stories about friends, officers, and what they found back home upon return. Some survivors debated the role in the war of the Japanese politicians and generals and even the emperor. After all the speeches and talk, one statement from a former Imperial Army soldier stood out to Laura. "Fifty years ago, we fought against each other," said Teruo Nishijama. "It does not matter now who won or who lost. The question is, what have we really learned?"

For much of the reunion, the veterans circled around Laura. They were anxious to meet the daughter of the man who provided the only surviving written account of the Japanese loss at Attu. Most wanted to learn more about Laura's father. Some were interested in Laura's life in the United States. Few veterans seemed bitter. Most were wiser.

In Japan, Laura tried to visit her father's family home in Hiroshima, but learned it had been destroyed by the American atomic bomb. She visited the Hiroshima Peace Memorial Museum, and was taken aback when she met a man who had become a living exhibit on the consequences of nuclear war. When the man lifted his shirt to show visitors the awful bomb burns across his torso, Laura gasped. She knew the Japanese government caused much pain in World War II, but the Japanese people had suffered much, too.

Laura had learned a lot about war. The most powerful lesson to her, though, was about the aftermath. She had many reasons to hate the man who killed her father. But he was a man, too, with his own flaws and insecurities. Even if Dick Laird's words and manners were rough, his heart was right. He had a conscience. He wanted to do better. Like Laura's father, Laird was an ordinary person thrust into an extraordinary circumstance. He did the best he could in a situation no one should ever face. As Taeko said, "I understand that it happened during the war, and Mr. Laird, too, was ordered to fight against his enemy by his superior officer. War killed so many bright young people who could have tremendously contributed to the future of the countries. It's totally a waste of talents."

The mere logistics of war were daunting to Laura. To travel to Attu Island for the ceremony marking the fiftieth anniversary of the battle there, Laura had to fly from Los Angeles to Seattle to Anchorage, where she switched to another plane for the 1,100-mile trip to Adak Island in the Aleutians. From Adak she flew another 450 miles to Attu.

She could not get over the remoteness of Attu. The island was so far from anything. In 1993, the only inhabitants of the island were the twenty U.S. Coast Guard employees running a long-range radio station for ships navigating the North Pacific and Bering Sea. What Attu lacked in population, it made up for with wind and fog and cold.

Laura was struck by the raw feeling of the place. It was wild. Mountains towered, waves crashed, and willows whipped. The ground was so mushy that it moved with each step. The air was dank. She had never been so far from civilization. Few others had, either.

She looked around and could not imagine

why anyone would fight over such a place. She could not believe her father died here. What was the point? Who gained anything? What were the generals thinking? What was anybody thinking?

On her flights to Attu, Laura had worked on her speech. At home in Los Angeles, she had written, "How ironic that my father was killed in combat against his beloved America while in loyal service to his Japanese homeland. . . . Like my father, I, too, have a great love for Japan and America." When she arrived in Alaska, she reversed the order of the countries so that her speech said, "America and Japan."

With a quivering voice, in front of American veterans and dignitaries, Laura read her speech first in English, then repeated it in Japanese.

"Beginning May 11, 1943, a terrible and agonizing battle raged for eighteen days where we now stand," Laura began. "My father, a physician, died here at Attu on May 29th, the last day of the battle. I was only three months old and we never had a chance to meet, which grieved me throughout my childhood and even as an adult. And then, through the process of reading his diary, which survived the war, from researching his family history, I began to find the missing pieces of life's puzzle."

She described her father's life and how he had been torn between two countries. She told how he was born in Japan but learned to be a doctor in the United States, and how she and her sister had both followed him into the medical profession as nurses.

"Today, I place this wreath in honor of all the American and Japanese fathers, sons, husbands, and friends who died and were buried in this soil," Laura said. "On behalf of all their loved ones who were left behind, but have never been forgotten, and finally in memory of my father, Dr. Paul Nobuo Tatsuguchi, who died, as he lived, in the act of healing."

After speaking, Laura was approached by a California woman, Tempe Robinson. Her father, an American soldier, had been killed on Attu the same day as Laura's father. At the time, Tempe was six months old and Laura was three months old. The two women hugged. Though born on opposite sides of the world, and opposite sides of the war, each fatherless daughter said she knew how the other must feel. Laura's heart swelled.

Laura's speech was received warmly by some veterans and coolly by others. Some told Laura they were moved by her father's circumstance, and admired his courage under the worst possible circumstances. Other American veterans, however, remained upset that their government had allowed Japan to erect an eighteen-foot titanium sculpture on Attu with an inscription in both Japanese and English: "In memory of all those who sacrificed their lives in the islands and seas of the North Pacific during World War II and in dedication to world peace." Some American veterans believed that Attu was sacred ground for the 549 Americans killed and 3,280 hurt there, and that the Japanese had no right to be building any monument to a battle they had started.

Fifty years after her father was killed in the Battle of Attu, Laura could see that some people would never allow some wounds to heal. Several months later, however, she was startled to be greeted with a sign of hope.

When Ed Dickinson, an American veteran of Attu, wrote a report on the Attu memorial trip for the newsletter of the U.S. Army's 7th Infantry Division, he was contacted by another vet who read it and was moved by Laura's speech. That vet requested Laura's home address.

In the summer of 1994, Laura received a

surprise package in the mail. It was a Bible. Laura opened the black leather cover. Inside was a pressed wildflower, handwriting in the margins — and a picture of her sister, Joy, as a toddler.

Laura and Taeko could not believe it. In their hands was the Attu Bible of Paul Nobuo Tatsuguchi.

The sender was Alvin H. Koeppe of Wayne, Michigan. Like Dick Laird, Koeppe was a soldier who had fought on Attu, Kwajalein, Leyte, and Okinawa. For fifty years this stranger had kept one of her family's most treasured possessions and then returned it. The man was unclear about exactly how he had come to acquire the Bible, and Laura was not going to press him about it. She was so grateful just to have the tangible evidence of the faith of her father. She thanked the soldier profusely. Just a few months later, on May 3, 1995 — fifty-two years to the day that he, Laird, and other American troops had boarded their ships to fight in the Aleutians — Alvin Koeppe died. Laura prayed that he died in peace.

When Laura had returned home from Attu it was with a new appreciation of veterans. It had been difficult enough just to visit the

Aleutians. She couldn't imagine trying to survive in a swampy Alaskan foxhole with shells and bullets exploding around her.

She wondered how Laird was doing. On her next trip to visit her son at the University of Arizona, she called Laird and took him to lunch. His mind was sharp and he seemed to enjoy seeing her. She told him about her trips to Attu and Hokkaido; he told her about his grandchildren and photography and orchids.

A few months after Laura took Laird out to lunch, she and her mother sent him a Christmas card. He sent one in return.

The next time she visited her son in college, Laura took Laird to lunch again. They ran out of things to say about Attu. Instead, they talked about life — the joys of raising children, the difficulty of balancing work and family, the decisions that had set them on their current paths.

On the next visit after that, they did not talk about Attu at all. Nor on the visit after that, or after that.

Amid the lunchtime bustle of a restaurant, they wondered what the other patrons would make of them, he the frail old man in a Western bolo tie, she the middle-age Japanese woman in fashionable black slacks and blouse. He had taken her father's life.

She had given him forgiveness.

Laura would never know exactly what had happened to her father on Attu, but she knew enough.

AFTERWORD

In the spring of 2011, after several phone interviews, Laura Tatsuguchi Davis invited me to Los Angeles to meet her mother. Taeko was ninety-eight years old and living with Laura. You should come soon, Laura told me. She didn't have to spell out the reason why.

I met Taeko in the hospital bed Laura had set up in the first floor of their home. Taeko could not sit up by herself. She drifted in and out of sleep. Laura said her mother still wanted to meet me.

When I introduced myself, Taeko nodded and whispered. I leaned in closer, but understood little of what she said. Her breathing was louder than her words.

Laura told me that she and her mother had lived together for more than three decades. For much of that time Taeko had been strong enough to help care for Laura's twins, but now it was Laura's turn to care for her. As a career nurse, Laura had an unvarnished view of what the days ahead would look like for her mother. Adjusting her mother's pillow, Laura spoke in a voice with the timbre of someone accustomed to being heard above the din of a busy hospital. Yet her eyes were dewy. She left us alone.

I sat next to Taeko and felt like I was sharing the room with greatness. She had been confronted with so much in life. She had loved and lost and scrapped through war and its ruin to raise two young daughters who were now strong, smart, and loving women. She did not seek anyone's pity or attention, though Laura and Joy did assure me she thought more people should know about her husband's story. I asked Taeko if she could hear me, but received no response. Her spirit was stronger than her body.

In the course of my reporting I had come to view Taeko as a symbol — someone who had never fought in war, but still suffered one of its deepest wounds. What happened to her was not fair. She could have been bitter. Instead, she pushed on with dignity. She gave hope to her daughters. She gave peace to the man who killed her husband.

Her breaths deepened and slowed. Taeko

fell into a sleep. I felt honored to sit with her.

Outside Taeko's room, Laura showed me the photo albums and walls of pictures documenting the family's life. Her father's Bible had been donated to the Japanese American museum in Los Angeles. Laura wanted it to be part of history for others to see.

I checked in the next day with Laura, who told me that her mother was happy to have met me, and was hoping my research would help illuminate her husband's story. Still, Taeko had not slept well that night. Laura thought her mother's tossing and turning might have been caused by the rekindling of old memories. She doesn't like to think about anything sad, Laura told me. Wanting to respect her, I decided against trying to talk with Taeko again.

A few weeks later, on June 1, 2011, Taeko died.

Dick Laird was a lonely man by the time Taeko and Laura had started sending him Christmas cards. His beloved Rose had died of a stroke on Thanksgiving Day of 1998. According to their surviving daughters, Peggy of Tucson and Ellie of Las Cruces, New Mexico, Laird seemed lost without Rose. He channeled his remaining energy into cultivating unusual orchids in his greenhouse, photographing cactus in the wilds of southern Arizona, and puttering around the house. A former neighbor described Laird as quiet and meticulous. He was the kind of guy, the neighbor told me, who looked you in the eye and kept his word. He was the kind of guy, the neighbor said, you'd never want to cross.

Laird died on January 14, 2005.

As for Attu Island, it never became anyone's military prize. After the Japanese were vanquished in the spring of 1943, the U.S. military succeeded in building a runway on Attu, but williwaws, fog, and the never-ending torrents of ice, snow, and rain prevented much use of the island. In December 1943, the Navy and Coast Guard began trying to build a LORAN navigation station for ships on Attu. The first shipment of construction materials was ruined after a storm smashed the delivery barges onto the rocks. Another storm killed nine workers when vast waves capsized their tugboat 200 feet from shore. In the succeeding weeks, the Army lost another forty-one men to high seas and avalanches. The war in the Aleutians was over, but Attu would not stop killing men. The navigation station was finally up and operating on Attu by February 1944.

A crew of twenty or so men operated the LORAN station through the Cold War. Attu was the nightmare job assignment of the U.S. Coast Guard. The isolation was extreme; the weather was worse. Even the peacetime veterans of Attu Island expressed amazement that they survived it.

By 2010, advances in GPS navigation technology made LORAN obsolete. The Coast Guard finally called it quits on Attu. In a fitting tribute, the official decommissioning ceremony was delayed for a day when a storm and thick fog prevented the Coast Guard plane from landing on the island. The last Coast Guardsman left Attu on August 27, 2010.

Today there are no permanent residents of Attu. The island receives only a handful of visitors a year, mainly federal biologists checking the status of colonies of nesting seabirds, and amateur birders spending thousands of dollars to spot rare Asiatic species blown off course by storms during migration. The island remains a majestic but eerie sight: Snowcapped peaks and rocky shores are strewn with the planes, weaponry, and vehicles destroyed six decades earlier. Visiting biologists and birders are cautioned to hike only in established areas to avoid detonating unexploded bombs.

The bodies of Americans killed during the Battle of Attu have been transferred to other cemeteries across the United States, but hundreds of Japanese are buried on the island, mostly in mass graves now covered by tundra. A few old Coast Guard buildings survive. Storms knock down more roofs and walls every year. The current government plan is for Attu Island to revert to nature and remain uninhabited by man.

ACKNOWLEDGMENTS

First and foremost, I thank the families of Dick Laird and Paul Nobuo Tatsuguchi.

For the Laird family, daughters Peggy Laird and Elinor McGonigle opened their homes — and countless family documents and photo albums — for me during the reporting of this book. Many stories about the early lives of Dick and Rose Laird came from diaries and letters provided to me by Peggy and Ellie. Other key insights about Dick and Rose Laird came from Bill, Essence, and Charlie McGonigle.

At the Tatsuguchi family, Taeko, Laura, and Joy answered my endless phone calls, supplied boxes of records, and let me copy family photos from the walls. Meeting Taeko was one of the high points of my career as a journalist. It is hard to overstate the patience of the Tatsuguchi family, and I am grateful.

I was lucky to have a wonderful team of editors at Simon & Schuster. Leslie Meredith inspired me. Rakesh Satyal and Loan Le worked the manuscript to cut fat and add muscle. Once again my agent, Jody Rein, was a big-hearted pro. David Brown and Paul Olsewski gave this book a big push forward.

Many researchers and librarians spent much time helping me to chase down obscure records and interview transcripts.

At Elmendorf Air Force Base in Anchorage, Doug Beckstead and Joe Orr set me up in a room of file cabinets and let me dig into reams of War Department records. John Haile Cloe, a former Air Force historian with encyclopedic knowledge of the military history of Alaska, helped me put those records in perspective. Faydra Lampshire guided me through National Archives documents in Alaska. Rachel Mason of the National Park Service and Steve Delehanty of the U.S. Fish and Wildlife Service taught me about the cultural and natural history of the Aleutians. George Darrow and Mike Phillips at the Alaska Veterans Museum helped me gain access to World War II records. Sara Piasecki of the Anchorage Museum helped me find photos and written accounts of Attu Island before and after the Japanese invasion. Mary Breu offered terrific insight to the lives of Attu settlers

Etta and Foster Jones. Jerry Sherard gave guidance on the history and safety record of the Appalachian coal mining business. Dr. Stephen Jaffe helped secure key background information.

The Steny H. Hoyer Research Complex at the National Archives of College Park, Maryland, is a vast and intimidating place, but archivist Megan Dwyre showed me how to navigate it, or at least part of it. Researchers at the Western History Collection of the Denver Public Library served up unexpected records about the U.S. Army equipment, rations, and training.

At Emory University in Atlanta, home of the archives of Professor Floyd Watkins, I was helped greatly with documents and interview recordings by Kathy Shoemaker, Liz Chase, Sara Logue, and Trey Bunn. Bruce Tabb of the University of Oregon libraries in Eugene helped me find my way through the Brian Garfield collection.

For help with photographs, I am grateful to Lisa Hupp of the U.S. Fish and Wildlife Service, Gwen Higgins and Arlene Schmuland of the University of Alaska Anchorage, Becky Butler and Rose Speranza of the University of Alaska Fairbanks, Sandra Johnston of the Alaska State Library in

Juneau, and Ted Spencer of Wings Over Alaska.

Christina Whiting, Marianne Aplin, and Poppy Benson of Homer, Alaska, helped me greatly with an initial reporting trip to Alaska. Draggan Mihailovich, Chris Everson, and Jeff McMillan put me on the camping trip of a lifetime on Attu Island. No thanks whatsoever to Wendelin Sachtler.

For readers interested in learning more about the overall war in the Aleutians, the best single source, especially from the perspective of generals and admirals, is Brian Garfield's 1969 book, *The Thousand-Mile War.* I also learned much from the official battle summary, *Infantry Operations in the Aleutians: The Battle for Attu,* written by Colonel Lamar Tooke and published in 1990 by the US Army War College. The best account from the view of soldiers on the ground is the 1944 War Department book, *The Capture of Attu,* which was written partially by Dashiell Hammett. "Modern armies had never fought before on any field that was like the Aleutians," Hammett wrote. "We could borrow no knowledge from the past. We would have to learn as we went along, how to live and fight and win in this land, the least-known part of our America."

My family put up with a lot during my reporting and writing of this project. Our sons, Cass, Max, and Wesley, lifted me from my deepest funks. My wife, Merrill, always gave strength and love. I am a lucky man.

This book taught me many lessons, but one that really hit home was about the sacrifices of soldiers. My father, John Obmascik, served as a U.S. Marine. This book is dedicated to him.

BIBLIOGRAPHY

Bix, Herbert P. *Hirohito and the Making of Modern Japan.* New York: HarperCollins, 2000.

Breu, Mary. *Last Letters from Attu: The True Story of Etta Jones, Alaska Pioneer and Japanese POW.* Anchorage, Alaska: Northwest Books, 2009.

Cloe, John Haile. *The Aleutian Warriors: A History of the 11th Air Force & Fleet Air Wing 4.* Missoula, Montana: Anchorage Chapter — Air Force Association and Pictorial Histories Publishing Co., 1990.

Cohen, Stan. *The Forgotten War: A Pictorial History of World War II in Alaska and Northwestern Canada.* Missoula, Montana: Pictorial Histories Publishing Co., 1988.

Garfield, Brian. *The Thousand-Mile War: World War II in Alaska and the Aleutians.* Garden City, N.Y.: Doubleday, 1969.

Golodoff, Nick, edited by Rachel Mason.

Attu Boy. Anchorage, Alaska: National Park Service, 2012.

Hane, Mikiso. *Japan: A Short History.* London: Oneworld Publications, 2000.

Hays, Otis Jr. *Alaska's Hidden Wars: Secret Campaigns on the North Pacific Rim.* Fairbanks, Alaska: University of Alaska Press, 2004.

Ienaga, Saburo. *The Pacific War: 1931–1945.* New York: Pantheon, 1978.

Kohlhoff, Dean. *When the Wind Was a River.* Seattle: University of Washington Press, 1995.

LaFeber, Walter. *The Clash: U.S.-Japanese Relations Throughout History.* New York: W.W. Norton, 1998.

Leckie, Robert. *Okinawa: The Last Battle of World War II.* New York: Viking, 1995.

Morison, Samuel Eliot, *History of United States Naval Operations in World War II.* Boston: Little, Brown, 1947–62.

Oliver, Ethel Ross. *Journal of an Aleutian Year.* Seattle: University of Washington Press, 1988.

Prange, Gordon W., with Donald M. Goldstein and Katherine V. Dillon. *Miracle at Midway.* New York: Penguin, 1982.

Seiple, Samantha. *Ghosts in the Fog: The Untold Story of Alaska's WWII Invasion.*

New York: Scholastic Press, 2011.

Spector, Ronald H. *Eagle Against the Sun: The American War with Japan.* New York: Free Press, 1985.

Toland, John. *The Rising Sun: The Decline and Fall of the Japanese Empire, 1936–1945.* New York: Random House, 1970.

United States War Department. *The Capture of Attu: As Told by the Men Who Fought There.* Washington, D.C.: The Infantry Journal, 1944.

Woodward, C. Vann. *The Battle for Leyte Gulf.* New York: Macmillan, 1947.

Yahara, Hiromichi. *The Battle for Okinawa.* New York: J. Wiley, c. 1995.

ILLUSTRATION CREDITS

1. Laird family
2. Laird family
3. Laird family
4. Laird family
5. Laura Tatsuguchi Davis
6. Laura Tatsuguchi Davis
7. Laura Tatsuguchi Davis
8. Laura Tatsuguchi Davis
9. Elmendorf Air Force Base History Office / US Army Signal Corps
10. Wings Over Alaska / Ted Spencer Collection
11. US Navy
12. Alan G. May papers, Archives and Special Collections, Consortium Library, University of Alaska Anchorage
13. US Navy
14. Alaska State Library Historical Collections
15. US Army Signal Corps
16. Joint Base Elmendorf-Richardson His-

tory Office

17. University of Alaska Fairbanks, Alaska and Polar Regions Collections and Archives

18. University of Alaska Fairbanks, Alaska and Polar Regions Collections and Archives

19. Alaska State Library Historical Collections

20. US Army Signal Corps

21. US Army Signal Corps

22. US Army Signal Corps

23. US Navy

24. Wings Over Alaska / Ted Spencer Collection

25. US Army Signal Corps

26. Wings Over Alaska / Ted Spencer Collection

27. Alaska State Library Historical Collections

28. US Army Air Force

29. US Army Signal Corps

30. US Navy

31. Wings Over Alaska / Ted Spencer Collection

32. US Coast Guard

33. Lisa Hupp, Alaska region, US Fish and Wildlife Service

34. Photo by Mark Obmascik

35. Photo by Mark Obmascik

ABOUT THE AUTHOR

Mark Obmascik is a Pulitzer Prize–winning journalist and bestselling author. His first nonfiction book, *The Big Year,* was named a best book of the year by five major media and turned into a Hollywood movie. His second, *Halfway to Heaven,* was winner of the National Outdoor Book Award for Outdoor Literature. He lives in Denver. He and his wife have three sons.